SPARK L

BANKRUPTCY

McLaren Legal Publishers LLC
New York

ALSO AVAILABLE IN THIS SERIES:

Agency & Partnership
Antitrust
Bankruptcy
Civil Procedure
Family Law
Federal Income Tax
Labor Law
Wills & Trusts

SPARK LAW SERIES®

BANKRUPTCY

First Edition

John Anderson, Esq.
New York University School of Law

ISBN 10: 0-9801482-2-7
ISBN 13: 978-0-9801482-2-0

Published by
McLaren Legal Publishers LLC
136 West 21st Street, 8th Floor
New York, NY 10011

Web: www.mclarenpublishing.com
Email: contact@mclarenpublishing.com

Printed in the United States of America

HOW TO USE THIS BOOK

This law school study aid is a non-keyed book. While it includes many of the key critical cases in the subject addressed, it is meant to provide an overall rigorous review of the topic indicated and convey key concepts and points of law for general study. For a keyed book linked to a specific casebook, please use our Legal Path Series® of keyed books.

"All of what you need, none of what you don't"

Our law school study guides give you exactly what you need to understand the key principles of the subject, including the sometimes elusive Black Letter law. We are not a replacement for an in depth legal analysis of the subject matter covered; however, we do present what is absolutely critical in a very concise format.

Abbreviations used in this book

Use of the word "his" in this book is gender neutral and encompasses both "his" and "her."

Pay particular attention to sections with this symbol: ☞

TABLE OF CONTENTS

Bankruptcy

28 U.S.C. § 157. Procedures

(a) Each district court may provide that any or all cases under title 11 and any or all proceedings arising under title 11 or arising in or related to a case under title 11 shall be referred to the bankruptcy judges for the district.

(b) (1) Bankruptcy judges may hear and determine all cases under title 11 and all core proceedings arising under title 11, or arising in a case under title 11, referred under subsection (a) of this section, and may enter appropriate orders and judgments, subject to review under section 158 of this title.

(2) Core proceedings include, but are not limited to—

(A) matters concerning the administration of the estate;

(B) allowance or disallowance of claims against the estate or exemptions from property of the estate, and estimation of claims or interests for the purposes of confirming a plan under chapter 11, 12, or 13 of title 11 but not the liquidation or estimation of contingent or unliquidated personal injury tort or wrongful death claims against the estate for purposes of distribution in a case under title 11;

(C) counterclaims by the estate against persons filing claims against the estate;

(D) orders in respect to obtaining credit;

(E) orders to turn over property of the estate;

(F) proceedings to determine, avoid, or recover preferences;

(G) motions to terminate, annul, or modify the automatic stay;

(H) proceedings to determine, avoid, or recover fraudulent conveyances;

(I) determinations as to the dischargeability of particular debts;

(J) objections to discharges;

(K) determinations of the validity, extent, or priority of liens;

(L) confirmations of plans;

(M) orders approving the use or lease of property, including the use of cash collateral;

(N) orders approving the sale of property other than property resulting from claims brought by the estate against persons who have not filed claims against the estate;

(O) other proceedings affecting the liquidation of the assets of the estate or the adjustment of the debtor-creditor or the equity security holder relationship, except personal injury tort or wrongful death claims~~.~~; and

(P) recognition of foreign proceedings and other matters under chapter 15 of title 11.

(3) The bankruptcy judge shall determine, on the judge's own motion or on timely motion of a party, whether a proceeding is a core proceeding under this subsection or is a proceeding that is otherwise related to a case under title 11. A determination that a proceeding is not a core proceeding shall not be made solely on the basis that its resolution may be affected by State law.

(4) Non-core proceedings under section 157(b)(2)(B) of title 28, United States Code, shall not be subject to the mandatory abstention provisions of section 1334(c)(2).

(5) The district court shall order that personal injury tort and wrongful death claims shall be tried in the district court in which the bankruptcy case is pending, or in the district court in the district in which the claim arose, as determined by the district court in which the bankruptcy case is pending.

(c) (1) A bankruptcy judge may hear a proceeding that is not a core proceeding but that is otherwise related to a case under title 11. In such proceeding, the bankruptcy judge shall submit proposed findings of fact and conclusions of law to the district court, and any final order or judgment shall be entered by the district judge after considering the bankruptcy judge's proposed findings and conclusions and after reviewing de novo those matters to which any party has timely and specifically objected.

(2) Notwithstanding the provisions of paragraph (1) of this subsection, the district court, with the consent of all the parties to the proceeding, may refer a proceeding related to a case under title 11 to a bankruptcy judge to hear and determine and to enter appropriate orders and judgments, subject to review under section 158 of this title.

(d) The district court may withdraw, in whole or in part, any case or proceeding referred under this section, on its own motion or on timely motion of any party, for cause shown. The district court shall, on timely motion of a party, so withdraw a proceeding if the court determines that resolution of the proceeding requires consideration of both title 11 and other laws of the United States regulating organizations or activities affecting interstate commerce.

(e) If the right to a jury trial applies in a proceeding that may be heard under this section by a bankruptcy judge, the bankruptcy judge may conduct the jury trial if specially designated to exercise such jurisdiction by the district court and with the express consent of all the parties.

28 U.S.C. § 1334. Bankruptcy cases and proceedings

(a) Except as provided in subsection (b) of this section, the district courts shall have original and exclusive jurisdiction of all cases under title 11.

(b) Except as provided in subsection (e)(2), and notwithstanding any Act of Congress that confers exclusive jurisdiction on a court or courts other than the district courts, the district courts shall have original but not exclusive jurisdiction of all civil proceedings arising under title 11, or arising in or related to cases under title 11.

(c) (1) Except with respect to a case under chapter 15 of title 11, nothing in this section prevents a district court in the interest of justice, or in the interest of comity with State courts or respect for State law, from abstaining from hearing a particular proceeding arising under title 11 or arising in or related to a case under title 11.

(2) Upon timely motion of a party in a proceeding based upon a State law claim or State law cause of action, related to a case under title 11 but not arising under title 11 or arising in a case under title 11, with respect to which an action could not have been commenced in a court of the United States absent jurisdiction under this section, the district court shall abstain from hearing such proceeding if an action is commenced, and can be timely adjudicated, in a State forum of appropriate jurisdiction.

(d) Any decision to abstain or not to abstain made under subsection (c) (other than a decision not to abstain in a proceeding described in subsection (c)(2)) is not reviewable by appeal or otherwise by the court of appeals under section 158(d), 1291, or 1292 of this title or by the Supreme Court of the United States under section 1254 of this title. Subsection (c) and this subsection shall not be construed to limit the applicability of the stay provided for by section 362 of title 11, United States Code, as such section applies to an action affecting the property of the estate in bankruptcy.

(e) The district court in which a case under title 11 is commenced or is pending shall have exclusive jurisdiction—

(1) of all the property, wherever located, of the debtor as of the commencement of such case, and of property of the estate; and

(2) over all claims or causes of action that involve construction of section 327 of title 11, United States Code, or rules relating to disclosure requirements under section 327.[1]

- *Flow chart (pages 9 – 10)*
- Bankruptcy court can only hear cases arising in or under bankruptcy
- Bankruptcy court has no jurisdiction to hear:

[1] Applicable only to cases under the Bankruptcy Code commenced after the date of enactment of the Act. Pub. L. No. 109-8, 119 Stat. 23, Sec. 324(b).

    - Personal injury
    - No relating to... - cannot piggy-back on other claims
- *Wood v. Wood* – "We hold, therefore, that a proceeding is core under §157 if it invokes a substantive right provided by Title 11 or if it is a proceeding that, by its nature, could arise only in the context of a bankruptcy case. The proceeding before us does not meet this test and, accordingly, is a non-core proceeding. The plaintiff's suit is not based on any right created by the federal bankruptcy law. It is based on state created rights. Moreover, this suit is not a proceeding that could arise only in the context of a bankruptcy. It is simply a state contract action that, had there been no bankruptcy, could have proceeded in state court."
- **Sovereign Immunity**
    - *U.S. Constitution Article I, clause 8; Amendment XI*
        - *See page 19*
    - *Tenn. Student Assistance Corp. v Hood (syllabus)*
        - Student loan owed to state but Supreme Court found that this was an *in rem* proceeding because it was a suit against the state and not a suit against a person
        - It was the way the court chose to uphold the bankruptcy power against the 11th amendment with respect to student loans
        - Even though there is a state guarantee for student loans there is not an issue of dischargability of those student loans in bankruptcy

28 U.S.C. § 1409. Venue

- Venue designates the particular geographic area in which a particular court who has jurisdiction may hear a case
- *28 U.S.C.§1408*
    - A case under Title 11 May be commenced in the district court for the district:
    - In which the domicile, residence, principal place of business in the United States or the principal assets
    - Look to the 180 days prior
    - "If one of those four things was in that district for all of more of those days than any other district then venue is proper there"
    - Hillman- just more than elsewhere
- *28 U.S.C.§1409* – been amended
    - Consumer cases
    - "Have to chase them to where they live"

§ 1409. Venue of proceedings arising under title 11 or arising in or related to cases under title 11

(a) Except as otherwise provided in subsections (b) and (d), a proceeding arising under title 11 or arising in or related to a case under title 11 may be commenced in the district court in which such case is pending.

(b) Except as provided in subsection (d) of this section, a trustee in a case under title 11 may commence a proceeding arising in or related to such case to recover a money judgment of or property worth less than $1,000 or a consumer debt of less than $15,000, or a debt (excluding a consumer debt) against a noninsider of less than $10,000, only in the district court for the district in which the defendant resides.

(c) Except as provided in subsection (b) of this section, a trustee in a case under title 11 may commence a proceeding arising in or related to such case as statutory successor to the debtor or creditors under section 541 or 544(b) of title 11 in the district court for the district where the State or Federal court sits in which, under applicable nonbankruptcy venue provisions, the debtor or creditors, as the case may be, may have commenced an action on which such proceeding is based if the case under title 11 had not been commenced.

(d) A trustee may commence a proceeding arising under title 11 or arising in or related to a case under title 11 based on a claim arising after the commencement of such case from the operation of the business of the debtor only in the district court for the district where a State or Federal court sits in which, under applicable nonbankruptcy venue provisions, an action on such claim may have been brought.

(e) A proceeding arising under title 11 or arising in or related to a case under title 11, based on a claim arising after the commencement of such case from the operation of the business of the debtor, may be commenced against the representative of the estate in such case in the district court for the district where the State or Federal court sits in which the party commencing such proceeding may, under applicable nonbankruptcy venue provisions, have brought an action on such claim, or in the district court in which such case is pending.

- *In re Pettit*
    - Issue is where defendant is domiciled
    - Domicile- is a person's legal home, place where you have your true fixed permanent home - domicile is not residency
    - **Domicile / residence –** domicile is a home, or where one intends to return regardless of where they may be at the time / residence is where you are living at the time
        - Ex. law student from FL going to law school in MA – domiciled in FL but resided in MA

- "When you no longer have the intention of returning to what was your domicile then you no longer are domiciled in the former place of residence"
- Corporation's domicile is in the state of incorporation – doesn't matter where assets or principal place of business is
- Presumption is that the district where the bankruptcy petition is filed is proper

11 U.S.C. §109 Eligibility

Who may be a debtor:

(a) Notwithstanding any other provision of this section, only a person that resides or has a domicile, a place of business, or property in the United States, or a municipality, may be a debtor under this title.

(b) A person may be a debtor under chapter 7 of this title only if such person is not—

(1) a railroad;

(2) a domestic insurance company, bank, savings bank, cooperative bank, savings and loan association, building and loan association, homestead association, a New Markets Venture Capital company as defined in section 351 of the Small Business Investment Act of 1958, a small business investment company licensed by the Small Business Administration under section 301 of the Small Business Investment Act of 1958, credit union, or industrial bank or similar institution which is an insured bank as defined in section 3(h) of the Federal Deposit Insurance Act, except that an uninsured State member bank, or a corporation organized under section 25A of the Federal Reserve Act, which operates, or operates as, a multilateral clearing organization pursuant to section 409 of the Federal Deposit Insurance Corporation Improvement Act of 1991 may be a debtor if a petition is filed at the direction of the Board of Governors of the Federal Reserve System; or

(3) (A) a foreign insurance company, engaged in such business in the United States; or

(B) a foreign bank, savings bank, cooperative bank, savings and loan association, building and loan association, or credit union, that has a branch or agency (as defined in section 1(b) of the International Banking Act of 1978[2] in the United States.

(c) An entity may be a debtor under chapter 9 of this title if and only if such entity—

(1) is a municipality;

[2] *Sic.* There should probably be a closing parenthesis here.

(2) is specifically authorized, in its capacity as a municipality or by name, to be a debtor under such chapter by State law, or by a governmental officer or organization empowered by State law to authorize such entity to be a debtor under such chapter;

(3) is insolvent;

(4) desires to effect a plan to adjust such debts; and

(5) (A) has obtained the agreement of creditors holding at least a majority in amount of the claims of each class that such entity intends to impair under a plan in a case under such chapter;

(B) has negotiated in good faith with creditors and has failed to obtain the agreement of creditors holding at least a majority in amount of the claims of each class that such entity intends to impair under a plan in a case under such chapter;

(C) is unable to negotiate with creditors because such negotiation is impracticable; or

(D) reasonably believes that a creditor may attempt to obtain a transfer that is avoidable under section 547 of this title.

(d) Only a railroad, a person that may be a debtor under chapter 7 of this title, (except a stockbroker or a commodity broker), and an uninsured State member bank, or a corporation organized under section 25A of the Federal Reserve Act, which operates, or operates as, a multilateral clearing organization pursuant to section 409 of the Federal Deposit Insurance Corporation Improvement Act of 1991 may be a debtor under chapter 11 of this title.

(e) Only an individual with regular income that owes, on the date of the filing of the petition, noncontingent, liquidated, unsecured debts of less than $307,675 and noncontingent, liquidated, secured debts of less than $922,975, or an individual with regular income and such individual's spouse, except a stockbroker or a commodity broker, that owe, on the date of the filing of the petition, noncontingent, liquidated, unsecured debts that aggregate less than $307,675 and noncontingent, liquidated, secured debts of less than $922,975 may be a debtor under chapter 13 of this title.

(f) Only a family farmer or family fisherman with regular annual income may be a debtor under chapter 12 of this title.

(g) Notwithstanding any other provision of this section, no individual or family farmer may be a debtor under this title who has been a debtor in a case pending under this title at any time in the preceding 180 days if—

(1) the case was dismissed by the court for willful failure of the debtor to abide by orders of the court, or to appear before the court in proper prosecution of the case; or

(2) the debtor requested and obtained the voluntary dismissal of the case following the filing of a request for relief from the automatic stay provided by section 362 of this title.

(h) (1) Subject to paragraphs (2) and (3), and notwithstanding any other provision of this section, an individual may not be a debtor under this title unless such individual has, during the 180-day period preceding the date of filing of the petition by such individual, received from an approved nonprofit budget and credit counseling agency described in section 111(a) an individual or group briefing (including a briefing conducted by telephone or on the Internet) that outlined the opportunities for available credit counseling and assisted such individual in performing a related budget analysis.

(2) (A) Paragraph (1) shall not apply with respect to a debtor who resides in a district for which the United States trustee (or the bankruptcy administrator, if any) determines that the approved nonprofit budget and credit counseling agencies for such district are not reasonably able to provide adequate services to the additional individuals who would otherwise seek credit counseling from such agencies by reason of the requirements of paragraph (1).

(B) The United States trustee (or the bankruptcy administrator, if any) who makes a determination described in subparagraph (A) shall review such determination not later than 1 year after the date of such determination, and not less frequently than annually thereafter. Notwithstanding the preceding sentence, a nonprofit budget and credit counseling agency may be disapproved by the United States trustee (or the bankruptcy administrator, if any) at any time.

(3) (A) Subject to subparagraph (B), the requirements of paragraph (1) shall not apply with respect to a debtor who submits to the court a certification that—

(i) describes exigent circumstances that merit a waiver of the requirements of paragraph (1);

(ii) states that the debtor requested credit counseling services from an approved nonprofit budget and credit counseling agency, but was unable to obtain the services referred to in paragraph (1) during the 5-day period beginning on the date on which the debtor made that request; and

(iii) is satisfactory to the court.

(B) With respect to a debtor, an exemption under subparagraph (A) shall cease to apply to that debtor on the date on which the debtor meets the requirements of paragraph (1), but in no case may the exemption apply to that debtor after the date that is 30 days after the debtor files a petition, except that the court, for cause, may order an additional 15 days.

(4) The requirements of paragraph (1) shall not apply with respect to a debtor whom the court determines, after notice and hearing, is unable to complete those requirements because of incapacity, disability, or active military duty in a military combat zone. For the purposes of this paragraph, incapacity means that the debtor is impaired by reason of mental illness or mental deficiency so that he is incapable of realizing and making rational decisions with respect to his financial responsibilities; and 'disability' means that the debtor is so physically impaired as to be unable, after reasonable effort, to participate in an in person, telephone, or Internet briefing required under paragraph (1).

11 U.S.C. §707. Dismissal

Dismissal of a case or conversion to a case under chapter 11 or 13

(a) The court may dismiss a case under this chapter only after notice and a hearing and only for cause, including—

(1) unreasonable delay by the debtor that is prejudicial to creditors;

(2) nonpayment of any fees or charges required under chapter 123 of title 28; and

(3) failure of the debtor in a voluntary case to file, within fifteen days or such additional time as the court may allow after the filing of the petition commencing such case, the information required by paragraph (1) of section 521, but only on a motion by the United States trustee.

(b) (1) After notice and a hearing, the court, on its own motion or on a motion by the United States trustee, trustee (or bankruptcy administrator, if any), or any party in interest, may dismiss a case filed by an individual debtor under this chapter whose debts are primarily consumer debts, or, with the debtor's consent, convert such a case to a case under chapter 11 or 13 of this title, if it finds that the granting of relief would be an abuse of the provisions of this chapter. In making a determination whether to dismiss a case under this section, the court may not take into consideration whether a debtor has made, or continues to make, charitable contributions (that meet the definition of "charitable contribution" under section 548(d)(3)) to any qualified religious or charitable entity or organization (as that term is defined in section 548(d)(4)).

(2) (A) (i) In considering under paragraph (1) whether the granting of relief would be an abuse of the provisions of this chapter, the court shall presume abuse exists if the debtor's current monthly income reduced by the amounts determined under clauses (ii), (iii), and (iv), and multiplied by 60 is not less than the lesser of—

(I) 25 percent of the debtor's nonpriority unsecured claims in the case, or $6,000, whichever is greater; or

(II) $10,000.

(ii) (I) The debtor's monthly expenses shall be the debtor's applicable monthly expense amounts specified under the National Standards and Local Standards, and the debtor's actual monthly expenses for the categories specified as Other Necessary Expenses issued by the Internal Revenue Service for the area in which the debtor resides, as in effect on the date of the order for relief, for the debtor, the dependents of the debtor, and the spouse of the debtor in a joint case, if the spouse is not otherwise a dependent. Such expenses shall include reasonably necessary health insurance, disability insurance, and health savings account expenses for the debtor, the spouse of the debtor, or the dependents of the debtor. Notwithstanding any other provision of this clause, the monthly expenses of the debtor shall not include any payments for debts. In addition, the debtor's monthly expenses shall include the debtor's reasonably necessary expenses incurred to maintain the safety of the debtor and the family of the debtor from family violence as identified under section 309 of the Family Violence Prevention and Services Act, or other applicable Federal law. The expenses included in the debtor's monthly expenses described in the preceding sentence shall be kept confidential by the court. In addition, if it is demonstrated that it is reasonable and necessary, the debtor's monthly expenses may also include an additional allowance for food and clothing of up to 5 percent of the food and clothing categories as specified by the National Standards issued by the Internal Revenue Service.

(II) In addition, the debtor's monthly expenses may include, if applicable, the continuation of actual expenses paid by the debtor that are reasonable and necessary for care and support of an elderly, chronically ill, or disabled household member or member of the debtor's immediate family (including parents, grandparents, siblings, children, and grandchildren of the debtor, the dependents of the debtor, and the spouse of the debtor in a joint case who is not a dependent) and who is unable to pay for such reasonable and necessary expenses.

(III) In addition, for a debtor eligible for chapter 13, the debtor's monthly expenses may include the actual administrative expenses of administering a chapter 13 plan for the district in which the debtor resides, up to an amount of 10 percent of the projected plan payments, as determined under schedules issued by the Executive Office for United States Trustees.

(IV) In addition, the debtor's monthly expenses may include the actual expenses for each dependent child less than 18 years of age, not to exceed $1,500 per year per child, to attend a private or public elementary or secondary school if the debtor provides documentation of such expenses and a detailed explanation of why such expenses are reasonable and necessary, and why such expenses are not already accounted for in the National Standards, Local Standards, or Other Necessary Expenses referred to in subclause (I).

(V) In addition, the debtor's monthly expenses may include an allowance for housing and utilities, in excess of the allowance specified by the Local Standards for housing and utilities issued by the Internal Revenue Service, based on the actual expenses for home energy costs if the debtor provides documentation of such actual expenses and demonstrates that such actual expenses are reasonable and necessary.

(iii) The debtor's average monthly payments on account of secured debts shall be calculated as the sum of—

(I) the total of all amounts scheduled as contractually due to secured creditors in each month of the 60 months following the date of the petition; and

(II) any additional payments to secured creditors necessary for the debtor, in filing a plan under chapter 13 of this title, to maintain possession of the debtor's primary residence, motor vehicle, or other property necessary for the support of the debtor and the debtor's dependents, that serves as collateral for secured debts;

divided by 60.

(iv) The debtor's expenses for payment of all priority claims (including priority child support and alimony claims) shall be calculated as the total amount of debts entitled to priority, divided by 60.

(B) (i) In any proceeding brought under this subsection, the presumption of abuse may only be rebutted by demonstrating special circumstances, such as a serious medical condition or a call or order to active duty in the Armed Forces, to the extent such special circumstances that justify additional expenses or adjustments of current monthly income for which there is no reasonable alternative.

(ii) In order to establish special circumstances, the debtor shall be required to itemize each additional expense or adjustment of income and to provide—

(I) documentation for such expense or adjustment to income; and

(II) a detailed explanation of the special circumstances that make such expenses or adjustment to income necessary and reasonable.

(iii) The debtor shall attest under oath to the accuracy of any information provided to demonstrate that additional expenses or adjustments to income are required.

(iv) The presumption of abuse may only be rebutted if the additional expenses or adjustments to income referred to in clause (i) cause the product of the debtor's current monthly income reduced by the amounts determined under clauses (ii), (iii), and (iv) of subparagraph (A) when multiplied by 60 to be less than the lesser of—

(I) 25 percent of the debtor's nonpriority unsecured claims, or $6,000, whichever is greater; or

(II) $10,000.

(C) As part of the schedule of current income and expenditures required under section 521, the debtor shall include a statement of the debtor's current monthly income, and the calculations that determine whether a presumption arises under subparagraph (A)(i), that show how each such amount is calculated.

(D) Subparagraphs (A) through (C) shall not apply, and the court may not dismiss or convert a case based on any form of means testing, if the debtor is a disabled veteran (as defined in section 3741(1) of title 38), and the indebtedness occurred primarily during a period during which he or she was—

(i) on active duty (as defined in section 101(d)(1) of title 10); or

(ii) performing a homeland defense activity (as defined in section 901(1) of title 32).

(3) In considering under paragraph (1) whether the granting of relief would be an abuse of the provisions of this chapter in a case in which the presumption in subparagraph (A)(i) of such paragraph does not arise or is rebutted, the court shall consider—

(A) whether the debtor filed the petition in bad faith; or

(B) the totality of the circumstances (including whether the debtor seeks to reject a personal services contract and the financial need for such rejection as sought by the debtor) of the debtor's financial situation demonstrates abuse.

(4) (A) The court, on its own initiative or on the motion of a party in interest, in accordance with the procedures described in rule 9011 of the Federal Rules of Bankruptcy Procedure, may order the attorney for the debtor to reimburse the trustee for all reasonable costs in prosecuting a motion filed under section 707(b), including reasonable attorneys' fees, if—

(i) a trustee files a motion for dismissal or conversion under this subsection; and

(ii) the court—

(I) grants such motion; and

(II) finds that the action of the attorney for the debtor in filing a case under this chapter violated rule 9011 of the Federal Rules of Bankruptcy Procedure.

(B) If the court finds that the attorney for the debtor violated rule 9011 of the Federal Rules of Bankruptcy Procedure, the court, on its own initiative or on the motion of a party in interest, in accordance with such procedures, may order—

(i) the assessment of an appropriate civil penalty against the attorney for the debtor; and

(ii) the payment of such civil penalty to the trustee, the United States trustee (or the bankruptcy administrator, if any).

(C) The signature of an attorney on a petition, pleading, or written motion shall constitute a certification that the attorney has—

(i) performed a reasonable investigation into the circumstances that gave rise to the petition, pleading, or written motion; and

(ii) determined that the petition, pleading, or written motion—

(I) is well grounded in fact; and

(II) is warranted by existing law or a good faith argument for the extension, modification, or reversal of existing law and does not constitute an abuse under paragraph (1).

(D) The signature of an attorney on the petition shall constitute a certification that the attorney has no knowledge after an inquiry that the information in the schedules filed with such petition is incorrect.

(5) (A) Except as provided in subparagraph (B) and subject to paragraph (6), the court, on its own initiative or on the motion of a party in interest, in accordance with the procedures described in rule 9011 of the Federal

Rules of Bankruptcy Procedure, may award a debtor all reasonable costs (including reasonable attorneys' fees) in contesting a motion filed by a party in interest (other than a trustee or United States trustee (or bankruptcy administrator, if any)) under this subsection if—

(i) the court does not grant the motion; and

(ii) the court finds that—

(I) the position of the party that filed the motion violated rule 9011 of the Federal Rules of Bankruptcy Procedure; or

(II) the attorney (if any) who filed the motion did not comply with the requirements of clauses (i) and (ii) of paragraph (4)(c), and the motion was made solely for the purpose of coercing a debtor into waiving a right guaranteed to the debtor under this title.

(B) A small business that has a claim of an aggregate amount less than $1,000 shall not be subject to subparagraph (A)(ii)(I).

(C) For purposes of this paragraph—

(i) the term 'small business' means an unincorporated business, partnership, corporation, association, or organization that—

(I) has fewer than 25 full-time employees as determined on the date on which the motion is filed; and

(II) is engaged in commercial or business activity; and

(ii) the number of employees of a wholly owned subsidiary of a corporation includes the employees of—

(I) a parent corporation; and

(II) any other subsidiary corporation of the parent corporation.

(6) Only the judge or United States trustee (or bankruptcy administrator, if any) may file a motion under section 707(b), if the current monthly income of the debtor, or in a joint case, the debtor and the debtor's spouse, as of the date of the order for relief, when multiplied by 12, is equal to or less than—

(A) in the case of a debtor in a household of 1 person, the median family income of the applicable State for 1 earner;

(B) in the case of a debtor in a household of 2, 3, or 4 individuals, the highest median family income of the applicable State for a family of the same number or fewer individuals; or

(C) in the case of a debtor in a household exceeding 4 individuals, the highest median family income of the applicable State for a family of 4 or fewer individuals, plus $525 per month for each individual in excess of 4.

(7) (A) No judge, United States trustee (or bankruptcy administrator, if any), trustee, or other party in interest may file a motion under paragraph (2) if the current monthly income of the debtor, including a veteran (as that term is defined in section 101 of title 38), and the debtor's spouse combined, as of the date of the order for relief when multiplied by 12, is equal to or less than—

(i) in the case of a debtor in a household of 1 person, the median family income of the applicable State for 1 earner;

(ii) in the case of a debtor in a household of 2, 3, or 4 individuals, the highest median family income of the applicable State for a family of the same number or fewer individuals; or

(iii) in the case of a debtor in a household exceeding 4 individuals, the highest median family income of the applicable State for a family of 4 or fewer individuals, plus $525 per month for each individual in excess of 4.

(B) In a case that is not a joint case, current monthly income of the debtor's spouse shall not be considered for purposes of subparagraph (A) if—

(i) (I) the debtor and the debtor's spouse are separated under applicable nonbankruptcy law; or

(II) the debtor and the debtor's spouse are living separate and apart, other than for the purpose of evading subparagraph (A); and

(ii) the debtor files a statement under penalty of perjury—

(I) specifying that the debtor meets the requirement of subclause (I) or (II) of clause (i); and

(II) disclosing the aggregate, or best estimate of the aggregate, amount of any cash or money payments received from the debtor's spouse attributed to the debtor's current monthly income.

(c) (1) In this subsection—

(A) the term 'crime of violence' has the meaning given such term in section 16 of title 18; and

(B) the term 'drug trafficking crime' has the meaning given such term in section 924(c)(2) of title 18.

(2) Except as provided in paragraph (3), after notice and a hearing, the court, on a motion by the victim of a crime of violence or a drug trafficking crime, may when it is in the best interest of the victim dismiss a voluntary case filed under

this chapter by a debtor who is an individual if such individual was convicted of such crime.

(3) The court may not dismiss a case under paragraph (2) if the debtor establishes by a preponderance of the evidence that the filing of a case under this chapter is necessary to satisfy a claim for a domestic support obligation.

- *First U.S.A. v. Lamanna (In re Lamanna)*
    - Debtor able to pay 100% of debts within 3 years if he was under Chapter 13, but he filed under Chapter 7
        - Court found this to be "substantial abuse"
    - The test for *substantial abuse* is *"totality of the circumstances"*
        - No longer "substantial abuse" – now it is just "abuse"

11 U.S.C. §303. Involuntary Petitions

Involuntary cases

(a) An involuntary case may be commenced only under chapter 7 or 11 of this title, and only against a person, except a farmer, family farmer, or a corporation that is not a moneyed, business, or commercial corporation, that may be a debtor under the chapter under which such case is commenced.

(b) An involuntary case against a person is commenced by the filing with the bankruptcy court of a petition under chapter 7 or 11 of this title

(1) by three or more entities, each of which is either a holder of a claim against such person that is not contingent as to liability or the subject of a bona fide dispute as to liability or amount, or an indenture trustee representing such a holder, if such noncontingent, undisputed claims aggregate at least $10,000[3] more than the value of any lien on property of the debtor securing such claims held by the holders of such claims;[4]

(2) if there are fewer than 12 such holders, excluding any employee or insider of such person and any transferee of a transfer that is voidable under section 544, 545, 547, 548, 549, or 724(a) of this title, by one or more of such holders that hold in the aggregate at least $10,000[5] of such claims;

(3) if such person is a partnership—

[3] Currently $12,300.

[4] Effective as of the date of enactment of the Act; applicable to any case under the Bankruptcy Code pending or commenced on or after such date. Pub. L. No. 109-8, 119 Stat. 23, Sec. 1234(b).

[5] Currently $12,300.

(A) by fewer than all of the general partners in such partnership; or

(B) if relief has been ordered under this title with respect to all of the general partners in such partnership, by a general partner in such partnership, the trustee of such a general partner, or a holder of a claim against such partnership; or

(4) by a foreign representative of the estate in a foreign proceeding concerning such person.

(c) After the filing of a petition under this section but before the case is dismissed or relief is ordered, a creditor holding an unsecured claim that is not contingent, other than a creditor filing under subsection (b) of this section, may join in the petition with the same effect as if such joining creditor were a petitioning creditor under subsection (b) of this section.

(d) The debtor, or a general partner in a partnership debtor that did not join in the petition, may file an answer to a petition under this section.

(e) After notice and a hearing, and for cause, the court may require the petitioners under this section to file a bond to indemnify the debtor for such amounts as the court may later allow under subsection (i) of this section.

(f) Notwithstanding section 363 of this title, except to the extent that the court orders otherwise, and until an order for relief in the case, any business of the debtor may continue to operate, and the debtor may continue to use, acquire, or dispose of property as if an involuntary case concerning the debtor had not been commenced.

(g) At any time after the commencement of an involuntary case under chapter 7 of this title but before an order for relief in the case, the court, on request of a party in interest, after notice to the debtor and a hearing, and if necessary to preserve the property of the estate or to prevent loss to the estate, may order the United States trustee to appoint an interim trustee under section 701 of this title to take possession of the property of the estate and to operate any business of the debtor. Before an order for relief, the debtor may regain possession of property in the possession of a trustee ordered appointed under this subsection if the debtor files such bond as the court requires, conditioned on the debtor's accounting for and delivering to the trustee, if there is an order for relief in the case, such property, or the value, as of the date the debtor regains possession, of such property.

(h) If the petition is not timely controverted, the court shall order relief against the debtor in an involuntary case under the chapter under which the petition was filed. Otherwise, after trial, the court shall order relief against the debtor in an involuntary case under the chapter under which the petition was filed, only if—

(1) the debtor is generally not paying such debtor's debts as such debts become due unless such debts are the subject of a bona fide dispute as to liability or amount;[6] or

(2) within 120 days before the date of the filing of the petition, a custodian, other than a trustee, receiver, or agent appointed or authorized to take charge of less than substantially all of the property of the debtor for the purpose of enforcing a lien against such property, was appointed or took possession.

(i) If the court dismisses a petition under this section other than on consent of all petitioners and the debtor, and if the debtor does not waive the right to judgment under this subsection, the court may grant judgment—

(1) against the petitioners and in favor of the debtor for—

(A) costs; or

(B) a reasonable attorney's fee; or

(2) against any petitioner that filed the petition in bad faith, for—

(A) any damages proximately caused by such filing; or

(B) punitive damages.

(j) Only after notice to all creditors and a hearing may the court dismiss a petition filed under this section—

(1) on the motion of a petitioner;

(2) on consent of all petitioners and the debtor; or

(3) for want of prosecution.

~~(k) Notwithstanding subsection (a) of this section, an involuntary case may be commenced against a foreign bank that is not engaged in such business in the United States only under chapter 7 of this title and only if a foreign proceeding concerning such bank is pending.~~

(l) (1) if—

(A) the petition under this section is false or contains any materially false, fictitious, or fraudulent statement;

(B) the debtor is an individual; and

(C) the court dismisses such petition,

[6] Effective as of the date of enactment of the Act; applicable to any case under the Bankruptcy Code pending or commenced on or after such date. Pub. L. No. 109-8, 119 Stat. 23, Sec. 1234(b).

the court, upon the motion of the debtor, shall seal all the records of the court relating to such petition, and all references to such petition.

(2) If the debtor is an individual and the court dismisses the petition under this section, the court may enter an order prohibiting all consumer reporting agencies (as defined in section 603(f) of the Fair Credit Reporting Act (15 U.S.C. 1681a(f))) from making any consumer report (as defined in section 603(d) of that Act) that contains any information relating to such petition or to the case commenced by the filing of such petition.

(3) Upon the expiration of the statute of limitations described in section 3282 of title 18, for a violation of section 152 or 157 of such title, the court, upon the motion of the debtor and for good cause, may expunge any records relating to a petition filed under this section.

- Involuntary petition can be filed by claimaints with no contingency with respect to liability or Not subject to a bona fide dispute
- *In re Lough*
  - Bank put her into involuntary
  - She disputed that she was liable under either the note or under the guaranty
  - Court dismissed the involuntary petition
  - Hillman- Guaranties live forever
  - Important to keep track of the guarantee and when the need
  - Need three creditors to file unless there are less than 12 creditors
- *Basin Elec. Power Coop. v. Midwest Procession Company*
  - Basin filed the petition knowing there were more than 12 creditors
  - Given the opportunity to amend and pulled in two other creditor
  - Done in bad faith
  - If you know there are less than twelve and file with less than three then it is a fraudulent attempt to confer jurisdiction onto the bankruptcy court
  - If the answer to an involuntary petition filed by fewer than three creditors avers the existence of twelve or more creditors the debtor shall file with the answer a list of all creditors
  - Invols are normally filed when there is a fear that the debtor will take the money and run

11 U.S.C. §541. Property of the Estate

Property of the estate

(a) The commencement of a case under section 301, 302, or 303 of this title creates an estate. Such estate is comprised of all the following property, wherever located and by whomever held:

(1) Except as provided in subsections (b) and (c)(2) of this section, all legal or equitable interests of the debtor in property as of the commencement of the case.

(2) All interests of the debtor and the debtor's spouse in community property as of the commencement of the case that is—

(A) under the sole, equal, or joint management and control of the debtor; or

(B) liable for an allowable claim against the debtor, or for both an allowable claim against the debtor and an allowable claim against the debtor's spouse, to the extent that such interest is so liable.

(3) Any interest in property that the trustee recovers under section 329(b), 363(n), 543, 550, 553, or 723 of this title.

(4) Any interest in property preserved for the benefit of or ordered transferred to the estate under section 510(c) or 551 of this title.

(5) Any interest in property that would have been property of the estate if such interest had been an interest of the debtor on the date of the filing of the petition, and that the debtor acquires or becomes entitled to acquire within 180 days after such date—

(A) by bequest, devise, or inheritance;

(B) as a result of a property settlement agreement with the debtor's spouse, or of an interlocutory or final divorce decree; or

(C) as a beneficiary of a life insurance policy or of a death benefit plan.

(6) Proceeds, product, offspring, rents, or profits of or from property of the estate, except such as are earnings from services performed by an individual debtor after the commencement of the case.

(7) Any interest in property that the estate acquires after the commencement of the case.

(b) Property of the estate does not include—

(1) any power that the debtor may exercise solely for the benefit of an entity other than the debtor;

(2) any interest of the debtor as a lessee under a lease of nonresidential real property that has terminated at the expiration of the stated term of such lease before the commencement of the case under this title, and ceases to include any interest of the debtor as a lessee under a lease of nonresidential real

property that has terminated at the expiration of the stated term of such lease during the case;

(3) any eligibility of the debtor to participate in programs authorized under the Higher Education Act of 1965(20 U.S.C. 1001 et seq.; 42 U.S.C. 2751 et seq.), or any accreditation status or State licensure of the debtor as an educational institution;

(4) any interest of the debtor in liquid or gaseous hydrocarbons to the extent that—

(A) (i) the debtor has transferred or has agreed to transfer such interest pursuant to a farmout agreement or any written agreement directly related to a farmout agreement; and

(ii) but for the operation of this paragraph, the estate could include the interest referred to in clause (i) only by virtue of section 365 or 544(a)(3) of this title; ~~or~~

(B) (i) the debtor has transferred such interest pursuant to a written conveyance of a production payment to an entity that does not participate in the operation of the property from which such production payment is transferred; and

(ii) but for the operation of this paragraph, the estate could include the interest referred to in clause (i) only by virtue of section 365 or 542 of this title;

(5) funds placed in an education individual retirement account (as defined in section 530(b)(1) of the Internal Revenue Code of 1986) not later than 365 days before the date of the filing of the petition in a case under this title, but—

(A) only if the designated beneficiary of such account was a child, stepchild, grandchild, or stepgrandchild of the debtor for the taxable year for which funds were placed in such account;

(B) only to the extent that such funds—

(i) are not pledged or promised to any entity in connection with any extension of credit; and

(ii) are not excess contributions (as described in section 4973(e) of the Internal Revenue Code of 1986); and

(C) in the case of funds placed in all such accounts having the same designated beneficiary not earlier than 720 days nor later than 365 days before such date, only so much of such funds as does not exceed $5,000;

(6) funds used to purchase a tuition credit or certificate or contributed to an account in accordance with section 529(b)(1)(A) of the Internal Revenue Code

of 1986 under a qualified State tuition program (as defined in section 529(b)(1) of such Code) not later than 365 days before the date of the filing of the petition in a case under this title, but—

(A) only if the designated beneficiary of the amounts paid or contributed to such tuition program was a child, stepchild, grandchild, or stepgrandchild of the debtor for the taxable year for which funds were paid or contributed;

(B) with respect to the aggregate amount paid or contributed to such program having the same designated beneficiary, only so much of such amount as does not exceed the total contributions permitted under section 529(b)(7) of such Code with respect to such beneficiary, as adjusted beginning on the date of the filing of the petition in a case under this title by the annual increase or decrease (rounded to the nearest tenth of 1 percent) in the education expenditure category of the Consumer Price Index prepared by the Department of Labor; and

(C) in the case of funds paid or contributed to such program having the same designated beneficiary not earlier than 720 days nor later than 365 days before such date, only so much of such funds as does not exceed $5,000;

(7) any amount—

(A) withheld by an employer from the wages of employees for payment as contributions—

(i) to—

(I) an employee benefit plan that is subject to title I of the Employee Retirement Income Security Act of 1974 or under an employee benefit plan which is a governmental plan under section 414(d) of the Internal Revenue Code of 1986;

(II) a deferred compensation plan under section 457 of the Internal Revenue Code of 1986; or

(III) a tax-deferred annuity under section 403(b) of the Internal Revenue Code of 1986;

except that such amount under this subparagraph shall not constitute disposable income as defined in section 1325(b)(2); or

(ii) to a health insurance plan regulated by State law whether or not subject to such title; or

(B) received by an employer from employees for payment as contributions—

(i) to—

(I) an employee benefit plan that is subject to title I of the Employee Retirement Income Security Act of 1974 or under an employee benefit plan which is a governmental plan under section 414(d) of the Internal Revenue Code of 1986;

(II) a deferred compensation plan under section 457 of the Internal Revenue Code of 1986; or

(III) a tax-deferred annuity under section 403(b) of the Internal Revenue Code of 1986;

except that such amount under this subparagraph shall not constitute disposable income, as defined in section 1325(b)(2); or

(ii) to a health insurance plan regulated by State law whether or not subject to such title;

(8) subject to subchapter III of chapter 5, any interest of the debtor in property where the debtor pledged or sold tangible personal property (other than securities or written or printed evidences of indebtedness or title) as collateral for a loan or advance of money given by a person licensed under law to make such loans or advances, where—

(A) the tangible personal property is in the possession of the pledgee or transferee;

(B) the debtor has no obligation to repay the money, redeem the collateral, or buy back the property at a stipulated price; and

(C) neither the debtor nor the trustee have exercised any right to redeem provided under the contract or State law, in a timely manner as provided under State law and section 108(b); or

(9) any interest in cash or cash equivalents that constitute proceeds of a sale by the debtor of a money order that is made—

(A) on or after the date that is 14 days prior to the date on which the petition Is filed; and

(B) under an agreement with a money order issuer that prohibits the commingling of such proceeds with property of the debtor (notwithstanding that, contrary to the agreement, the proceeds may have been commingled with property of the debtor), unless the money order issuer had not taken action, prior to the filing of the petition, to require compliance with the prohibition. Paragraph (4) shall not be construed to exclude from the estate any consideration the debtor retains, receives, or is entitled to receive for transferring an interest in liquid or gaseous hydrocarbons pursuant to a farmout agreement.

(c) (1) Except as provided in paragraph (2) of this subsection, an interest of the debtor in property becomes property of the estate under subsection (a)(1), (a)(2), or (a)(5) of this section notwithstanding any provision in an agreement, transfer instrument, or applicable nonbankruptcy law—

(A) that restricts or conditions transfer of such interest by the debtor; or

(B) that is conditioned on the insolvency or financial condition of the debtor, on the commencement of a case under this title, or on the appointment of or taking possession by a trustee in a case under this title or a custodian before such commencement, and that effects or gives an option to effect a forfeiture, modification, or termination of the debtor's interest in property.

(2) A restriction on the transfer of a beneficial interest of the debtor in a trust that is enforceable under applicable nonbankruptcy law is enforceable in a case under this title.

(d) Property in which the debtor holds, as of the commencement of the case, only legal title and not an equitable interest, such as a mortgage secured by real property, or an interest in such a mortgage, sold by the debtor but as to which the debtor retains legal title to service or supervise the servicing of such mortgage or interest, becomes property of the estate under subsection (a)(1) or (2) of this section only to the extent of the debtor's legal title to such property, but not to the extent of any equitable interest in such property that the debtor does not hold.

(e) In determining whether any of the relationships specified in paragraph (5)(A) or (6)(A) of subsection (b) exists, a legally adopted child of an individual (and a child who is a member of an individual's household, if placed with such individual by an authorized placement agency for legal adoption by such individual), or a foster child of an individual (if such child has as the child's principal place of abode the home of the debtor and is a member of the debtor's household) shall be treated as a child of such individual by blood.

(f) Notwithstanding any other provision of this title, property that is held by a debtor that is a corporation described in section 501(c)(3) of the Internal Revenue Code of 1986 and exempt from tax under section 501(a) of such Code may be transferred to an entity that is not such a corporation, but only under the same conditions as would apply if the debtor had not filed a case under this title.[7]

- The commencement of a case creates an estate
- POE- a snapshot of what the debtor possesses at the time of the petition
- Look at all the debtor has. Then make some exclusions to get to POE
- Some things are excluded from the estate (ERISA)
- What is left after the exclusions is POE

[7] Effective as of the date of enactment of the Act; applicable to any case under the Bankruptcy Code pending or commenced on or after such date. The Act further provides, however, that "the court shall not confirm a plan under chapter 11 of title 11, United States Code, without considering whether this section would substantially affect the rights of a party in interest who first acquired rights with respect to the debtor after the date of the filing of the petition." Pub. L. No. 109-8, 119 Stat. 23, Sec. 1221(d).

- POE is what the trustee or debtor in possession deals with in the bankruptcy
- Trustee will gather the POE and reduce it to cash and distribute it according to the code priorities
- Debtor is entitled to some things- these are exemptions
- "All of the rest minus the exclusions and the exemptions is what is POE
- "Hillman- it is easy if it is an asset that the debtor owns
- Have to go to state law to determine what the nature of the interest is in assets. It is only when we are look at the state law that we can determine what is property of the estate
- Unless those state law rules are displaced by bankruptcy law, then state law rules
- Trying to determine what state law rules would say is POE

11 U.S.C. §544. Trustee as a Lien Creditor

Trustee as lien creditor and as successor to certain creditors and purchasers

(a) The trustee shall have, as of the commencement of the case, and without regard to any knowledge of the trustee or of any creditor, the rights and powers of, or may avoid any transfer of property of the debtor or any obligation incurred by the debtor that is voidable by—

(1) a creditor that extends credit to the debtor at the time of the commencement of the case, and that obtains, at such time and with respect to such credit, a judicial lien on all property on which a creditor on a simple contract could have obtained such a judicial lien, whether or not such a creditor exists;

(2) a creditor that extends credit to the debtor at the time of the commencement of the case, and obtains, at such time and with respect to such credit, an execution against the debtor that is returned unsatisfied at such time, whether or not such a creditor exists; or

(3) a bona fide purchaser of real property, other than fixtures, from the debtor, against whom applicable law permits such transfer to be perfected, that obtains the status of a bona fide purchaser and has perfected such transfer at the time of the commencement of the case, whether or not such a purchaser exists.

(b) (1) Except as provided in paragraph (2), the trustee may avoid any transfer of an interest of the debtor in property or any obligation incurred by the debtor that is voidable under applicable law by a creditor holding an unsecured claim that is allowable under section 502 of this title or that is not allowable only under section 502(e) of this title.

(2) Paragraph (1) shall not apply to a transfer of a charitable contribution (as that term is defined in section 548(d)(3)) that is not covered under section 548(a)(1)(B), by reason of section 548(a)(2). Any claim by any person to recover a transferred contribution described in the preceding sentence under Federal or State law in a Federal or State court shall be preempted by the commencement of the case.

- *United Sates v. Whiting Pools, Inc.* (IRS tax lien on property)
    - Notwithstanding the federal tax lien on the property, the debtor still has some interest in the property and it is POE and it has to go back to the trustee of the debtor in possession
    - Not held to be any higher than any other secured creditors
    - When property seized prior to the filing of a petition is draw into the Chapter 11 reorganization estate, the Service's tax lien is not dissolved, nor is its status as a secured creditor
- *Patterson v. Shumate (syllabus)* (Pension funds not admitted in bankruptcy)
    - The plain language of the Bankruptcy Code and ERISA establishes that an antialienation provision in a qualified pension plan constitutes a restriction on transfer enforceable under "applicable nonbankruptcy law" for purposes of §541(c)(2)
- *In re Herzig* (spend-thrift trust)
    - Father knew that his son was a spendthrift- experimental filmmaker
    - Wanted to protect James from himself
    - James was not happy with William being his trustee
    - Created a mechanism whereby he could get rid of William
    - Added this extra language to the will and the effect of it was to destroy the spendthrift trust
    - Because of this painless process, could dissolve the trust
    - Because it was not a spendthrift trust it became POE
    - Moving out, and forcing William resign would automatically make the trust dissolve
    - Hillman- can either make a spendthrift trust spendthrift, or not spendthrift
- Mortgage example prior to the 1980's:
    - Mortgage can be considered *equity of redemption*
    - Seller sells you a house – you pay bank a mortgage – bank pays the seller the money for the house – you pay off the mortgage to the bank
    - Post 1980's:
        - Now there are things called *mortgage bankers* (not just your normal neighborhood bank)

- One difference is that mortgage bankers didn't have any money – how could they fund it?
  - They sold the mortgage before they got it
  - They would sell mortgage to the bank
- Now you make your monthly payments to the mortgage banker, who is now a *servicer* – they take an amount out of your check as a servicing fee and sends the rest to the bank

- Problem arises:
  - The bank doesn't have the money to cover the mortgage so the mortgage banker borrows the money from a *warehousing bank* – they pay off the house and when the bank gets enough money they buy the mortgage from the mortgage banker – now the mortgage banker pays off the warehouse banker
  - Real problem arises when mortgage bankers started going bankrupt
  - The mortgages become property of the estate (POE)
  - 541(d) says that the only thing that is POE is the servicing right

Matrimonial Issues

- When you have two or more owners of property, they both own it
  - Two possibilities if not married:
    - Tenants in common – each have an undivided one-half interest which you can sell
      - If one of the two dies, the property will go to the heirs – look to the will
    - Joint-tenancy – still have undivided interest in property, but they are connected
      - Biggest difference is that if one dies, the other owns the whole things
      - If one sells his interest, he destroys the joint-tenancy – now there is a tenancy in common

- It can even be broken by selling interest to a buyer and having the buyer sell it back – this breaks the joint-tenancy
- If married:
  - Tenancy by the entirety – like a joint-tenancy with two basic differences:
    - Parties have to be married – when either dies, the other owns it
    - Tenants by the entirety are a unit – have to act together – one tenant can't transfer interest – it takes two
    - In most states, a tenancy by the entirety can't be reached by a creditor of only one of the partners

- *Attachment* – a lien on the property
  - Once the creditor gets a judgment, they can get an *execution*
  - In MA, tenancy by the entirety will be POEed just as if it was a joint-tenancy
    - Creditor can put an attachment on a property – which essentially doesn't give it the power to do anything
      - However, once there is a divorce, or the non-debtor spouse dies, or it is not the non-debtor spouse's principle place of residence, it can be seized
- *Peebles v. Minnis* (removal of the defendants' attachment on property he owns with his wife)
  - Under the statute you cannot seize or execute, but you can attach
  - Cannot do anything with the attachment
  - Hillman- you can put your attachment on the property. Someday something will happen: death divorce, or will no longer be the principal residence and then you can execute on your attachment

        - These future possibilities are sufficient to support attachment
    - Hillman- are a result of this case- in Mass property that is owned by T by E will be POE just as it would in JT and T in C
- *Mass. Gen. Laws ch. 209 §1 – Domestic Relations – Husband and Wife General Provisions*
        - "The interest of a debtor spouse in property held as tenants by the entirety shall not be subject to seizure or execution by a creditor of such debtor spouse so long as such property is the principal residence of the nondebtor spouse."
- *In re Perry*
    - *In re Cox*
    - *In re Keiter*

Constructive Trusts

- *In re DVI, Inc.*
    - Court found that a constructive trust could not be avoided.
    - How did the court determine whether there was a constructive trust?
    - Went to Illinois law- under Illinois law this would be a constructive trust
    - H- will find cited in DVI- whether a constructive trust wins or loses
    - 541 v. 547 battle
    - Majority of courts conclude that 541(d) is subject to the rights of the debtor to avoid an unperfected interest in the property under other provisions of the bankruptcy Code
    - In re Omegas group- held that a constructive trust only beats the 544 powers of a trustee only if it has been judicially determined before the bankruptcy to be a constructive trust
    - ALR note 96 ALR fed 100, Power of trustee in bankruptcy to defeat rights of beneficiary under the bankruptcy code
    - Property is in the name of one party and another party is claiming an interest
    - H- this battle rages to this day

- Hot cases are divorce cases, but the other cases have more change involved

- **Post-petition Earnings**
  - *Jess v. Carey (In re Jess)* (attorney fee as asset under pre-petition Chapter 7)
    - Issue is whether work done prior to the filing of a bankruptcy petition can be claimed as pre-petition or post petition assets?
    - Trustee sought turnover of a portion of a contingency fee payment attributable to pre-petition work performed by the Debtor, an attorney
    - The bankruptcy court granted the request and the Debtor appeals
      - Court concludes that a portion of the fee earned prior to the Debtor's filing is an asset of the chapter 7 estate
    - "The Tully court recognized the policy implications of its result: 'a reversal of the bankruptcy court would allow [real estate] brokers to file bankruptcy petitions immediately before the close of escrow and have the commission deemed a post-petition earning, not property of the estate."
    - "Here, as the bankruptcy court pointed out, Jess performed work per-petition for which he was paid post-petition. Although he had only a contingent interest in the fee, he had some interest which can be included in the bankruptcy estate."

11 U.S.C. §522. Exemptions

Exemptions

(a) In this section—

(1) "dependent" includes spouse, whether or not actually dependent; and

(2) "value" means fair market value as of the date of the filing of the petition or, with respect to property that becomes property of the estate after such date, as of the date such property becomes property of the estate.

(b) (1) Notwithstanding section 541 of this title, an individual debtor may exempt from property of the estate the property listed in either paragraph (2) or, in the alternative, paragraph (3) of this subsection. In joint cases filed under section 302 of this title and individual cases filed under section 301 or 303 of this title by or against debtors who are husband and wife, and whose estates are ordered to be jointly administered under Rule 1015(b) of the Federal Rules of Bankruptcy Procedure, one debtor may not elect to exempt property listed in paragraph (2) and the other debtor elect to exempt property listed in paragraph (3) of this subsection. If the parties cannot agree on the alternative to be elected, they shall be deemed to elect paragraph (2), where such election is permitted under the law of the jurisdiction where the case is filed.

(2) Property listed in this paragraph is property that is specified under subsection (d), unless the State law that is applicable to the debtor under paragraph (3)(A) specifically does not so authorize.

(3) Property listed in this paragraph is—

(A) subject to subsections (o) and (p),[8] any property that is exempt under Federal law, other than subsection (d) of this section, or State or local law that is applicable on the date of the filing of the petition at the place in which the debtor's domicile has been located for the 730 days immediately preceding the date of the filing of the petition or if the debtor's domicile has not been located at a single State for such 730-day period, the place in which the debtor's domicile was located for 180 days immediately preceding the 730-day period or for a longer portion of such 180-day period than in any other place;

(B) any interest in property in which the debtor had, immediately before the commencement of the case, an interest as a tenant by the entirety or joint tenant to the extent that such interest as a tenant by the entirety or joint tenant is exempt from process under applicable nonbankruptcy law.; and

(C) retirement funds to the extent that those funds are in a fund or account that is exempt from taxation under section 401, 403, 408, 408A, 414, 457, or 501(a) of the Internal Revenue Code of 1986.

If the effect of the domiciliary requirement under subparagraph (A) is to render the debtor ineligible for any exemption, the debtor may elect to exempt property that is specified under subsection (d).

(4) For purposes of paragraph (3)(c) and subsection (d)(12), the following shall apply:

[8] Effective 180 days after the date of enactment of the Act; applicable to any case under the Bankruptcy Code commenced on or after the date of enactment. Pub. L. No. 109-8, 119 Stat. 23, Sec. 1501(2).

(A) If the retirement funds are in a retirement fund that has received a favorable determination under section 7805 of the Internal Revenue Code of 1986, and that determination is in effect as of the date of the filing of the petition in a case under this title, those funds shall be presumed to be exempt from the estate.

(B) If the retirement funds are in a retirement fund that has not received a favorable determination under such section 7805, those funds are exempt from the estate if the debtor demonstrates that—

(i) no prior determination to the contrary has been made by a court or the Internal Revenue Service; and

(ii) (I) the retirement fund is in substantial compliance with the applicable requirements of the Internal Revenue Code of 1986; or

(II) the retirement fund fails to be in substantial compliance with the applicable requirements of the Internal Revenue Code of 1986 and the debtor is not materially responsible for that failure.

(C) A direct transfer of retirement funds from 1 fund or account that is exempt from taxation under section 401, 403, 408, 408A, 414, 457, or 501(a) of the Internal Revenue Code of 1986, under section 401(a)(31) of the Internal Revenue Code of 1986, or otherwise, shall not cease to qualify for exemption under paragraph (3)(C) or subsection (d)(12) by reason of such direct transfer.

(D) (i) Any distribution that qualifies as an eligible rollover distribution within the meaning of section 402(c) of the Internal Revenue Code of 1986 or that is described in clause (ii) shall not cease to qualify for exemption under paragraph (3)(c) or subsection (d)(12) by reason of such distribution.

(ii) A distribution described in this clause is an amount that—

(I) has been distributed from a fund or account that is exempt from taxation under section 401, 403, 408, 408A, 414, 457, or 501(a) of the Internal Revenue Code of 1986; and

(II) to the extent allowed by law, is deposited in such a fund or account not later than 60 days after the distribution of such amount.

(c) Unless the case is dismissed, property exempted under this section is not liable during or after the case for any debt of the debtor that arose, or that is determined under section 502 of this title as if such debt had arisen, before the commencement of the case, except—

(1) a debt of a kind specified in paragraph (1) or (5) of section 523(a) (in which case, notwithstanding any provision of applicable nonbankruptcy law to the contrary, such property shall be liable for a debt of a kind specified in section 523(a)(5));

(2) a debt secured by a lien that is—

(A) (i) not avoided under subsection (f) or (g) of this section or under section 544, 545, 547, 548, 549, or 724(a) of this title; and

(ii) not void under section 506(d) of this title; or

(B) a tax lien, notice of which is properly filed;

(3) a debt of a kind specified in section 523(a)(4) or 523(a)(6) of this title owed by an institution-affiliated party of an insured depository institution to a Federal depository institutions regulatory agency acting in its capacity as conservator, receiver, or liquidating agent for such institution; or

(4) a debt in connection with fraud in the obtaining or providing of any scholarship, grant, loan, tuition, discount, award, or other financial assistance for purposes of financing an education at an institution of higher education (as that term is defined in section 101 of the Higher Education Act of 1965(20 U.S.C. 1001)).

(d) The following property may be exempted under subsection (b)(~~1~~2) of this section:

(1) The debtor's aggregate interest, not to exceed $15,000[9] in value, in real property or personal property that the debtor or a dependent of the debtor uses as a residence, in a cooperative that owns property that the debtor or a dependent of the debtor uses as a residence, or in a burial plot for the debtor or a dependent of the debtor.

(2) The debtor's interest, not to exceed $2,400[10] in value, in one motor vehicle.

(3) The debtor's interest, not to exceed $400[11] in value in any particular item or $8,000[12] in aggregate value, in household furnishings, household goods, wearing apparel, appliances, books, animals, crops, or musical instruments, that are held primarily for the personal, family, or household use of the debtor or a dependent of the debtor.

(4) The debtor's aggregate interest, not to exceed $1,000[13] in value, in jewelry held primarily for the personal, family, or household use of the debtor or a dependent of the debtor.

---

9 Currently $18,450.
10 Currently $2,950.
11 Currently $475.
12 Currently $9,850.
13 Currently $1,225.

(5) The debtor's aggregate interest in any property, not to exceed in value $800[14] plus up to $7,500[15] of any unused amount of the exemption provided under paragraph (1) of this subsection.

(6) The debtor's aggregate interest, not to exceed $1,500[16] in value, in any implements, professional books, or tools, of the trade of the debtor or the trade of a dependent of the debtor.

(7) Any unmatured life insurance contract owned by the debtor, other than a credit life insurance contract.

(8) The debtor's aggregate interest, not to exceed in value $8,000[17] less any amount of property of the estate transferred in the manner specified in section 542(d) of this title, in any accrued dividend or interest under, or loan value of, any unmatured life insurance contract owned by the debtor under which the insured is the debtor or an individual of whom the debtor is a dependent.

(9) Professionally prescribed health aids for the debtor or a dependent of the debtor.

(10) The debtor's right to receive—

(A) a social security benefit, unemployment compensation, or a local public assistance benefit;

(B) a veterans' benefit;

(C) a disability, illness, or unemployment benefit;

(D) alimony, support, or separate maintenance, to the extent reasonably necessary for the support of the debtor and any dependent of the debtor;

(E) a payment under a stock bonus, pension, profitsharing, annuity, or similar plan or contract on account of illness, disability, death, age, or length of service, to the extent reasonably necessary for the support of the debtor and any dependent of the debtor, unless—

(i) such plan or contract was established by or under the auspices of an insider that employed the debtor at the time the debtor's rights under such plan or contract arose;

(ii) such payment is on account of age or length of service; and (iii) such plan or contract does not qualify under section 401(a), 403(a), 403(b), or 408 of the Internal Revenue Code of 1986.

---

[14] Currently $975.
[15] Currently $9,250.
[16] Currently $1,850.
[17] Currently $9,850.

(11) The debtor's right to receive, or property that is traceable to—

(A) an award under a crime victim's reparation law;

(B) a payment on account of the wrongful death of an individual of whom the debtor was a dependent, to the extent reasonably necessary for the support of the debtor and any dependent of the debtor;

(C) a payment under a life insurance contract that insured the life of an individual of whom the debtor was a dependent on the date of such individual's death, to the extent reasonably necessary for the support of the debtor and any dependent of the debtor;

(D) a payment, not to exceed $15,000,[18] on account of personal bodily injury, not including pain and suffering or compensation for actual pecuniary loss, of the debtor or an individual of whom the debtor is a dependent; or

(E) a payment in compensation of loss of future earnings of the debtor or an individual of whom the debtor is or was a dependent, to the extent reasonably necessary for the support of the debtor and any dependent of the debtor.

<u>(12) Retirement funds to the extent that those funds are in a fund or account that is exempt from taxation under section 401, 403, 408, 408A, 414, 457, or 501(a) of the Internal Revenue Code of 1986.</u>

(e) A waiver of an exemption executed in favor of a creditor that holds an unsecured claim against the debtor is unenforceable in a case under this title with respect to such claim against property that the debtor may exempt under subsection (b) of this section. A waiver by the debtor of a power under subsection (f) or (h) of this section to avoid a transfer, under subsection (g) or (i) of this section to exempt property, or under subsection (i) of this section to recover property or to preserve a transfer, is unenforceable in a case under this title.

(f) (1) Notwithstanding any waiver of exemptions but subject to paragraph (3), the debtor may avoid the fixing of a lien on an interest of the debtor in property to the extent that such lien impairs an exemption to which the debtor would have been entitled under subsection (b) of this section, if such lien is—

(A) a judicial lien, other than a judicial lien that secures a debt—<u>of a kind that is specified in section 523(a)(5); or</u>

(B) a nonpossessory, nonpurchase-money security interest in any—

(i) household furnishings, household goods, wearing apparel, appliances, books, animals, crops, musical instruments, or jewelry that are held primarily for the personal, family, or household use of the debtor or a dependent of the debtor;

[18] Currently $18,450.

(ii) implements, professional books, or tools, of the trade of the debtor or the trade of a dependent of the debtor; or

(iii) professionally prescribed health aids for the debtor or a dependent of the debtor.

(2) (A) For the purposes of this subsection, a lien shall be considered to impair an exemption to the extent that the sum of—

(i) the lien;

(ii) all other liens on the property; and

(iii) the amount of the exemption that the debtor could claim if there were no liens on the property; exceeds the value that the debtor's interest in the property would have in the absence of any liens.

(B) In the case of a property subject to more than 1 lien, a lien that has been avoided shall not be considered in making the calculation under subparagraph (A) with respect to other liens.

(C) This paragraph shall not apply with respect to a judgment arising out of a mortgage foreclosure.

(3) In a case in which State law that is applicable to the debtor—

(A) permits a person to voluntarily waive a right to claim exemptions under subsection (d) or prohibits a debtor from claiming exemptions under subsection (d); and

(B) either permits the debtor to claim exemptions under State law without limitation in amount, except to the extent that the debtor has permitted the fixing of a consensual lien on any property or prohibits avoidance of a consensual lien on property otherwise eligible to be claimed as exempt property; the debtor may not avoid the fixing of a lien on an interest of the debtor or a dependent of the debtor in property if the lien is a nonpossessory, nonpurchase-money security interest in implements, professional books, or tools of the trade of the debtor or a dependent of the debtor or farm animals or crops of the debtor or a dependent of the debtor to the extent the value of such implements, professional books, tools of the trade, animals, and crops exceeds $5,000.

(4) (A) Subject to subparagraph (B), for purposes of paragraph (1)(B), the term 'household goods' means—

(i) clothing;

(ii) furniture;

(iii) appliances;

(iv) 1 radio;

(v) 1 television;

(vi) 1 VCR;

(vii) linens;

(viii) china;

(ix) crockery;

(x) kitchenware;

(xi) educational materials and educational equipment primarily for the use of minor dependent children of the debtor;

(xii) medical equipment and supplies;

(xiii) furniture exclusively for the use of minor children, or elderly or disabled dependents of the debtor;

(xiv) personal effects (including the toys and hobby equipment of minor dependent children and wedding rings) of the debtor and the dependents of the debtor; and

(xv) 1 personal computer and related equipment.

(B) The term "household goods" does not include—

(i) works of art (unless by or of the debtor, or any relative of the debtor);

(ii) electronic entertainment equipment with a fair market value of more than $500 in the aggregate (except 1 television, 1 radio, and 1 VCR);

(iii) items acquired as antiques with a fair market value of more than $500 in the aggregate;

(iv) jewelry with a fair market value of more than $500 in the aggregate (except wedding rings); and

(v) a computer (except as otherwise provided for in this section), motor vehicle (including a tractor or lawn tractor), boat, or a motorized recreational device, conveyance, vehicle, watercraft, or aircraft.

(g) Notwithstanding sections 550 and 551 of this title, the debtor may exempt under subsection (b) of this section property that the trustee recovers under section 510(c)(2), 542, 543, 550, 551, or 553 of this title, to the extent that the debtor could have exempted such property under subsection (b) of this section if such property had not been transferred, if—

(1) (A) such transfer was not a voluntary transfer of such property by the debtor; and

(B) the debtor did not conceal such property; or

(2) the debtor could have avoided such transfer under subsection (f)(1)(B) of this section.

(h) The debtor may avoid a transfer of property of the debtor or recover a setoff to the extent that the debtor could have exempted such property under subsection (g)(1) of this section if the trustee had avoided such transfer, if—

(1) such transfer is avoidable by the trustee under section 544, 545, 547, 548, 549, or 724(a) of this title or recoverable by the trustee under section 553 of this title; and

(2) the trustee does not attempt to avoid such transfer.

(i) (1) If the debtor avoids a transfer or recovers a setoff under subsection (f) or (h) of this section, the debtor may recover in the manner prescribed by, and subject to the limitations of, section 550 of this title, the same as if the trustee had avoided such transfer, and may exempt any property so recovered under subsection (b) of this section.

(2) Notwithstanding section 551 of this title, a transfer avoided under section 544, 545, 547, 548, 549, or 724(a) of this title, under subsection (f) or (h) of this section, or property recovered under section 553 of this title, may be preserved for the benefit of the debtor to the extent that the debtor may exempt such property under subsection (g) of this section or paragraph (1) of this subsection.

(j) Notwithstanding subsections (g) and (i) of this section, the debtor may exempt a particular kind of property under subsections (g) and (i) of this section only to the extent that the debtor has exempted less property in value of such kind than that to which the debtor is entitled under subsection (b) of this section.

(k) Property that the debtor exempts under this section is not liable for payment of any administrative expense except—

(1) the aliquot share of the costs and expenses of avoiding a transfer of property that the debtor exempts under subsection (g) of this section, or of recovery of such property, that is attributable to the value of the portion of such property exempted in relation to the value of the property recovered; and

(2) any costs and expenses of avoiding a transfer under subsection (f) or (h) of this section, or of recovery of property under subsection (i)(1) of this section, that the debtor has not paid.

(l) The debtor shall file a list of property that the debtor claims as exempt under subsection (b) of this section. If the debtor does not file such a list, a dependent of the debtor may file such a list, or may claim property as exempt from property of the estate on behalf of the debtor. Unless a party in interest objects, the property claimed as exempt on such list is exempt.

(m) Subject to the limitation in subsection (b), this section shall apply separately with respect to each debtor in a joint case.

(n) For assets in individual retirement accounts described in section 408 or 408A of the Internal Revenue Code of 1986, other than a simplified employee pension under section 408(k) of such Code or a simple retirement account under section 408(p) of such Code, the aggregate value of such assets exempted under this section, without regard to amounts attributable to rollover contributions under section 402(c), 402(e)(6), 403(a)(4), 403(a)(5), and 403(b)(8) of the Internal Revenue Code of 1986, and earnings thereon, shall not exceed $1,000,000 in a case filed by a debtor who is an individual, except that such amount may be increased if the interests of justice so require.

(o) For purposes of subsection (b)(3)(A), and notwithstanding subsection (a), the value of an interest in—

(1) real or personal property that the debtor or a dependent of the debtor uses as a residence;

(2) a cooperative that owns property that the debtor or a dependent of the debtor uses as a residence;

(3) a burial plot for the debtor or a dependent of the debtor; or

(4) real or personal property that the debtor or a dependent of the debtor claims as a homestead;

shall be reduced to the extent that such value is attributable to any portion of any property that the debtor disposed of in the 10-year period ending on the date of the filing of the petition with the intent to hinder, delay, or defraud a creditor and that the debtor could not exempt, or that portion that the debtor could not exempt, under subsection (b), if on such date the debtor had held the property so disposed of.[19]

(p) (1) Except as provided in paragraph (2) of this subsection and sections 544 and 548, as a result of electing under subsection (b)(3)(A) to exempt property under State or local law, a debtor may not exempt any amount of interest that was acquired by the debtor during the 1215-day period preceding the date of the filing of the petition that exceeds in the aggregate $125,000 in value in—

(A) real or personal property that the debtor or a dependent of the debtor uses as a residence;

(B) a cooperative that owns property that the debtor or a dependent of the debtor uses as a residence;

[19] Effective 180 days after the date of enactment of Act; applicable to any case under the Bankruptcy Code commenced on or after the date of enactment. Pub. L. No. 109-8, 119 Stat. 23, Sec. 1501(2).

(C) a burial plot for the debtor or a dependent of the debtor; or

(D) real or personal property that the debtor or dependent of the debtor claims as a homestead.

(2) (A) The limitation under paragraph (1) shall not apply to an exemption claimed under subsection (b)(3)(A) by a family farmer for the principal residence of such farmer.

(B) For purposes of paragraph (1), any amount of such interest does not include any interest transferred from a debtor's previous principal residence (which was acquired prior to the beginning of such 1215-day period) into the debtor's current principal residence, if the debtor's previous and current residences are located in the same State.[20]

(q) (1) As a result of electing under subsection (b)(3)(A) to exempt property under State or local law, a debtor may not exempt any amount of an interest in property described in subparagraphs (A), (B), (C), and (D) of subsection (p)(1) which exceeds in the aggregate $125,000 if—

(A) the court determines, after notice and a hearing, that the debtor has been convicted of a felony (as defined in section 3156 of title 18), which under the circumstances, demonstrates that the filing of the case was an abuse of the provisions of this title; or

(B) the debtor owes a debt arising from—

(i) any violation of the Federal securities laws (as defined in section 3(a)(47) of the Securities Exchange Act of 1934), any State securities laws, or any regulation or order issued under Federal securities laws or State securities laws;

(ii) fraud, deceit, or manipulation in a fiduciary capacity or in connection with the purchase or sale of any security registered under section 12 or 15(d) of the Securities Exchange Act of 1934 or under section 6 of the Securities Act of 1933;

(iii) any civil remedy under section 1964 of title 18; or

(iv) any criminal act, intentional tort, or willful or reckless misconduct that caused serious physical injury or death to another individual in the preceding 5 years.

(2) Paragraph (1) shall not apply to the extent the amount of an interest in property described in subparagraphs (A), (B), (C), and (D) of subsection (p)(1)

[20] Effective 180 days after the date of enactment of the Act; applicable to any case under the Bankruptcy Code commenced on or after the date of enactment. Pub. L. No. 109-8, 119 Stat. 23, Sec. 1501(2).

<u>is reasonably necessary for the support of the debtor and any dependent of the debtor.</u>

- *Fed. R. Bankr. P. 4003*
    - *Taylor v. Freeland & Kronz* (validity of exemption after 30 day period)
        - Court read 4003(b)- objections must be filed with 30 days after the creditors meeting unless an extension is granted
        - Even though the exemption claimed was incorrect, the debtor got away with it because no one timely objected
        - Trustee wanted to reopen the debtor's petition to get the award money from an employment discrimination settlement
        - Taylor is trustee of Davis
        - Davis had a pending lawsuit against TWA in which she believed she would receive some money – she claimed this future settlement as exempt
        - Taylor never objected to this exemption within the specified period of time
        - After the 30 day limit, and after Davis received her money, Taylor claimed that the settlement money was part of the POE – the court did not agree
        - Theoretically, the exempt assets are what gives the debtor a fresh start
        - Pre-bankruptcy planning – convert non-exempt assets into exempt assets
        - If you fail to object to the exemption within the 30 days, you are out of luck
- *Hanson v. First National Bank* (sold everything at fair market value and bought life insurance)
    - Debtors, Hansons, converted non-exempt assets into exempt assets
    - Creditors argue that the Hansons acted with intent to defraud the creditors – need to find extringent evidence to prove this
    - Debtors sold assets to family members and friends, bought life insurance equaling just under $20,000, and prepaid mortgage – these are all exempt from seizure
    - Court did not find that there was extringent evidence to prove an intent to defraud – decisions such as this one

            would not be overturned unless the court was "clearly erroneous" in deciding
        - Where the debtor acts with actual intent to defraud creditors, his exemptions will be denied them
    - *Norwest Bank v. Tveten* (doctor being a "pig")
        - Physician owed 19,000,000 and put 700,000 into exempt property
        - Trial court found that there was an intent to defraud and the appeals court affirmed
        - Reason for the difference
        - Unless the decision below is clearly erroneous it will be sustained
        - Hillman- can do pre bankruptcy planning but cannot be a pig about it
        - So long as the numbers make you think of a fresh start you are okay
    - **Massachusetts Homestead**
        - *Mass. Gen. L. Ch. 188, §§1 –2, 4 – 7* (see page 93)
            - Homestead is not automatic in MA – have to declare
            - Does not exempt you from property taxes
            - May be acquired by owner or owners of a home, or one who rightfully possesses the premise by lease or otherwise and who occupy or intend to occupy homestead as principle place of residence
        - *Patriot Portfolio, LLC v. Weinstein (In re Weinstein)* (Bankruptcy Code preempting State)
            - Question in appeal is whether, under 11 U.S.C. §522, a Chapter 7 debtor may assert a homestead exemption for his residence acquired after a debt and attachment of a lien, despite the Massachusetts statute excepting the preexisting lien and debt from the homestead protection
            - Held that Bankruptcy Code §§522(f) and 522(c) preempt the Massachusetts provisions excepting preexisting liens and prior contracted debts from homestead protection
                - The courts allowed the homestead protection because Bankruptcy Code §522 preemtped the state exceptions

Executory Contracts

- Executory contract – definition offered by Professor Countryman - A contract under which the obligation of both the bankrupt and the other party to the contract are so far unperformed that the failure of either to complete performance would constitute a material breach excusing the performance of the other.
  - Leases are always executory contracts
- New statute elminated discretion in extending the time to assume or reject
- Only one extension
- H- will force debtor tenants to make the decision to assume or reject earlier than they earlier would have done. Some of these elections will be inappropriate. Will find that leases that they thought were good to assume in fact are not as they move closer to reorganization
- You can reject a contract that you previously assumed
- Hypos:
  - Non-executory
    - Pay 5 agree to give bushel next week. During the week File for bankruptcy. First party already performed so account receivable
    - If opposite would not be executory but have a claim against the estate for $5
  - Executory
    - Make a deal next week bushel of wheat pay when get it.
    - File during week. This is executory because it follows def.

11 U.S.C. §365. Executory contracts & unexpired leases

Executory contracts and unexpired leases

(a) Except as provided in sections 765 and 766 of this title and in subsections (b), (c), and (d) of this section, the trustee, subject to the court's approval, may assume or reject any executory contract or unexpired lease of the debtor.

(b) (1) If there has been a default in an executory contract or unexpired lease of the debtor, the trustee may not assume such contract or lease unless, at the time of assumption of such contract or lease, the trustee—

(A) cures, or provides adequate assurance that the trustee will promptly cure, such default other than a default that is a breach of a provision relating to the satisfaction of any provision (other than a penalty rate or penalty provision) relating to a default arising from any failure to perform nonmonetary obligations under an unexpired lease of real property, if it is impossible for the trustee to cure such default by performing nonmonetary acts at and after the time of assumption, except that if

<u>such default arises from a failure to operate in accordance with a nonresidential real property lease, then such default shall be cured by performance at and after the time of assumption in accordance with such lease, and pecuniary losses resulting from such default shall be compensated in accordance with the provisions of this paragraph</u>;

(B) compensates, or provides adequate assurance that the trustee will promptly compensate, a party other than the debtor to such contract or lease, for any actual pecuniary loss to such party resulting from such default; and

(C) provides adequate assurance of future performance under such contract or lease.

(2) Paragraph (1) of this subsection does not apply to a default that is a breach of a provision relating to—

(A) the insolvency or financial condition of the debtor at any time before the closing of the case;

(B) the commencement of a case under this title;

(C) the appointment of or taking possession by a trustee in a case under this title or a custodian before such commencement; or

(D) the satisfaction of any penalty rate or <u>penalty</u> provision relating to a default arising from any failure by the debtor to perform nonmonetary obligations under the executory contract or unexpired lease.

(3) For the purposes of paragraph (1) of this subsection and paragraph (2)(B) of subsection (f), adequate assurance of future performance of a lease of real property in a shopping center includes adequate assurance—

(A) of the source of rent and other consideration due under such lease, and in the case of an assignment, that the financial condition and operating performance of the proposed assignee and its guarantors, if any, shall be similar to the financial condition and operating performance of the debtor and its guarantors, if any, as of the time the debtor became the lessee under the lease;

(B) that any percentage rent due under such lease will not decline substantially;

(C) that assumption or assignment of such lease is subject to all the provisions thereof, including (but not limited to) provisions such as a radius, location, use, or exclusivity provision, and will not breach any such provision contained in any other lease, financing agreement, or master agreement relating to such shopping center; and

(D) that assumption or assignment of such lease will not disrupt any tenant mix or balance in such shopping center.

(4) Notwithstanding any other provision of this section, if there has been a default in an unexpired lease of the debtor, other than a default of a kind specified in paragraph (2) of this subsection, the trustee may not require a lessor to provide services or supplies incidental to such lease before assumption of such lease unless the lessor is compensated under the terms of such lease for any services and supplies provided under such lease before assumption of such lease.

(c) The trustee may not assume or assign any executory contract or unexpired lease of the debtor, whether or not such contract or lease prohibits or restricts assignment of rights or delegation of duties, if—

(1) (A) applicable law excuses a party, other than the debtor, to such contract or lease from accepting performance from or rendering performance to an entity other than the debtor or the debtor in possession, whether or not such contract or lease prohibits or restricts assignment of rights or delegation of duties; and

(B) such party does not consent to such assumption or assignment; or

(2) such contract is a contract to make a loan, or extend other debt financing or financial accommodations, to or for the benefit of the debtor, or to issue a security of the debtor; or

(3) such lease is of nonresidential real property and has been terminated under applicable nonbankruptcy law prior to the order for relief~~; or~~.

(d) (1) In a case under chapter 7 of this title, if the trustee does not assume or reject an executory contract or unexpired lease of residential real property or of personal property of the debtor within 60 days after the order for relief, or within such additional time as the court, for cause, within such 60- day period, fixes, then such contract or lease is deemed rejected.

(2) In a case under chapter 9, 11, 12, or 13 of this title, the trustee may assume or reject an executory contract or unexpired lease of residential real property or of personal property of the debtor at any time before the confirmation of a plan but the court, on the request of any party to such contract or lease, may order the trustee to determine within a specified period of time whether to assume or reject such contract or lease.

(3) The trustee shall timely perform all the obligations of the debtor, except those specified in section 36(b)(2), arising from and after the order for relief under any unexpired lease of nonresidential real property, until such lease is assumed or rejected, notwithstanding section 503((b)(1) of this title. The court may extend, for cause, the time for performance of any such obligation that arises within 60 days after the date of the order for relief, but the time for performance shall not be extended beyond such 60-day period. This subsection shall not be deemed to affect the trustee's obligations under the provisions of subsection (b) or (f) of this section. Acceptance of any such

performance does not constitute waiver or relinquishment of the lessor's rights under such lease or under this title.

(4)-(A) Subject to subparagraph (B), an unexpired lease of nonresidential real property under which the debtor is the lessee shall be deemed rejected, and the trustee shall immediately surrender that nonresidential real property to the lessor, if the trustee does not assume or reject the unexpired lease by the earlier of—

(i) the date that is 120 days after the date of the order for relief; or

(ii) the date of the entry of an order confirming a plan.

(B) (i) The court may extend the period determined under subparagraph (A), prior to the expiration of the 120-day period, for 90 days on the motion of the trustee or lessor for cause.

(ii) If the court grants an extension under clause (i), the court may grant a subsequent extension only upon prior written consent of the lessor in each instance.

(5) The trustee shall timely perform all of the obligations of the debtor, except those specified in section 365(b)(2), first arising from or after 60 days after the order for relief in a case under chapter 11 of this title under an unexpired lease of personal property (other than personal property leased to an individual primarily for personal, family, or household purposes), until such lease is assumed or rejected notwithstanding section 503(b)(1) of this title, unless the court, after notice and a hearing and based on the equities of the case, orders otherwise with respect to the obligations or timely performance thereof. This subsection shall not be deemed to affect the trustee's obligations under the provisions of subsection (b) or (f). Acceptance of any such performance does not constitute waiver or relinquishment of the lessor's rights under such lease or under this title.

(e) (1) Notwithstanding a provision in an executory contract or unexpired lease, or in applicable law, an executory contract or unexpired lease of the debtor may not be terminated or modified, and any right or obligation under such contract or lease may not be terminated or modified, at any time after the commencement of the case solely because of a provision in such contract or lease that is conditioned on—

(A) the insolvency or financial condition of the debtor at any time before the closing of the case;

(B) the commencement of a case under this title; or

(C) the appointment of or taking possession by a trustee in a case under this title or a custodian before such commencement.

(2) Paragraph (1) of this subsection does not apply to an executory contract or unexpired lease of the debtor, whether or not such contract or lease prohibits or restricts assignment of rights or delegation of duties, if—

(A) (i) applicable law excuses a party, other than the debtor, to such contract or lease from accepting performance from or rendering performance to the trustee or to an assignee of such contract or lease, whether or not such contract or lease prohibits or restricts assignment of rights or delegation of duties; and

(ii) such party does not consent to such assumption or assignment; or

(B) such contract is a contract to make a loan, or extend other debt financing or financial accommodations, to or for the benefit of the debtor, or to issue a security of the debtor.

(f) (1) Except as provided in subsections (b) and (c) of this section, notwithstanding a provision in an executory contract or unexpired lease of the debtor, or in applicable law, that prohibits, restricts, or conditions the assignment of such contract or lease, the trustee may assign such contract or lease under paragraph (2) of this subsection.

(2) The trustee may assign an executory contract or unexpired lease of the debtor only if—

(A) the trustee assumes such contract or lease in accordance with the provisions of this section; and

(B) adequate assurance of future performance by the assignee of such contract or lease is provided, whether or not there has been a default in such contract or lease.

(3) Notwithstanding a provision in an executory contract or unexpired lease of the debtor, or in applicable law that terminates or modifies, or permits a party other than the debtor to terminate or modify, such contract or lease or a right or obligation under such contract or lease on account of an assignment of such contract or lease, such contract, lease, right, or obligation may not be terminated or modified under such provision because of the assumption or assignment of such contract or lease by the trustee.

(g) Except as provided in subsections (h)(2) and (i)(2) of this section, the rejection of an executory contract or unexpired lease of the debtor constitutes a breach of such contract or lease—

(1) if such contract or lease has not been assumed under this section or under a plan confirmed under chapter 9, 11, 12, or 13 of this title, immediately before the date of the filing of the petition; or

(2) if such contract or lease has been assumed under this section or under a plan confirmed under chapter 9, 11, 12, or 13 of this title—

(A) if before such rejection the case has not been converted under section 1112, 1208, or 1307 of this title, at the time of such rejection; or

(B) if before such rejection the case has been converted under section 1112, 1208, or 1307 of this title—

(i) immediately before the date of such conversion, if such contract or lease was assumed before such conversion; or

(ii) at the time of such rejection, if such contract or lease was assumed after such conversion.

(h) (1) (A) If the trustee rejects an unexpired lease of real property under which the debtor is the lessor and—

(i) if the rejection by the trustee amounts to such a breach as would entitle the lessee to treat such lease as terminated by virtue of its terms, applicable nonbankruptcy law, or any agreement made by the lessee, then the lessee under such lease may treat such lease as terminated by the rejection; or

(ii) if the term of such lease has commenced, the lessee may retain its rights under such lease (including rights such as those relating to the amount and timing of payment of rent and other amounts payable by the lessee and any right of use, possession, quiet enjoyment, subletting, assignment, or hypothecation) that are in or appurtenant to the real property for the balance of the term of such lease and for any renewal or extension of such rights to the extent that such rights are enforceable under applicable nonbankruptcy law.

(B) If the lessee retains its rights under subparagraph (A)(ii), the lessee may offset against the rent reserved under such lease for the balance of the term after the date of the rejection of such lease and for the term of any renewal or extension of such lease, the value of any damage caused by the nonperformance after the date of such rejection, of any obligation of the debtor under such lease, but the lessee shall not have any other right against the estate or the debtor on account of any damage occurring after such date caused by such nonperformance.

(C) The rejection of a lease of real property in a shopping center with respect to which the lessee elects to retain its rights under subparagraph (A)(ii) does not affect the enforceability under applicable nonbankruptcy law of any provision in the lease pertaining to radius, location, use, exclusivity, or tenant mix or balance.

(D) In this paragraph, "lessee" includes any successor, assign, or mortgagee permitted under the terms of such lease.

(2) (A) If the trustee rejects a timeshare interest under a timeshare plan under which the debtor is the timeshare interest seller and—

(i) if the rejection amounts to such a breach as would entitle the timeshare interest purchaser to treat the timeshare plan as terminated under its terms, applicable nonbankruptcy law, or any agreement made by timeshare interest purchaser, the timeshare interest purchaser under the timeshare plan may treat the timeshare plan as terminated by such rejection; or

(ii) if the term of such timeshare interest has commenced, then the timeshare interest purchaser may retain its rights in such timeshare interest for the balance of such term and for any term of renewal or extension of such timeshare interest to the extent that such rights are enforceable under applicable nonbankruptcy law.

(B) If the timeshare interest purchaser retains its rights under subparagraph (A), such timeshare interest purchaser may offset against the moneys due for such timeshare interest for the balance of the term after the date of the rejection of such timeshare interest, and the term of any renewal or extension of such timeshare interest, the value of any damage caused by the nonperformance after the date of such rejection, of any obligation of the debtor under such timeshare plan, but the timeshare interest purchaser shall not have any right against the estate or the debtor on account of any damage occurring after such date caused by such nonperformance.

(i) (1) If the trustee rejects an executory contract of the debtor for the sale of real property or for the sale of a timeshare interest under a timeshare plan, under which the purchaser is in possession, such purchaser may treat such contract as terminated, or, in the alternative, may remain in possession of such real property or timeshare interest.

(2) If such purchaser remains in possession—

(A) such purchaser shall continue to make all payments due under such contract, but may, offset against such payments any damages occurring after the date of the rejection of such contract caused by the nonperformance of any obligation of the debtor after such date, but such purchaser does not have any rights against the estate on account of any damages arising after such date from such rejection, other than such offset; and

(B) the trustee shall deliver title to such purchaser in accordance with the provisions of such contract, but is relieved of all other obligations to perform under such contract.

(j) A purchaser that treats an executory contract as terminated under subsection (i) of this section, or a party whose executory contract to purchase real property from the debtor is rejected and under which such party is not in possession, has a lien on the interest of the debtor in such property for the recovery of any portion of the purchase price that such purchaser or party has paid.

(k) Assignment by the trustee to an entity of a contract or lease assumed under this section relieves the trustee and the estate from any liability for any breach of such contract or lease occurring after such assignment.

(l) If an unexpired lease under which the debtor is the lessee is assigned pursuant to this section, the lessor of the property may require a deposit or other security for the performance of the debtor's obligations under the lease substantially the same as would have been required by the landlord upon the initial leasing to a similar tenant.

(m) For purposes of this section 365 and sections 541(b)(2) and 362(b)(10), leases of real property shall include any rental agreement to use real property.

(n) (1) If the trustee rejects an executory contract under which the debtor is a licensor of a right to intellectual property, the licensee under such contract may elect—

(A) to treat such contract as terminated by such rejection if such rejection by the trustee amounts to such a breach as would entitle the licensee to treat such contract as terminated by virtue of its own terms, applicable nonbankruptcy law, or an agreement made by the licensee with another entity; or

(B) to retain its rights (including a right to enforce any exclusivity provision of such contract, but excluding any other right under applicable nonbankruptcy law to specific performance of such contract) under such contract and under any agreement supplementary to such contract, to such intellectual property (including any embodiment of such intellectual property to the extent protected by applicable nonbankruptcy law), as such rights existed immediately before the case commenced, for—

(i) the duration of such contract; and

(ii) any period for which such contract may be extended by the licensee as of right under applicable nonbankruptcy law.

(2) If the licensee elects to retain its rights, as described in paragraph (1)(B) of this subsection, under such contract—

(A) the trustee shall allow the licensee to exercise such rights;

(B) the licensee shall make all royalty payments due under such contract for the duration of such contract and for any period described in paragraph (1)(B) of this subsection for which the licensee extends such contract; and

(C) the licensee shall be deemed to waive—

(i) any right of setoff it may have with respect to such contract under this title or applicable nonbankruptcy law; and

(ii) any claim allowable under section 503(b) of this title arising from the performance of such contract.

(3) If the licensee elects to retain its rights, as described in paragraph (1)(B) of this subsection, then on the written request of the licensee the trustee shall—

(A) to the extent provided in such contract, or any agreement supplementary to such contract, provide to the licensee any intellectual property (including such embodiment) held by the trustee; and

(B) not interfere with the rights of the licensee as provided in such contract, or any agreement supplementary to such contract, to such intellectual property (including such embodiment) including any right to obtain such intellectual property (or such embodiment) from another entity.

(4) Unless and until the trustee rejects such contract, on the written request of the licensee the trustee shall—

(A) to the extent provided in such contract or any agreement supplementary to such contract—

(i) perform such contract; or

(ii) provide to the licensee such intellectual property (including any embodiment of such intellectual property to the extent protected by applicable nonbankruptcy law) held by the trustee; and

(B) not interfere with the rights of the licensee as provided in such contract, or any agreement supplementary to such contract, to such intellectual property (including such embodiment), including any right to obtain such intellectual property (or such embodiment) from another entity.

(o) In a case under chapter 11 of this title, the trustee shall be deemed to have assumed (consistent with the debtor's other obligations under section 507), and shall immediately cure any deficit under, any commitment by the debtor to a Federal depository institutions regulatory agency (or predecessor to such agency) to maintain the capital of an insured depository institution, and any claim for a subsequent breach of the obligations thereunder shall be entitled to priority under section 507. This subsection shall not extend any commitment that would otherwise be terminated by any act of such an agency.

<u>(p) (1) If a lease of personal property is rejected or not timely assumed by the trustee under subsection (d), the leased property is no longer property of the estate and the stay under section 362(a) is automatically terminated.</u>

<u>(2) (A) If the debtor in a case under chapter 7 is an individual, the debtor may notify the creditor in writing that the debtor desires to assume the lease. Upon being so notified, the creditor may, at its option, notify the debtor that it is willing to have the lease assumed by the debtor and may</u>

condition such assumption on cure of any outstanding default on terms set by the contract.

(B) If, not later than 30 days after notice is provided under subparagraph (A), the debtor notifies the lessor in writing that the lease is assumed, the liability under the lease will be assumed by the debtor and not by the estate.

(C) The stay under section 362 and the injunction under section 524(a)(2) shall not be violated by notification of the debtor and negotiation of cure under this subsection.

(3) In a case under chapter 11 in which the debtor is an individual and in a case under chapter 13, if the debtor is the lessee with respect to personal property and the lease is not assumed in the plan confirmed by the court, the lease is deemed rejected as of the conclusion of the hearing on confirmation. If the lease is rejected, the stay under section 362 and any stay under section 1301 is automatically terminated with respect to the property subject to the lease.

- *Burger King Corp v. Rovine Corp. (In re Rovine Corp.)* (non-compete clause rejected)
    - Burger King said that by rejecting the executory contract, the defendant also rejected the non-compete covenant
    - Issue is non compete clause
    - Is it exucatory contract or Franchise
    - The contract was unfulfilled as of Chapter 11
    - 365 Subject to rejection
    - The Contract was Rejected
    - And BK still wanted non compete clause followed
    - Since under 365 cannot force Non compete clause
- *Sir Speedy, Inc. v. Morse* (non-compete clause not rejected)
    - Sir Speedy said that rejecting the executory contract, the defendant does not reject the non-compete covenant
    - Non compete clause
    - Dude filed chapter 7 and changed the name of his store from sir speedy to morse printing
    - Appeals ct reversed bankruptcy ct ruling that non-compete does not give rise to right of payment and thus not a claim under 101(5)(B)
    - Franchise agreement rejected the day he filed for bankruptcy
    - In many other decisions the court has held non compete clauses to be valid even if the debtor has rejected the franchise agreement
    - While the non compete is not a claim can seek injunctive relief
    - Here rejected contract but non compete is allowed

- There is a completely opposite case to sir Speedy in MA called Maids
- Hillman Likes Sir Speedy

- Lessor / Lesee
    - When the person who is bankrupt is the lessor (landlord) we look at §365(h)
    - When the person who is bankrupt is the lessee (tenant) we look at §365(i) and (j)
    - When the lease is rejected the non-debtor has the option of retaining his property
- *Thinking Machines Corp. v. Mellon Financial Serv. (In re Thinking Machines Corp.)* (rejection of lease)
    - Issue: Is court approval a condition precedent or subsequent to the effective rejection of a nonresidential lease pursuant to section 365(a)?
    - Court concluded that the statute is most propitiously read to make court approval a condition precedent to an effective rejection of a nonresidential lease
    - Court can make it retroactive
- *In re Microvideo Learning Systems, Inc.* (
    - Debtor did not pay rent from January 1, 1999 to the lease rejection date, February 8, 1999
    - Creditor argues that it is entitled to immediate payment for that period
    - Debtor argues that if its assets were liquidated today, its proceeds would not be sufficient to pay the estate's administrative expense claims in full – thus, it would be inequitable to pay creditor 100% of its administrative expense claim, while other administrative expense creditors, including professionals, would receive less than full payment of their claims
    - If representing the landlord do not sit around and wait, Come in quick like a bunny and file a motion to have the rent paid timely. Cause not going to get super priority
    - Pre-rejection lease payment was denied
- Time limit – if your dealing with residential property and your in Chapter 7, within 60 days

11 U.S.C. §521. Reaffirmation and Redemption

Debtor's duties

(a) The debtor shall—

(1) file—

(A) a list of creditors,; and

(B) unless the court orders otherwise,—

(i) a schedule of assets and liabilities,;

(ii) a schedule of current income and current expenditures;

(iii) a statement of the debtor's financial affairs and, if section 342(b) applies, a certificate—

(I) of an attorney whose name is indicated on the petition as the attorney for the debtor, or a bankruptcy petition preparer signing the petition under section 110(b)(1), indicating that such attorney or the bankruptcy petition preparer delivered to the debtor the notice required by section 342(b); or

(II) if no attorney is so indicated, and no bankruptcy petition preparer signed the petition, of the debtor that such notice was received and read by the debtor;

(iv) copies of all payment advices or other evidence of payment received within 60 days before the date of the filing of the petition, by the debtor from any employer of the debtor;

(v) a statement of the amount of monthly net income, itemized to show how the amount is calculated; and

(vi) a statement disclosing any reasonably anticipated increase in income or expenditures over the 12-month period following the date of the filing of the petition;

(2) if an individual debtor's schedule of assets and liabilities includes debts which are secured by property of the estate—

(A) within thirty days after the date of the filing of a petition under chapter 7 of this title or on or before the date of the meeting of creditors, whichever is earlier, or within such additional time as the court, for cause, within such period fixes, the debtor shall file with the clerk a statement of his intention with respect to the retention or surrender of such property and, if applicable, specifying that such property is claimed as exempt, that the debtor intends to redeem such property, or that the debtor intends to reaffirm debts secured by such property;

(B) 30 days after the first date set for the meeting of creditors under section 341(a), or within such additional time as the court, for cause, within such 30-day period fixes, the debtor shall perform his intention with respect to such property, as specified by subparagraph (A) of this paragraph; and

(C) nothing in subparagraphs (A) and (B) of this paragraph shall alter the debtor's or the trustee's rights with regard to such property under this title, except as provided in section 362(h);

(3) if a trustee is serving in the case or an auditor serving under section 586(f) of title 28, cooperate with the trustee as necessary to enable the trustee to perform the trustee's duties under this title;

(4) if a trustee is serving in the case or an auditor serving under section 586(f) of title 28, surrender to the trustee all property of the estate and any recorded information, including books, documents, records, and papers, relating to property of the estate, whether or not immunity is granted under section 344 of this title;

(5) appear at the hearing required under section 524(d) of this title.;

(6) in a case under chapter 7 of this title in which the debtor is an individual, not retain possession of personal property as to which a creditor has an allowed claim for the purchase price secured in whole or in part by an interest in such personal property unless the debtor, not later than 45 days after the first meeting of creditors under section 341(a), either—

(A) enters into an agreement with the creditor pursuant to section 524(c) with respect to the claim secured by such property; or

(B) redeems such property from the security interest pursuant to section 722.

If the debtor fails to so act within the 45-day period referred to in paragraph (6), the stay under section 362(a) is terminated with respect to the personal property of the estate or of the debtor which is affected, such property shall no longer be property of the estate, and the creditor may take whatever action as to such property as is permitted by applicable nonbankruptcy law, unless the court determines on the motion of the trustee filed before the expiration of such 45-day period, and after notice and a hearing, that such property is of consequential value or benefit to the estate, orders appropriate adequate protection of the creditor's interest, and orders the debtor to deliver any collateral in the debtor's possession to the trustee; and

(7) unless a trustee is serving in the case, continue to perform the obligations required of the administrator (as defined in section 3 of the Employee Retirement Income Security Act of 1974) of an employee benefit plan if at the time of the commencement of the case the debtor (or any entity designated by the debtor) served as such administrator.

(b) In addition to the requirements under subsection (a), a debtor who is an individual shall file with the court—

(1) a certificate from the approved nonprofit budget and credit counseling agency that provided the debtor services under section 109(h) describing the services provided to the debtor; and

(2) a copy of the debt repayment plan, if any, developed under section 109(h) through the approved nonprofit budget and credit counseling agency referred to in paragraph (1); or

(3) a sworn statement that sets forth exigent circumstances that preclude the filing of a certificate including –

(A) the debtor is facing foreclosure, garnishment, attachment, eviction, levy of execution, utility shutoff, or similar claim enforcement procedure that would deprive the debtor of property or necessary services before the debtor could obtain counseling;

(B) the debtor is unable to obtain counseling services due to lack of transportation, incapacity, or disability;

(C) the debtor attempted to obtain counseling within the five-day period immediately before filing bankruptcy but was unsuccessful in obtaining counseling for circumstances beyond the debtor's control;

(D) the debtor cannot afford costs associated with the counseling program; or

(E) the debtor met the requirements of section 109(h)(1) and a certificate was unavailable, lost, or unreasonably denied.

(c) In addition to meeting the requirements under subsection (a), a debtor shall file with the court a record of any interest that a debtor has in an education individual retirement account (as defined in section 530(b)(1) of the Internal Revenue Code of 1986) or under a qualified State tuition program (as defined in section 529(b)(1) of such Code).

(d) If the debtor fails timely to take the action specified in subsection (a)(6) of this section, or in paragraphs (1) and (2) of section 362(h), with respect to property which a lessor or bailor owns and has leased, rented, or bailed to the debtor or as to which a creditor holds a security interest not otherwise voidable under section 522(f), 544, 545, 547, 548, or 549, nothing in this title shall prevent or limit the operation of a provision in the underlying lease or agreement that has the effect of placing the debtor in default under such lease or agreement by reason of the occurrence, pendency, or existence of a proceeding under this title or the insolvency of the debtor. Nothing in this subsection shall be deemed to justify limiting such a provision in any other circumstance.

(e) (1) If the debtor in a case under chapter 7 or 13 is an individual and if a creditor files with the court at any time a request to receive a copy of the petition, schedules, and statement of financial affairs filed by the debtor, then the court shall make such petition, such schedules, and such statement available to such creditor.

(2) (A) The debtor shall provide—

(i) not later than 7 days before the date first set for the first meeting of creditors, to the trustee a copy of the Federal income tax return required under applicable law (or at the election of the debtor, a transcript of such return) for the most recent tax year ending immediately before the commencement of the case and for which a Federal income tax return was filed; and

(ii) at the same time the debtor complies with clause (i), a copy of such return (or if elected under clause (i), such transcript) to any creditor that timely requests such copy.

(B) If the debtor fails to comply with clause (i) or (ii) of subparagraph (A), the court shall dismiss the case unless the debtor demonstrates that the failure to so comply is due to circumstances beyond the control of the debtor.

(C) If a creditor requests a copy of such tax return or such transcript and if the debtor fails to provide a copy of such tax return or such transcript to such creditor at the time the debtor provides such tax return or such transcript to the trustee, then the court shall dismiss the case unless the debtor demonstrates that the failure to provide a copy of such tax return or such transcript is due to circumstances beyond the control of the debtor.

(3) If a creditor in a case under chapter 13 files with the court at any time a request to receive a copy of the plan filed by the debtor, then the court shall make available to such creditor a copy of the plan—

(A) at a reasonable cost; and

(B) not later than 5 days after such request is filed.

(f) At the request of the court, the United States trustee, or any party in interest in a case under chapter 7, 11, or 13, a debtor who is an individual shall file with the court—

(1) at the same time filed with the taxing authority, a copy of each Federal income tax return required under applicable law (or at the election of the debtor, a transcript of such tax return) with respect to each tax year of the debtor ending while the case is pending under such chapter;

(2) at the same time filed with the taxing authority, each Federal income tax return required under applicable law (or at the election of the debtor, a transcript of such tax return) that had not been filed with such authority as of the date of the commencement of the case and that was subsequently filed

for any tax year of the debtor ending in the 3-year period ending on the date of the commencement of the case;

(3) a copy of each amendment to any Federal income tax return or transcript filed with the court under paragraph (1) or (2); and

(4) in a case under chapter 13—

(A) on the date that is either 90 days after the end of such tax year or 1 year after the date of the commencement of the case, whichever is later, if a plan is not confirmed before such later date; and

(B) annually after the plan is confirmed and until the case is closed, not later than the date that is 45 days before the anniversary of the confirmation of the plan;

a statement, under penalty of perjury, of the income and expenditures of the debtor during the tax year of the debtor most recently concluded before such statement is filed under this paragraph, and of the monthly income of the debtor, that shows how income, expenditures, and monthly income are calculated.

(g) (1) A statement referred to in subsection (f)(4) shall disclose—

(A) the amount and sources of the income of the debtor;

(B) the identity of any person responsible with the debtor for the support of any dependent of the debtor; and

(C) the identity of any person who contributed, and the amount contributed, to the household in which the debtor resides.

(2) The tax returns, amendments, and statement of income and expenditures described in subsections (e)(2)(A) and (f) shall be available to the United States trustee (or the bankruptcy administrator, if any), the trustee, and any party in interest for inspection and copying, subject to the requirements of section 315(c) of the Bankruptcy Abuse Prevention and Consumer Protection Act of 2005.

(h) If requested by the United States trustee or by the trustee, the debtor shall provide—

(1) a document that establishes the identity of the debtor, including a driver's license, passport, or other document that contains a photograph of the debtor; or

(2) such other personal identifying information relating to the debtor that establishes the identity of the debtor.

(i) (1) Subject to paragraphs (2) and (4) and notwithstanding section 707(a), if an individual debtor in a voluntary case under chapter 7 or 13 fails to file all of the information required under subsection (a)(1) within 45 days after the date of the filing of the petition, the case shall be automatically dismissed effective on the 46th day after the date of the filing of the petition.

(2) Subject to paragraph (4) and with respect to a case described in paragraph (1), any party in interest may request the court to enter an order dismissing the case. If requested, the court shall enter an order of dismissal not later than 5 days after such request.

(3) Subject to paragraph (4) and upon request of the debtor made within 45 days after the date of the filing of the petition described in paragraph (1), the court may allow the debtor an additional period of not to exceed 45 days to file the information required under subsection (a)(1) if the court finds justification for extending the period for the filing.

(4) Notwithstanding any other provision of this subsection, on the motion of the trustee filed before the expiration of the applicable period of time specified in paragraph (1), (2), or (3), and after notice and a hearing, the court may decline to dismiss the case if the court finds that the debtor attempted in good faith to file all the information required by subsection (a)(1)(B)(iv) and that the best interests of creditors would be served by administration of the case.

(j) (1) Notwithstanding any other provision of this title, if the debtor fails to file a tax return that becomes due after the commencement of the case or to properly obtain an extension of the due date for filing such return, the taxing authority may request that the court enter an order converting or dismissing the case.

(2) If the debtor does not file the required return or obtain the extension referred to in paragraph (1) within 90 days after a request is filed by the taxing authority under that paragraph, the court shall convert or dismiss the case, whichever is in the best interests of creditors and the estate.

11 U.S.C. §524. Effect of discharge

(a) A discharge in a case under this title—

(1) voids any judgment at any time obtained, to the extent that such judgment is a determination of the personal liability of the debtor with respect to any debt discharged under section 727, 944, 1141, 1228, or 1328 of this title, whether or not discharge of such debt is waived;

(2) operates as an injunction against the commencement or continuation of an action, the employment of process, or an act, to collect, recover or offset any such debt as a personal liability of the debtor, whether or not discharge of such debt is waived; and

(3) operates as an injunction against the commencement or continuation of an action, the employment of process, or an act, to collect or recover from, or offset against, property of the debtor of the kind specified in section 541(a)(2) of this title that is acquired after the commencement of the case, on account

of any allowable community claim, except a community claim that is excepted from discharge under section 523, 1228(a)(1), or 1328(a)(1), or that would be so excepted, determined in accordance with the provisions of sections 523(c) and 523(d) of this title, in a case concerning the debtor's spouse commenced on the date of the filing of the petition in the case concerning the debtor, whether or not discharge of the debt based on such community claim is waived.

(b) Subsection (a)(3) of this section does not apply if—

(1) (A) the debtor's spouse is a debtor in a case under this title, or a bankrupt or a debtor in a case under the Bankruptcy Act, commenced within six years of the date of the filing of the petition in the case concerning the debtor; and

(B) the court does not grant the debtor's spouse a discharge in such case concerning the debtor's spouse; or

(2) (A) the court would not grant the debtor's spouse a discharge in a case under chapter 7 of this title concerning such spouse commenced on the date of the filing of the petition in the case concerning the debtor; and

(B) a determination that the court would not so grant such discharge is made by the bankruptcy court within the time and in the manner provided for a determination under section 727 of this title of whether a debtor is granted a discharge.

(c) An agreement between a holder of a claim and the debtor, the consideration for which, in whole or in part, is based on a debt that is dischargeable in a case under this title is enforceable only to any extent enforceable under applicable nonbankruptcy law, whether or not discharge of such debt is waived, only if—

(1) such agreement was made before the granting of the discharge under section 727, 1141, 1228, or 1328 of this title;

(2) the debtor received the disclosures described in subsection (k) at or before the time at which the debtor signed the agreement;

(3) such agreement has been filed with the court and, if applicable, accompanied by a declaration or an affidavit of the attorney that represented the debtor during the course of negotiating an agreement under this subsection, which states that—

(A) such agreement represents a fully informed and voluntary agreement by the debtor;

(B) such agreement does not impose an undue hardship on the debtor or a dependent of the debtor; and (c) the attorney fully advised the debtor of the legal effect and consequences of—

(i) an agreement of the kind specified in this subsection; and

(ii) any default under such an agreement;

(4) the debtor has not rescinded such agreement at any time prior to discharge or within sixty days after such agreement is filed with the court, whichever occurs later, by giving notice of rescission to the holder of such claim;

(5) the provisions of subsection (d) of this section have been complied with; and

(6) (A) in a case concerning an individual who was not represented by an attorney during the course of negotiating an agreement under this subsection, the court approves such agreement as—

(i) not imposing an undue hardship on the debtor or a dependent of the debtor; and

(ii) in the best interest of the debtor.

(B) Subparagraph (A) shall not apply to the extent that such debt is a consumer debt secured by real property.

(d) In a case concerning an individual, when the court has determined whether to grant or not to grant a discharge under section 727, 1141, 1228, or 1328 of this title, the court may hold a hearing at which the debtor shall appear in person. At any such hearing, the court shall inform the debtor that a discharge has been granted or the reason why a discharge has not been granted. If a discharge has been granted and if the debtor desires to make an agreement of the kind specified in subsection (c) of this section and was not represented by an attorney during the course of negotiating such agreement, then the court shall hold a hearing at which the debtor shall appear in person and at such hearing the court shall—

(1) inform the debtor—

(A) that such an agreement is not required under this title, under nonbankruptcy law, or under any agreement not made in accordance with the provisions of subsection (c) of this section; and

(B) of the legal effect and consequences of—

(i) an agreement of the kind specified in subsection (c) of this section; and

(ii) a default under such an agreement; and

(2) determine whether the agreement that the debtor desires to make complies with the requirements of subsection (c)(6) of this section, if the consideration for such agreement is based in whole or in part on a consumer debt that is not secured by real property of the debtor.

(e) Except as provided in subsection (a)(3) of this section, discharge of a debt of the debtor does not affect the liability of any other entity on, or the property of any other entity for, such debt.

(f) Nothing contained in subsection (c) or (d) of this section prevents a debtor from voluntarily repaying any debt.

(g) (1) (A) After notice and hearing, a court that enters an order confirming a plan of reorganization under chapter 11 may issue, in connection with such order, an injunction in accordance with this subsection to supplement the injunctive effect of a discharge under this section.

(B) An injunction may be issued under subparagraph (A) to enjoin entities from taking legal action for the purpose of directly or indirectly collecting, recovering, or receiving payment or recovery with respect to any claim or demand that, under a plan of reorganization, is to be paid in whole or in part by a trust described in paragraph (2)(B)(i), except such legal actions as are expressly allowed by the injunction, the confirmation order, or the plan of reorganization.

(2) (A) Subject to subsection (h), if the requirements of subparagraph (B) are met at the time an injunction described in paragraph (1) is entered, then after entry of such injunction, any proceeding that involves the validity, application, construction, or modification of such injunction, or of this subsection with respect to such injunction, may be commenced only in the district court in which such injunction was entered, and such court shall have exclusive jurisdiction over any such proceeding without regard to the amount in controversy.

(B) The requirements of this subparagraph are that—

(i) the injunction is to be implemented in connection with a trust that, pursuant to the plan of reorganization—

(I) is to assume the liabilities of a debtor which at the time of entry of the order for relief has been named as a defendant in personal injury, wrongful death, or property-damage actions seeking recovery for damages allegedly caused by the presence of, or exposure to, asbestos or asbestos- containing products;

(II) is to be funded in whole or in part by the securities of 1 or more debtors involved in such plan and by the obligation of such debtor or debtors to make future payments, including dividends;

(III) is to own, or by the exercise of rights granted under such plan would be entitled to own if specified contingencies occur, a majority of the voting shares of—

(aa) each such debtor;

(bb) the parent corporation of each such debtor; or

(cc) a subsidiary of each such debtor that is also a debtor; and

(IV) is to use its assets or income to pay claims and demands; and

(ii) subject to subsection (h), the court determines that—

(I) the debtor is likely to be subject to substantial future demands for payment arising out of the same or similar conduct or events that gave rise to the claims that are addressed by the injunction;

(II) the actual amounts, numbers, and timing of such future demands cannot be determined;

(III) pursuit of such demands outside the procedures prescribed by such plan is likely to threaten the plan's purpose to deal equitably with claims and future demands;

(IV) as part of the process of seeking confirmation of such plan—

(aa) the terms of the injunction proposed to be issued under paragraph (1)(A), including any provisions barring actions against third parties pursuant to paragraph (4)(A), are set out in such plan and in any disclosure statement supporting the plan; and

(bb) a separate class or classes of the claimants whose claims are to be addressed by a trust described in clause (i) is established and votes, by at least 75 percent of those voting, in favor of the plan; and

(V) subject to subsection (h), pursuant to court orders or otherwise, the trust will operate through mechanisms such as structured, periodic, or supplemental payments, pro rata distributions, matrices, or periodic review of estimates of the numbers and values of present claims and future demands, or other comparable mechanisms, that provide reasonable assurance that the trust will value, and be in a financial position to pay, present claims and future demands that involve similar claims in substantially the same manner.

(3) (A) If the requirements of paragraph (2)(B) are met and the order confirming the plan of reorganization was issued or affirmed by the district court that has jurisdiction over the reorganization case, then after the time for appeal of the order that issues or affirms the plan—

(i) the injunction shall be valid and enforceable and may not be revoked or modified by any court except through appeal in accordance with paragraph (6);

(ii) no entity that pursuant to such plan or thereafter becomes a direct or indirect transferee of, or successor to any assets of, a debtor or trust that is the subject of the injunction shall be liable with respect to any claim or demand made against such entity by reason of its becoming such a transferee or successor; and

(iii) no entity that pursuant to such plan or thereafter makes a loan to such a debtor or trust or to such a successor or transferee shall, by reason of making the loan, be liable with respect to any claim or demand made against such entity, nor shall any pledge of assets made in connection with such a loan be upset or impaired for that reason;

(B) Subparagraph (A) shall not be construed to—

(i) imply that an entity described in subparagraph (A)(ii) or (iii) would, if this paragraph were not applicable, necessarily be liable to any entity by reason of any of the acts described in subparagraph (A);

(ii) relieve any such entity of the duty to comply with, or of liability under, any Federal or State law regarding the making of a fraudulent conveyance in a transaction described in subparagraph (A)(ii) or (iii); or

(iii) relieve a debtor of the debtor's obligation to comply with the terms of the plan of reorganization, or affect the power of the court to exercise its authority under sections 1141 and 1142 to compel the debtor to do so.

(4) (A) (i) Subject to subparagraph (B), an injunction described in paragraph (1) shall be valid and enforceable against all entities that it addresses.

(ii) Notwithstanding the provisions of section 524(e), such an injunction may bar any action directed against a third party who is identifiable from the terms of such injunction (by name or as part of an identifiable group) and is alleged to be directly or indirectly liable for the conduct of, claims against, or demands on the debtor to the extent such alleged liability of such third party arises by reason of—

(I) the third party's ownership of a financial interest in the debtor, a past or present affiliate of the debtor, or a predecessor in interest of the debtor;

(II) the third party's involvement in the management of the debtor or a predecessor in interest of the debtor, or service as an officer, director or employee of the debtor or a related party;

(III) the third party's provision of insurance to the debtor or a related party; or

(IV) the third party's involvement in a transaction changing the corporate structure, or in a loan or other financial transaction affecting the financial condition, of the debtor or a related party, including but not limited to—

(aa) involvement in providing financing (debt or equity), or advice to an entity involved in such a transaction; or

(bb) acquiring or selling a financial interest in an entity as part of such a transaction.

(iii) As used in this subparagraph, the term "related party" means—

(I) a past or present affiliate of the debtor;

(II) a predecessor in interest of the debtor; or

(III) any entity that owned a financial interest in—

(aa) the debtor;

(bb) a past or present affiliate of the debtor; or

(cc) a predecessor in interest of the debtor.

(B) Subject to subsection (h), if, under a plan of reorganization, a kind of demand described in such plan is to be paid in whole or in part by a trust described in paragraph (2)(B)(i) in connection with which an injunction described in paragraph (1) is to be implemented, then such injunction shall be valid and enforceable with respect to a demand of such kind made, after such plan is confirmed, against the debtor or debtors involved, or against a third party described in subparagraph (A)(ii), if—

(i) as part of the proceedings leading to issuance of such injunction, the court appoints a legal representative for the purpose of protecting the rights of persons that might subsequently assert demands of such kind, and

(ii) the court determines, before entering the order confirming such plan, that identifying such debtor or debtors, or such third party (by name or as part of an identifiable group), in such injunction with respect to such demands for purposes of this subparagraph is fair and equitable with respect to the persons that might subsequently assert such demands, in light of the benefits provided, or to be provided, to such trust on behalf of such debtor or debtors or such third party.

(5) In this subsection, the term "demand" means a demand for payment, present or future, that—

(A) was not a claim during the proceedings leading to the confirmation of a plan of reorganization;

(B) arises out of the same or similar conduct or events that gave rise to the claims addressed by the injunction issued under paragraph (1); and

(C) pursuant to the plan, is to be paid by a trust described in paragraph (2)(B)(i).

(6) Paragraph (3)(A)(i) does not bar an action taken by or at the direction of an appellate court on appeal of an injunction issued under paragraph (1) or of the order of confirmation that relates to the injunction.

(7) This subsection does not affect the operation of section 1144 or the power of the district court to refer a proceeding under section 157 of title 28 or any reference of a proceeding made prior to the date of the enactment of this subsection.

(h) Application to Existing Injunctions.—For purposes of subsection (g)—

(1) subject to paragraph (2), if an injunction of the kind described in subsection (g)(1)(B) was issued before the date of the enactment of this Act, as part of a plan of reorganization confirmed by an order entered before such date, then the injunction shall be considered to meet the requirements of subsection (g)(2)(B) for purposes of subsection (g)(2)(A), and to satisfy subsection (g)(4)(A)(ii), if—

(A) the court determined at the time the plan was confirmed that the plan was fair and equitable in accordance with the requirements of section 1129(b);

(B) as part of the proceedings leading to issuance of such injunction and confirmation of such plan, the court had appointed a legal representative for the purpose of protecting the rights of persons that might subsequently assert demands described in subsection (g)(4)(B) with respect to such plan; and

(C) such legal representative did not object to confirmation of such plan or issuance of such injunction; and

(2) for purposes of paragraph (1), if a trust described in subsection (g)(2)(B)(i) is subject to a court order on the date of the enactment of this Act staying such trust from settling or paying further claims—

(A) the requirements of subsection (g)(2)(B)(ii)(V) shall not apply with respect to such trust until such stay is lifted or dissolved; and

(B) if such trust meets such requirements on the date such stay is lifted or dissolved, such trust shall be considered to have met such requirements continuously from the date of the enactment of this Act.

<u>(i) The willful failure of a creditor to credit payments received under a plan confirmed under this title, unless the order confirming the plan is revoked, the plan is in default, or the creditor has not received payments required to be made under the</u>

plan in the manner required by the plan (including crediting the amounts required under the plan), shall constitute a violation of an injunction under subsection (a)(2) if the act of the creditor to collect and failure to credit payments in the manner required by the plan caused material injury to the debtor.

(j) Subsection (a)(2) does not operate as an injunction against an act by a creditor that is the holder of a secured claim, if—

(1) such creditor retains a security interest in real property that is the principal residence of the debtor;

(2) such act is in the ordinary course of business between the creditor and the debtor; and

(3) such act is limited to seeking or obtaining periodic payments associated with a valid security interest in lieu of pursuit of in rem relief to enforce the lien.

(k) (1) The disclosures required under subsection (c)(2) shall consist of the disclosure statement described in paragraph (3), completed as required in that paragraph, together with the agreement specified in subsection (c), statement, declaration, motion and order described, respectively, in paragraphs (4) through (8), and shall be the only disclosures required in connection with entering into such agreement.

(2) Disclosures made under paragraph (1) shall be made clearly and conspicuously and in writing. The terms "Amount Reaffirmed" and "Annual Percentage Rate" shall be disclosed more conspicuously than other terms, data or information provided in connection with this disclosure, except that the phrases "Before agreeing to reaffirm a debt, review these important disclosures" and "Summary of Reaffirmation Agreement" may be equally conspicuous. Disclosures may be made in a different order and may use terminology different from that set forth in paragraphs (2) through (8), except that the terms "Amount Reaffirmed" and "Annual Percentage Rate" must be used where indicated.

(3) The disclosure statement required under this paragraph shall consist of the following:

(A) The statement: "Part A: Before agreeing to reaffirm a debt, review these important disclosures:";

(B) Under the heading "Summary of Reaffirmation Agreement", the statement: "This Summary is made pursuant to the requirements of the Bankruptcy Code";

(C) The "Amount Reaffirmed", using that term, which shall be—

(i) the total amount of debt that the debtor agrees to reaffirm by entering into an agreement of the kind specified in subsection (c), and

(ii) the total of any fees and costs accrued as of the date of the disclosure statement, related to such total amount.

(D) In conjunction with the disclosure of the "Amount Reaffirmed", the statements—

(i) "The amount of debt you have agreed to reaffirm"; and

(ii) "Your credit agreement may obligate you to pay additional amounts which may come due after the date of this disclosure. Consult your credit agreement.".

(E) The "Annual Percentage Rate", using that term, which shall be disclosed as—

(i) if, at the time the petition is filed, the debt is an extension of credit under an open end credit plan, as the terms "credit" and "open end credit plan" are defined in section 103 of the Truth in Lending Act, then—

(I) the annual percentage rate determined under paragraphs (5) and (6) of section 127(b) of the Truth in Lending Act, as applicable, as disclosed to the debtor in the most recent periodic statement prior to entering into an agreement of the kind specified in subsection (c) or, if no such periodic statement has been given to the debtor during the prior 6 months, the annual percentage rate as it would have been so disclosed at the time the disclosure statement is given to the debtor, or to the extent this annual percentage rate is not readily available or not applicable, then

(II) the simple interest rate applicable to the amount reaffirmed as of the date the disclosure statement is given to the debtor, or if different simple interest rates apply to different balances, the simple interest rate applicable to each such balance, identifying the amount of each such balance included in the amount reaffirmed, or

(III) if the entity making the disclosure elects, to disclose the annual percentage rate under subclause (I) and the simple interest rate under subclause (II); or

(ii) if, at the time the petition is filed, the debt is an extension of credit other than under an open end credit plan, as the terms "credit" and "open end credit plan" are defined in section 103 of the Truth in Lending Act, then—

(I) the annual percentage rate under section 128(a)(4) of the Truth in Lending Act, as disclosed to the debtor in the most recent disclosure statement given to the debtor prior to the entering into an agreement of the kind specified in subsection (c) with respect to the debt, or, if no such disclosure statement was given to the debtor, the annual percentage rate as it would have been so disclosed at the time the disclosure statement is given to the debtor, or to the extent this annual percentage rate is not readily available or not applicable, then

(II) the simple interest rate applicable to the amount reaffirmed as of the date the disclosure statement is given to the debtor, or if different simple interest rates apply to different balances, the simple interest rate applicable to each such balance, identifying the amount of such balance included in the amount reaffirmed, or

(III) if the entity making the disclosure elects, to disclose the annual percentage rate under (I) and the simple interest rate under (II).

(F) If the underlying debt transaction was disclosed as a variable rate transaction on the most recent disclosure given under the Truth in Lending Act, by stating "The interest rate on your loan may be a variable interest rate which changes from time to time, so that the annual percentage rate disclosed here may be higher or lower.".

(G) If the debt is secured by a security interest which has not been waived in whole or in part or determined to be void by a final order of the court at the time of the disclosure, by disclosing that a security interest or lien in goods or property is asserted over some or all of the debts the debtor is reaffirming and listing the items and their original purchase price that are subject to the asserted security interest, or if not a purchase-money security interest then listing by items or types and the original amount of the loan.

(H) At the election of the creditor, a statement of the repayment schedule using 1 or a combination of the following—

(i) by making the statement: "Your first payment in the amount of $ is due on but the future payment amount may be different. Consult your reaffirmation agreement or credit agreement, as applicable.", and stating the amount of the first payment and the due date of that payment in the places provided;

(ii) by making the statement: "Your payment schedule will be:", and describing the repayment schedule with the number, amount, and due dates or period of payments scheduled to repay the debts reaffirmed to the extent then known by the disclosing party; or

(iii) by describing the debtor's repayment obligations with reasonable specificity to the extent then known by the disclosing party.

(I) The following statement: "Note: When this disclosure refers to what a creditor 'may' do, it does not use the word 'may' to give the creditor specific permission. The word 'may' is used to tell you what might occur if the law permits the creditor to take the action. If you have questions about your reaffirming a debt or what the law requires, consult with the attorney who helped you negotiate this agreement reaffirming a debt. If you don't have an attorney helping you, the judge will explain the effect of your reaffirming a debt when the hearing on the reaffirmation agreement is held.".

(J) (i) The following additional statements:

"Reaffirming a debt is a serious financial decision. The law requires you to take certain steps to make sure the decision is in your best interest. If these steps are not completed, the reaffirmation agreement is not effective, even though you have signed it.

1. Read the disclosures in this Part A carefully. Consider the decision to reaffirm carefully. Then, if you want to reaffirm, sign the reaffirmation agreement in Part B (or you may use a separate agreement you and your creditor agree on).

2. Complete and sign Part D and be sure you can afford to make the payments you are agreeing to make and have received a copy of the disclosure statement and a completed and signed reaffirmation agreement.

3. If you were represented by an attorney during the negotiation of your reaffirmation agreement, the attorney must have signed the certification in Part C.

4. If you were not represented by an attorney during the negotiation of your reaffirmation agreement, you must have completed and signed Part E.

5. The original of this disclosure must be filed with the court by you or your creditor. If a separate reaffirmation agreement (other than the one in Part B) has been signed, it must be attached.

6. If you were represented by an attorney during the negotiation of your reaffirmation agreement, your reaffirmation agreement becomes effective upon filing with the court unless the reaffirmation is presumed to be an undue hardship as explained in Part D.

7. If you were not represented by an attorney during the negotiation of your reaffirmation agreement, it will not be effective unless the court approves it. The court will notify you

of the hearing on your reaffirmation agreement. You must attend this hearing in bankruptcy court where the judge will review your reaffirmation agreement. The bankruptcy court must approve your reaffirmation agreement as consistent with your best interests, except that no court approval is required if your reaffirmation agreement is for a consumer debt secured by a mortgage, deed of trust, security deed, or other lien on your real property, like your home.

Your right to rescind (cancel) your reaffirmation agreement. You may rescind (cancel) your reaffirmation agreement at any time before the bankruptcy court enters a discharge order, or before the expiration of the 60-day period that begins on the date your reaffirmation agreement is filed with the court, whichever occurs later. To rescind (cancel) your reaffirmation agreement, you must notify the creditor that your reaffirmation agreement is rescinded (or canceled).

What are your obligations if you reaffirm the debt? A reaffirmed debt remains your personal legal obligation. It is not discharged in your bankruptcy case. That means that if you default on your reaffirmed debt after your bankruptcy case is over, your creditor may be able to take your property or your wages. Otherwise, your obligations will be determined by the reaffirmation agreement which may have changed the terms of the original agreement. For example, if you are reaffirming an open end credit agreement, the creditor may be permitted by that agreement or applicable law to change the terms of that agreement in the future under certain conditions.

Are you required to enter into a reaffirmation agreement by any law? No, you are not required to reaffirm a debt by any law. Only agree to reaffirm a debt if it is in your best interest. Be sure you can afford the payments you agree to make.

What if your creditor has a security interest or lien? Your bankruptcy discharge does not eliminate any lien on your property. A 'lien' is often referred to as a security interest, deed of trust, mortgage or security deed. Even if you do not reaffirm and your personal liability on the debt is discharged, because of the lien your creditor may still have the right to take the security property if you do not pay the debt or default on it. If the lien is on an item of personal property that is exempt under your State's law or that the trustee has abandoned, you may be able to redeem the item rather than reaffirm the debt. To redeem, you make a single payment to the creditor equal to the current value of the security property, as agreed by the parties or determined by the court.".

(ii) In the case of a reaffirmation under subsection (m)(2), numbered paragraph 6 in the disclosures required by clause (i) of this subparagraph shall read as follows:

"6. If you were represented by an attorney during the negotiation of your reaffirmation agreement, your reaffirmation agreement becomes effective upon filing with the court.".

(4) The form of such agreement required under this paragraph shall consist of the following:

"Part B: Reaffirmation Agreement. I (we) agree to reaffirm the debts arising under the credit agreement described below.

Brief description of credit agreement:

Description of any changes to the credit agreement made as part of this reaffirmation agreement:

Signature: Date:

Borrower:

Co-borrower, if also reaffirming these debts:

Accepted by creditor:

Date of creditor acceptance:".

(5) The declaration shall consist of the following:

(A) The following certification:

"Part C: Certification by Debtor's Attorney (If Any).

I hereby certify that (1) this agreement represents a fully informed and voluntary agreement by the debtor; (2) this agreement does not impose an undue hardship on the debtor or any dependent of the debtor; and (3) I have fully advised the debtor of the legal effect and consequences of this agreement and any default under this agreement.

Signature of Debtor's Attorney: Date:".

(B) If a presumption of undue hardship has been established with respect to such agreement, such certification shall state that in the opinion of the attorney, the debtor is able to make the payment.

(C) In the case of a reaffirmation agreement under subsection (m)(2), subparagraph (B) is not applicable.

(6) (A) The statement in support of such agreement, which the debtor shall sign and date prior to filing with the court, shall consist of the following:

"Part D: Debtor's Statement in Support of Reaffirmation Agreement.

1. I believe this reaffirmation agreement will not impose an undue hardship on my dependents or me. I can afford to make the payments on the reaffirmed debt because my monthly income (take home pay plus any other income received) is $ ________, and my actual current monthly expenses including monthly payments on post-bankruptcy debt and other reaffirmation agreements total $ ________, leaving $ ________ to make the required payments on this reaffirmed debt. I understand that if my income less my monthly expenses does not leave enough to make the payments, this reaffirmation agreement is presumed to be an undue hardship on me and must be reviewed by the court. However, this presumption may be overcome if I explain to the satisfaction of the court how I can afford to make the payments here: ________.

2. I received a copy of the Reaffirmation Disclosure Statement in Part A and a completed and signed reaffirmation agreement.".

(B) Where the debtor is represented by an attorney and is reaffirming a debt owed to a creditor defined in section 19(b)(1)(A)(iv) of the Federal Reserve Act, the statement of support of the reaffirmation agreement, which the debtor shall sign and date prior to filing with the court, shall consist of the following:

"I believe this reaffirmation agreement is in my financial interest. I can afford to make the payments on the reaffirmed debt. I received a copy of the Reaffirmation Disclosure Statement in Part A and a completed and signed reaffirmation agreement.".

(7) The motion that may be used if approval of such agreement by the court is required in order for it to be effective, shall be signed and dated by the movant and shall consist of the following:

"Part E: Motion for Court Approval (To be completed only if the debtor is not represented by an attorney.). I (we), the debtor(s), affirm the following to be true and correct:

I am not represented by an attorney in connection with this reaffirmation agreement.

I believe this reaffirmation agreement is in my best interest based on the income and expenses I have disclosed in my Statement in Support of this reaffirmation agreement, and because (provide any additional relevant reasons the court should consider):

Therefore, I ask the court for an order approving this reaffirmation agreement.".

(8) The court order, which may be used to approve such agreement, shall consist of the following:

"Court Order: The court grants the debtor's motion and approves the reaffirmation agreement described above.".

(l) Notwithstanding any other provision of this title the following shall apply:

(1) A creditor may accept payments from a debtor before and after the filing of an agreement of the kind specified in subsection (c) with the court.

(2) A creditor may accept payments from a debtor under such agreement that the creditor believes in good faith to be effective.

(3) The requirements of subsections (c)(2) and (k) shall be satisfied if disclosures required under those subsections are given in good faith.

(m) (1) Until 60 days after an agreement of the kind specified in subsection (c) is filed with the court (or such additional period as the court, after notice and a hearing and for cause, orders before the expiration of such period), it shall be presumed that such agreement is an undue hardship on the debtor if the debtor's monthly income less the debtor's monthly expenses as shown on the debtor's completed and signed statement in support of such agreement required under subsection (k)(6)(A) is less than the scheduled payments on the reaffirmed debt. This presumption shall be reviewed by the court. The presumption may be rebutted in writing by the debtor if the statement includes an explanation that identifies additional sources of funds to make the payments as agreed upon under the terms of such agreement. If the presumption is not rebutted to the satisfaction of the court, the court may disapprove such agreement. No agreement shall be disapproved without notice and a hearing to the debtor and creditor, and such hearing shall be concluded before the entry of the debtor's discharge.

(2) This subsection does not apply to reaffirmation agreements where the creditor is a credit union, as defined in section 19(b)(1)(A)(iv) of the Federal Reserve Act.

- Steps to take under reaffirmation
  - Take the new sections and cross off all the stuff that goes in the form
  - Just read the substantive provisions
  - Have to:
  - Sign a reafrrimation agreement
  - Sign a reaff disclosure statement
  - Signature of attorney
  - Signature of debtor
  - Motion
  - H- we are back to having the judge make the final call on whether the reaffirmation is appropriate

11 U.S.C. §722. Redemption

An individual debtor may, whether or not the debtor has waived the right to redeem under this section, redeem tangible personal property intended primarily for personal, family, or household use, from a lien securing a dischargeable consumer debt, if such property is exempted under section 522 of this title or has been abandoned under section 554 of this title, by paying the holder of such lien the amount of the allowed secured claim of such holder that is secured by such lien in full at the time of redemption.

- *Official Local Form 6*
- *11 U.S.C. 506*
    - 506
    - 506(a)(2) (2) - If the debtor is an individual in a case under chapter 7 or 13, such value with respect to personal property securing an allowed claim shall be determined based on the replacement value of such property as of the date of the filing of the petition without deduction for costs of sale or marketing. With respect to property acquired for personal, family, or household purposes, replacement value shall mean the price a retail merchant would charge for property of that kind considering the age and condition of the property at the time value is determined.
- Hillman notes - Redemption
    - Statement of intentions a debtor has to file with a petition- as to debts secured by the property of the estate that are consumer debts, my intention is either to: surrender the property, or reaffirm the debt, or redeem the property
    - Shall be based on the replacement value of the property at the time of the filing
    - With respect... replacement value shall mean the price that a retail merchant would charge for property of that kind...
    - Not an auction

11 U.S.C. §362. Automatic Stay

Automatic stay

(a) Except as provided in subsection (b) of this section, a petition filed under section 301, 302, or 303 of this title, or an application filed under section 5(a)(3) of the Securities Investor Protection Act of 1970, operates as a stay, applicable to all entities, of—

(1) the commencement or continuation, including the issuance or employment of process, of a judicial, administrative, or other action or proceeding against the debtor that was or could have been commenced before the commencement of the case under this title, or to recover a claim against the debtor that arose before the commencement of the case under this title;

(2) the enforcement, against the debtor or against property of the estate, of a judgment obtained before the commencement of the case under this title;

(3) any act to obtain possession of property of the estate or of property from the estate or to exercise control over property of the estate;

(4) any act to create, perfect, or enforce any lien against property of the estate;

(5) any act to create, perfect, or enforce against property of the debtor any lien to the extent that such lien secures a claim that arose before the commencement of the case under this title;

(6) any act to collect, assess, or recover a claim against the debtor that arose before the commencement of the case under this title;

(7) the setoff of any debt owing to the debtor that arose before the commencement of the case under this title against any claim against the debtor; and

(8) the commencement or continuation of a proceeding before the United States Tax Court concerning a corporate debtor's tax liability for a taxable period the bankruptcy court may determine or concerning the tax liability of a debtor who is an individual for a taxable period ending before the date of the order for relief under this title.

(b) The filing of a petition under section 301, 302, or 303 of this title, or of an application under section 5(a)(3) of the Securities Investor Protection Act of 1970, does not operate as a stay—

(1) under subsection (a) of this section, of the commencement or continuation of a criminal action or proceeding against the debtor;

(2) under subsection (a)

(A) of the commencement or continuation of a civil action or proceeding—

(i) for the establishment of paternity;

(ii) for the establishment or modification of an order for domestic support obligations;

(iii) concerning child custody or visitation;

(iv) for the dissolution of a marriage, except to the extent that such proceeding seeks to determine the division of property that is property of the estate; or

(v) regarding domestic violence;

(B) of the collection of a domestic support obligation from property that is not property of the estate;

(C) with respect to the withholding of income that is property of the estate or property of the debtor for payment of a domestic support obligation under a judicial or administrative order or a statute;

(D) of the withholding, suspension, or restriction of a driver's license, a professional or occupational license, or a recreational license, under State law, as specified in section 466(a)(16) of the Social Security Act;

(E) of the reporting of overdue support owed by a parent to any consumer reporting agency as specified in section 466(a)(7) of the Social Security Act;

(F) of the interception of a tax refund, as specified in sections 464 and 466(a)(3) of the Social Security Act or under an analogous State law; or

(G) of the enforcement of a medical obligation, as specified under title IV of the Social Security Act;

(3) under subsection (a) of this section, of any act to perfect, or to maintain or continue the perfection of, an interest in property to the extent that the trustee's rights and powers are subject to such perfection under section 546(b) of this title or to the extent that such act is accomplished within the period provided under section 547(e)(2)(A) of this title;

(4) under paragraph (1), (2), (3), or (6) of subsection (a) of this section, of the commencement or continuation of an action or proceeding by a governmental unit or any organization exercising authority under the Convention on the Prohibition of the Development, Production, Stockpiling and Use of Chemical Weapons and on Their Destruction, opened for signature on January 13, 1993, to enforce such governmental unit's or organization's police and regulatory power, including the enforcement of a judgment other than a money judgment, obtained in an action or proceeding by the governmental unit to enforce such governmental unit's or organization's police or regulatory power;

(5) [Repealed. Pub. L. No. 105-277, 112 Stat.2681, Sec. 603(1), Oct. 21, 1998]

(6) under subsection (a) of this section, of the setoff by a commodity broker, forward contract merchant, stockbroker, financial institutions, financial participant, or securities clearing agency of any mutual debt and claim under or in connection with commodity contracts, as defined in section 761 of this

title, forward contracts, or securities contracts, as defined in section 741 of this title, that constitutes the setoff of a claim against the debtor for a margin payment, as defined in section 101, 741, or 761 of this title, or settlement payment, as defined in section 101 or 741 of this title, arising out of commodity contracts, forward contracts, or securities contracts against cash, securities, or other property held by, pledged to, under the control of, or due from such commodity broker, forward contract merchant, stockbroker, financial institution, financial participant, or securities clearing agency to margin, guarantee, secure, or settle commodity contracts, forward contracts, or securities contracts;

(7) under subsection (a) of this section, of the setoff by a repo participant or financial participant, of any mutual debt and claim under or in connection with repurchase agreements that constitutes the setoff of a claim against the debtor for a margin payment, as defined in section 741 or 761 of this title, or settlement payment, as defined in section 741 of this title, arising out of repurchase agreements against cash, securities, or other property held by, pledged to, under the control of, or due from such repo participant or financial participant to margin, guarantee, secure or settle repurchase agreements;

(8) under subsection (a) of this section, of the commencement of any action by the Secretary of Housing and Urban Development to foreclose a mortgage or deed of trust in any case in which the mortgage or deed of trust held by the Secretary is insured or was formerly insured under the National Housing Act and covers property, or combinations of property, consisting of five or more living units;

(9) under subsection (a), of—

(A) an audit by a governmental unit to determine tax liability;

(B) the issuance to the debtor by a governmental unit of a notice of tax deficiency;

(C) a demand for tax returns; or

(D) the making of an assessment for any tax and issuance of a notice and demand for payment of such an assessment (but any tax lien that would otherwise attach to property of the estate by reason of such an assessment shall not take effect unless such tax is a debt of the debtor that will not be discharged in the case and such property or its proceeds are transferred out of the estate to, or otherwise revested in, the debtor).

(10) under subsection (a) of this section, of any act by a lessor to the debtor under a lease of nonresidential real property that has terminated by the expiration of the stated term of the lease before the commencement of or during a case under this title to obtain possession of such property;

(11) under subsection (a) of this section, of the presentment of a negotiable instrument and the giving of notice of and protesting dishonor of such an instrument;

(12) under subsection (a) of this section, after the date which is 90 days after the filing of such petition, of the commencement or continuation, and conclusion to the entry of final judgment, of an action which involves a debtor subject to reorganization pursuant to chapter 11 of this title and which was brought by the Secretary of Transportation under section 31325 of title 46(including distribution of any proceeds of sale) to foreclose a preferred ship or fleet mortgage, or a security interest in or relating to a vessel or vessel under construction, held by the Secretary of Transportation under section 207 or title XI of the Merchant Marine Act, 1936, or under applicable State law;

(13) under subsection (a) of this section, after the date which is 90 days after the filing of such petition, of the commencement or continuation, and conclusion to the entry of final judgment, of an action which involves a debtor subject to reorganization pursuant to chapter 11 of this title and which was brought by the Secretary of Commerce under section 31325 of title 46 (including distribution of any proceeds of sale) to foreclose a preferred ship or fleet mortgage in a vessel or a mortgage, deed of trust, or other security interest in a fishing facility held by the Secretary of Commerce under section 207 or title XI of the Merchant Marine Act, 1936;

(14) under subsection (a) of this section, of any action by an accrediting agency regarding the accreditation status of the debtor as an educational institution;

(15) under subsection (a) of this section, of any action by a State licensing body regarding the licensure of the debtor as an educational institution;

(16) under subsection (a) of this section, of any action by a guaranty agency, as defined in section 435(j) of the Higher Education Act of 1965 or the Secretary of Education regarding the eligibility of the debtor to participate in programs authorized under such Act;

(17) under subsection (a), of the setoff by a swap participant or financial participant of a mutual debt and claim under or in connection with one or more swap agreements that constitutes the setoff of a claim against the debtor for any payment or other transfer of property due from the debtor under or in connection with any swap agreement against any payment due to the debtor from the swap participant or financial participant under or in connection with any swap agreement or against cash, securities, or other property held by, pledged to, under the control of, or due from such swap participant or financial participant to margin, guarantee, secure, or settle any swap agreement;

(18) under subsection (a) of the creation or perfection of a statutory lien for an ad valorem property tax, or a special tax or special assessment on real property

whether or not ad valorem, imposed by a governmental unit, if such tax or assessment comes due after the date of the filing of the petition.;

(19) under subsection (a), of withholding of income from a debtor's wages and collection of amounts withheld, under the debtor's agreement authorizing that withholding and collection for the benefit of a pension, profit-sharing, stock bonus, or other plan established under section 401, 403, 408, 408A, 414, 457, or 501(c) of the Internal Revenue Code of 1986, that is sponsored by the employer of the debtor, or an affiliate, successor, or predecessor of such employer—

(A) to the extent that the amounts withheld and collected are used solely for payments relating to a loan from a plan under section 408(b)(1) of the Employee Retirement Income Security Act of 1974 or is subject to section 72(p) of the Internal Revenue Code of 1986; or

(B) a loan from a thrift savings plan permitted under subchapter III of chapter 84 of title 5, that satisfies the requirements of section 8433(g) of such title;

but nothing in this paragraph may be construed to provide that any loan made under a governmental plan under section 414(d), or a contract or account under section 403(b), of the Internal Revenue Code of 1986 constitutes a claim or a debt under this title;

(20) under subsection (a), of any act to enforce any lien against or security interest in real property following entry of the order under subsection (d)(4) as to such real property in any prior case under this title, for a period of 2 years after the date of the entry of such an order, except that the debtor, in a subsequent case under this title, may move for relief from such order based upon changed circumstances or for other good cause shown, after notice and a hearing;

(21) under subsection (a), of any act to enforce any lien against or security interest in real property—

(A) if the debtor is ineligible under section 109(g) to be a debtor in a case under this title; or

(B) if the case under this title was filed in violation of a bankruptcy court order in a prior case under this title prohibiting the debtor from being a debtor in another case under this title;

(22) subject to subsection (l), under subsection (a)(3), of the continuation of any eviction, unlawful detainer action, or similar proceeding by a lessor against a debtor involving residential property in which the debtor resides as a tenant under a lease or rental agreement and with respect to which the lessor has obtained before the date of the filing of the bankruptcy petition, a judgment for possession of such property against the debtor;

(23) subject to subsection (m), under subsection (a)(3), of an eviction action that seeks possession of the residential property in which the debtor resides as a tenant under a lease or rental agreement based on endangerment of such property or the illegal use of controlled substances on such property, but only if the lessor files with the court, and serves upon the debtor, a certification under penalty of perjury that such an eviction action has been filed, or that the debtor, during the 30-day period preceding the date of the filing of the certification, has endangered property or illegally used or allowed to be used a controlled substance on the property;

(24) under subsection (a), of any transfer that is not avoidable under section 544 and that is not avoidable under section 549;

(25) under subsection (a), of—

- (A) the commencement or continuation of an investigation or action by a securities self regulatory organization to enforce such organization's regulatory power;
- (B) the enforcement of an order or decision, other than for monetary sanctions, obtained in an action by such securities self regulatory organization to enforce such organization's regulatory power; or
- (C) any act taken by such securities self regulatory organization to delist, delete, or refuse to permit quotation of any stock that does not meet applicable regulatory requirements;

(26) under subsection (a), of the setoff under applicable nonbankruptcy law of an income tax refund, by a governmental unit, with respect to a taxable period that ended before the date of the order for relief against an income tax liability for a taxable period that also ended before the date of the order for relief, except that in any case in which the setoff of an income tax refund is not permitted under applicable nonbankruptcy law because of a pending action to determine the amount or legality of a tax liability, the governmental unit may hold the refund pending the resolution of the action, unless the court, on the motion of the trustee and after notice and a hearing, grants the taxing authority adequate protection (within the meaning of section 361) for the secured claim of such authority in the setoff under section 506(a);

(27) under subsection (a), of the setoff by a master netting agreement participant of a mutual debt and claim under or in connection with one or more master netting agreements or any contract or agreement subject to such agreements that constitutes the setoff of a claim against the debtor for any payment or other transfer of property due from the debtor under or in connection with such agreements or any contract or agreement subject to such agreements against any payment due to the debtor from such master netting agreement participant under or in connection with such agreements or any contract or agreement subject to such agreements or against cash, securities, or other property held by, pledged to, under the control of, or due from such master

netting agreement participant to margin, guarantee, secure, or settle such agreements or any contract or agreement subject to such agreements, to the extent that such participant is eligible to exercise such offset rights under paragraph (6), (7), or (17) for each individual contract covered by the master netting agreement in issue; and

(28) under subsection (a), of the exclusion by the Secretary of Health and Human Services of the debtor from participation in the medicare program or any other Federal health care program (as defined in section 1128B(f) of the Social Security Act pursuant to title XI or XVIII of such Act).

The provisions of paragraphs (12) and (13) of this subsection shall apply with respect to any such petition filed on or before December 31, 1989.

(c) Except as provided in subsections (d), (e), (f), and (h) of this section—

(1) the stay of an act against property of the estate under subsection (a) of this section continues until such property is no longer property of the estate;

(2) the stay of any other act under subsection (a) of this section continues until the earliest of

(A) the time the case is closed;

(B) the time the case is dismissed; or

(C) if the case is a case under chapter 7 of this title concerning an individual or a case under chapter 9, 11, 12, or 13 of this title, the time a discharge is granted or denied;

(3) if a single or joint case is filed by or against debtor who is an individual in a case under chapter 7, 11, or 13, and if a single or joint case of the debtor was pending within the preceding 1-year period but was dismissed, other than a case refiled under a chapter other than chapter 7 after dismissal under section 707(b)--

(A) the stay under subsection (a) with respect to any action taken with respect to a debt or property securing such debt or with respect to any lease shall terminate with respect to the debtor on the 30th day after the filing of the later case;

(B) on the motion of a party in interest for continuation of the automatic stay and upon notice and a hearing, the court may extend the stay in particular cases as to any or all creditors (subject to such conditions or limitations as the court may then impose) after notice and a hearing completed before the expiration of the 30-day period only if the party in interest demonstrates that the filing of the later case is in good faith as to the creditors to be stayed; and

(C) for purposes of subparagraph (B), a case is presumptively filed not in good faith (but such presumption may be rebutted by clear and convincing evidence to the contrary)--

(i) as to all creditors, if—

(I) more than 1 previous case under any of chapters 7, 11, and 13 in which the individual was a debtor was pending within the preceding 1-year period;

(II) a previous case under any of chapters 7, 11, and 13 in which the individual was a debtor was dismissed within such 1-year period, after the debtor failed to—

(aa) file or amend the petition or other documents as required by this title or the court without substantial excuse (but mere inadvertence or negligence shall not be a substantial excuse unless the dismissal was caused by the negligence of the debtor's attorney);

(bb) provide adequate protection as ordered by the court; or

(cc) perform the terms of a plan confirmed by the court; or

(III) there has not been a substantial change in the financial or personal affairs of the debtor since the dismissal of the next most previous case under chapter 7, 11, or 13 or any other reason to conclude that the later case will be concluded—

(aa) if a case under chapter 7, with a discharge; or

(bb) if a case under chapter 11 or 13, with a confirmed plan that will be fully performed; and

(ii) as to any creditor that commenced an action under subsection (d) in a previous case in which the individual was a debtor if, as of the date of dismissal of such case, that action was still pending or had been resolved by terminating, conditioning, or limiting the stay as to actions of such creditor; and

(4) (A) (i) if a single or joint case is filed by or against a debtor who is an individual under this title, and if 2 or more single or joint cases of the debtor were pending within the previous year but were dismissed, other than a case refiled under section 707(b), the stay under subsection (a) shall not go into effect upon the filing of the later case; and

(ii) on request of a party in interest, the court shall promptly enter an order confirming that no stay is in effect;

(B) if, within 30 days after the filing of the later case, a party in interest requests the court may order the stay to take effect in the case as to any or all creditors (subject to such conditions or limitations as the court may impose), after notice and a hearing, only if the party in interest demonstrates that the filing of the later case is in good faith as to the creditors to be stayed;

(C) a stay imposed under subparagraph (B) shall be effective on the date of the entry of the order allowing the stay to go into effect; and

(D) for purposes of subparagraph (B), a case is presumptively filed not in good faith (but such presumption may be rebutted by clear and convincing evidence to the contrary)--

(i) as to all creditors if—

(I) 2 or more previous cases under this title in which the individual was a debtor were pending within the 1-year period;

(II) a previous case under this title in which the individual was a debtor was dismissed within the time period stated in this paragraph after the debtor failed to file or amend the petition or other documents as required by this title or the court without substantial excuse (but mere inadvertence or negligence shall not be substantial excuse unless the dismissal was caused by the negligence of the debtor's attorney), failed to provide adequate protection as ordered by the court, or failed to perform the terms of a plan confirmed by the court; or

(III) there has not been a substantial change in the financial or personal affairs of the debtor since the dismissal of the next most previous case under this title, or any other reason to conclude that the later case will not be concluded, if a case under chapter 7, with a discharge, and if a case under chapter 11 or 13, with a confirmed plan that will be fully performed; or

(ii) as to any creditor that commenced an action under subsection (d) in a previous case in which the individual was a debtor if, as of the date of dismissal of such case, such action was still pending or had been resolved by terminating, conditioning, or limiting the stay as to such action of such creditor.

(d) On request of a party in interest and after notice and a hearing, the court shall grant relief from the stay provided under subsection (a) of this section, such as by terminating, annulling, modifying, or conditioning such stay—

(1) for cause, including the lack of adequate protection of an interest in property of such party in interest;

(2) with respect to a stay of an act against property under subsection (a) of this section, if—

(A) the debtor does not have an equity in such property; and

(B) such property is not necessary to an effective reorganization;

(3) with respect to a stay of an act against single asset real estate under subsection (a), by a creditor whose claim is secured by an interest in such real estate, unless, not later than the date that is 90 days after the entry of the order for relief (or such later date as the court may determine for cause by order entered within that 90-day period) or 30 days after the court determines that the debtor is subject to this paragraph, whichever is later—

(A) the debtor has filed a plan of reorganization that has a reasonable possibility of being confirmed within a reasonable time; or

(B) the debtor has commenced monthly payments that—

(i) may, in the debtor's sole discretion, notwithstanding section 363(c)(2), be made from rents or other income generated before, on, or after the date of the commencement of the case by or from the property to each creditor whose claim is secured by such real estate (other than a claim secured by a judgment lien or by an unmatured statutory lien); and

(ii) are in an amount equal to interest at the then applicable nondefault contract rate of interest on the value of the creditor's interest in the real estate; or

(4) with respect to a stay of an act against real property under subsection (a), by a creditor whose claim is secured by an interest in such real property, if the court finds that the filing of the petition was part of a scheme to delay, hinder, and defraud creditors that involved either—

(A) transfer of all or part ownership of, or other interest in, such real property without the consent of the secured creditor or court approval; or

(B) multiple bankruptcy filings affecting such real property.

If recorded in compliance with applicable State laws governing notices of interests or liens in real property, an order entered under paragraph (4) shall be binding in any other case under this title purporting to affect such real property filed not later than 2 years after the date of the entry of such order by the court, except that a debtor in a subsequent case under this title may move for relief from such order based upon changed circumstances or for good cause shown, after notice and a hearing. Any Federal, State, or local governmental unit that accepts notices of interests or liens in real property shall accept any certified copy of an order described in this subsection for indexing and recording.

(e) (1) Thirty days after a request under subsection (d) of this section for relief from the stay of any act against property of the estate under subsection (a) of this section, such stay is terminated with respect to the party in interest making such request, unless the court, after notice and a hearing, orders such stay continued in effect pending the conclusion of, or as a result of, a final hearing and determination under subsection (d) of this section. A hearing under this subsection may be a preliminary hearing, or may be consolidated with the final hearing under subsection (d) of this section. The court shall order such stay continued in effect pending the conclusion of the final hearing under subsection (d) of this section if there is a reasonable likelihood that the party opposing relief from such stay will prevail at the conclusion of such final hearing. If the hearing under this subsection is a preliminary hearing, then such final hearing shall be concluded not later than thirty days after the conclusion of such preliminary hearing, unless the 30-day period is extended with the consent of the parties in interest or for a specific time which the court finds is required by compelling circumstances.

(2) Notwithstanding paragraph (1), in a case under chapter 7, 11, or 13 in which the debtor is an individual, the stay under subsection (a) shall terminate on the date that is 60 days after a request is made by a party in interest under subsection (d), unless—

(A) a final decision is rendered by the court during the 60-day period beginning on the date of the request; or

(B) such 60-day period is extended—

(i) by agreement of all parties in interest; or

(ii) by the court for such specific period of time as the court finds is required for good cause, as described in findings made by the court.

(f) Upon request of a party in interest, the court, with or without a hearing, shall grant such relief from the stay provided under subsection (a) of this section as is necessary to prevent irreparable damage to the interest of an entity in property, if such interest will suffer such damage before there is an opportunity for notice and a hearing under subsection (d) or (e) of this section.

(g) In any hearing under subsection (d) or (e) of this section concerning relief from the stay of any act under subsection (a) of this section—

(1) the party requesting such relief has the burden of proof on the issue of the debtor's equity in property; and

(2) the party opposing such relief has the burden of proof on all other issues.

(h) (1) In a case in which the debtor is an individual, the stay provided by subsection (a) is terminated with respect to personal property of the estate or of the debtor securing in whole or in part a claim, or subject to an unexpired lease, and such personal property shall no longer be property of the estate if the debtor fails within the applicable time set by section 521(a)(2)--

(A) to file timely any statement of intention required under section 521(a)(2) with respect to such personal property or to indicate in such statement that the debtor will either surrender such personal property or retain it and, if retaining such personal property, either redeem such personal property pursuant to section 722, enter into an agreement of the kind specified in section 524(c) applicable to the debt secured by such personal property, or assume such unexpired lease pursuant to section 365(p) if the trustee does not do so, as applicable; and

(B) to take timely the action specified in such statement, as it may be amended before expiration of the period for taking action, unless such statement specifies the debtor's intention to reaffirm such debt on the original contract terms and the creditor refuses to agree to the reaffirmation on such terms.

(2) Paragraph (1) does not apply if the court determines, on the motion of the trustee filed before the expiration of the applicable time set by section 521(a)(2), after notice and a hearing, that such personal property is of consequential value or benefit to the estate, and orders appropriate adequate protection of the creditor's interest, and orders the debtor to deliver any collateral in the debtor's possession to the trustee. If the court does not so determine, the stay provided by subsection (a) shall terminate upon the conclusion of the hearing on the motion.

(i) If a case commenced under chapter 7, 11, or 13 is dismissed due to the creation of a debt repayment plan, for purposes of subsection (c)(3), any subsequent case commenced by the debtor under any such chapter shall not be presumed to be filed not in good faith.

(j) On request of a party in interest, the court shall issue an order under subsection (c) confirming that the automatic stay has been terminated.

(k) (1) Except as provided in paragraph (2), an individual injured by any willful violation of a stay provided by this section shall recover actual damages, including costs and attorneys' fees, and, in appropriate circumstances, may recover punitive damages.

(2) If such violation is based on an action taken by an entity in the good faith belief that subsection (h) applies to the debtor, the recovery under paragraph (1) of this subsection against such entity shall be limited to actual damages.

(l) (1) Except as otherwise provided in this subsection, subsection (b)(22) shall apply on the date that is 30 days after the date on which the bankruptcy petition is filed, if the debtor files with the petition and serves upon the lessor a certification under penalty of perjury that—

(A) under nonbankruptcy law applicable in the jurisdiction, there are circumstances under which the debtor would be permitted to cure the entire monetary default that gave rise to the judgment for possession, after that judgment for possession was entered; and

(B) the debtor (or an adult dependent of the debtor) has deposited with the clerk of the court, any rent that would become due during the 30-day period after the filing of the bankruptcy petition.

(2) If, within the 30-day period after the filing of the bankruptcy petition, the debtor (or an adult dependent of the debtor) complies with paragraph (1) and files with the court and serves upon the lessor a further certification under penalty of perjury that the debtor (or an adult dependent of the debtor) has cured, under nonbankrupcty law applicable in the jurisdiction, the entire monetary default that gave rise to the judgment under which possession is sought by the lessor, subsection (b)(22) shall not apply, unless ordered to apply by the court under paragraph (3).

(3) (A) If the lessor files an objection to any certification filed by the debtor under paragraph (1) or (2), and serves such objection upon the debtor, the court shall hold a hearing within 10 days after the filing and service of such objection to determine if the certification filed by the debtor under paragraph (1) or (2) is true.

(B) If the court upholds the objection of the lessor filed under subparagraph (A)--

(i) subsection (b)(22) shall apply immediately and relief from the stay provided under subsection (a)(3) shall not be required to enable the lessor to complete the process to recover full possession of the property; and

(ii) the clerk of the court shall immediately serve upon the lessor and the debtor a certified copy of the court's order upholding the lessor's objection.

(4) If a debtor, in accordance with paragraph (5), indicates on the petition that there was a judgment for possession of the residential rental property in which the debtor resides and does not file a certification under paragraph (1) or (2)--

(A) subsection (b)(22) shall apply immediately upon failure to file such certification, and relief from the stay provided under subsection (a)(3) shall not be required to enable the lessor to complete the process to recover full possession of the property; and

(B) the clerk of the court shall immediately serve upon the lessor and the debtor a certified copy of the docket indicating the absence of a filed certification and the applicability of the exception to the stay under subsection (b)(22).

(5) (A) Where a judgment for possession of residential property in which the debtor resides as a tenant under a lease or rental agreement has been obtained by the lessor, the debtor shall so indicate on the bankruptcy petition and shall provide the name and address of the lessor that obtained that pre-petition judgment on the petition and on any certification filed under this subsection.

(B) The form of certification filed with the petition, as specified in this subsection, shall provide for the debtor to certify, and the debtor shall certify—

(i) whether a judgment for possession of residential rental housing in which the debtor resides has been obtained against the debtor before the date of the filing of the petition; and

(ii) whether the debtor is claiming under paragraph (1) that under nonbankruptcy law applicable in the jurisdiction, there are circumstances under which the debtor would be permitted to cure the entire monetary default that gave rise to the judgment for possession, after that judgment of possession was entered, and has made the appropriate deposit with the court.

(C) The standard forms (electronic and otherwise) used in a bankruptcy proceeding shall be amended to reflect the requirements of this subsection.

(D) The clerk of the court shall arrange for the prompt transmittal of the rent deposited in accordance with paragraph (1)(B) to the lessor.

(m) (1) Except as otherwise provided in this subsection, subsection (b)(23) shall apply on the date that is 15 days after the date on which the lessor files and serves a certification described in subsection (b)(23).

(2) (A) If the debtor files with the court an objection to the truth or legal sufficiency of the certification described in subsection (b)(23) and serves such objection upon the lessor, subsection (b)(23) shall not apply, unless ordered to apply by the court under this subsection.

(B) If the debtor files and serves the objection under subparagraph (A), the court shall hold a hearing within 10 days after the filing and service of such objection to determine if the situation giving rise to the lessor's certification under paragraph (1) existed or has been remedied.

(C) If the debtor can demonstrate to the satisfaction of the court that the situation giving rise to the lessor's certification under paragraph (1) did not exist or has been remedied, the stay provided under subsection (a)(3) shall remain in effect until the termination of the stay under this section.

(D) If the debtor cannot demonstrate to the satisfaction of the court that the situation giving rise to the lessor's certification under paragraph (1) did not exist or has been remedied—

(i) relief from the stay provided under subsection (a)(3) shall not be required to enable the lessor to proceed with the eviction; and

(ii) the clerk of the court shall immediately serve upon the lessor and the debtor a certified copy of the court's order upholding the lessor's certification.

(3) If the debtor fails to file, within 15 days, an objection under paragraph (2)(A)--

(A) subsection (b)(23) shall apply immediately upon such failure and relief from the stay provided under subsection (a)(3) shall not be required to enable the lessor to complete the process to recover full possession of the property; and

(B) the clerk of the court shall immediately serve upon the lessor and the debtor a certified copy of the docket indicating such failure.

(n) (1) Except as provided in paragraph (2), subsection (a) does not apply in a case in which the debtor—

(A) is a debtor in a small business case pending at the time the petition is filed;

(B) was a debtor in a small business case that was dismissed for any reason by an order that became final in the 2-year period ending on the date of the order for relief entered with respect to the petition;

(C) was a debtor in a small business case in which a plan was confirmed in the 2-year period ending on the date of the order for relief entered with respect to the petition; or

(D) is an entity that has acquired substantially all of the assets or business of a small business debtor described in subparagraph (A), (B), or (C), unless such entity establishes by a preponderance of the evidence that such entity acquired substantially all of the assets or business of such small business debtor in good faith and not for the purpose of evading this paragraph.

(2) Paragraph (1) does not apply—

(A) to an involuntary case involving no collusion by the debtor with creditors; or

(B) to the filing of a petition if—

(i) the debtor proves by a preponderance of the evidence that the filing of the petition resulted from circumstances beyond the control of the debtor not foreseeable at the time the case then pending was filed; and

(ii) it is more likely than not that the court will confirm a feasible plan, but not a liquidating plan, within a reasonable period of time.

(o) The exercise of rights not subject to the stay arising under subsection (a) pursuant to paragraph (6), (7), (17), or (27) of subsection (b) shall not be stayed by any order of a court or administrative agency in any proceeding under this title.

- Automatic stay - 362(a):
  - The commencement or continuation, including the issuance or employment of process, of a judicial, administrative, or other action or proceeding against the debtor that was or could have been commenced before the commencement of the case under this title, or to recover a claim against the debtor that arose before the commencement of the case under this title;
- H- stops creditor from doing anything that would do them any good

- *Citizens Bank v. Strumpf* (administrative freeze on bank account)
  - Court held that the bank's actions were not a set off under 362(a)(7) and that it was not a permanent and absolute refusal to pay, but rather a temporary hold while it sought relief from the automatic stay
  - Have to act promptly- put on the freeze and immediately file for relief from stay

Relief from the Stay

- *Fed. R. Bankr. P. 4001(a)*
- *11 U.S.C. 362(d)*
- Get relief from stay by filing a motion
  - The party requesting relief has the burden of proof on the issue of the debtor's equity in property
    - The party opposing such relief has the burden of proof on all other issues
- Example - Property case problem – Black Acre
  Value → $100,000
  Real estate tax → $12,000 (increasing by $3,000/year)
  First mortgage → $40,000
  Second mortgage → $150,000

- First mortgagee – fully secured and entitled to interest – no risk – no relief of automatic stay
- Second mortgagee - $48,000 entitled and their position is eroding every minute – wants relief from stay or adequate protection
    - Entitled to adequate protection because its position is diminishing

- *Soares v. Brockton Credit Union (In re Soares)* (whether bankruptcy court may grant retroactive relief from automatic stay)
    - Retroactively relief should be the long odds exception
    - Each case should be done on its
    - When a creditor inadvertently violates the automatic stay in ignorance of a pending bankruptcy the courts have sometimes afforded retro relief
    - Debtors who act in bad faith may create situations that are ripe for retroactive relief
    - They illustrate that a rarely dispensed remedy like retroactive relieg from the automatic stay must rest on a set of facts that is both unusual and unusually compelling
- *United Savings Association of Texas v. Timbers of Inwood Forest Assoc.*
    - D(2) requires relief from stay unless a debtor provides a reasonable possibility of a successful reorganization within a reasonable time
    - Holding - Under secured creditors are not entitled to compensation under 362D1 for the delay caused by the automatic stay in foreclosing on their collateral
    - §362(d) authorizes the bankruptcy court to grant relief from the stay "(1) for cause, including the lack of adequate protection of an interest in property of...[a] party in interest," or "(2) with respect to a stay of an act against property," if the debtor does not have an equity in such property (i.e., the creditor is undersecured) and the property is "not necessary to an effective reorganization."
- *McMullen*
    - Real estate agent- never returned deposit from a real estate deal that fell through

- Without knowledge of the bankruptcy action pending wrote a letter to the board and asked them to take action
- The board decided that there was no violation and dismissed the action
- McMullen brought an action to assess liability against the sevigny's for a stay violation
- Only law at that time was Diamond
- Question was whether the activities that the Sevigny's took was a state violation?
- It was a not a stay violation

▪ *In re Diamond*
  - Real estate broker who went bankrupt. Lawyer for his creditors went to diamonds lawyer and said if you don't settle the debt with him he will go the licensing board to get the license
  - Issue was whether that action was a violation of the automatic stay by the creditor
  - C of Appeals- on those facts- the statement could be found to be coercive and it is possible that diamond could prove facts that would entitle him to receive relief under 362(h)

▪ Distinguishing *McMullen* and *Diamond*
  - H- can put them together on the strength of the threat
  - Diamond pay up or else
  - No evidence in McMullen of saying anything like that

11 U.S.C. §524(e). Third Party Injunctions

Except as provided in subsection (a)(3) of this section, discharge of a debt of the debtor does not affect the liability of any other entity on, or the property of any other entity for, such debt.

Subsection (a)(3) - operates as an injunction against the commencement or continuation of an action, the employment of process, or an act, to collect or recover from, or offset against, property of the debtor of the kind specified in section 541(a)(2) of this title that is acquired after the commencement of the case, on account of any allowable community claim, except a community claim that is excepted from discharge under section 523, 1228(a)(1), or 1328(a)(1), or that would be so excepted, determined in accordance with the provisions of sections 523(c) and 523(d) of this title, in a case concerning the debtor's spouse commenced on the date of the filing of the petition in the case concerning the debtor, whether or not discharge of the debt based on such community claim is waived.

The Trustee

- *28 U.S.C. §586(a)(1)*
    - United States trustee shall appoint a panel of private trustees
- *28 U.S.C. §959(b)*
    - Must operate the business subject to the rules where it is located as if he were a real person
- *28 U.S.C. §960*
    - Must pay any taxes that he would have to pay if he were a real person
- *11 U.S.C. §701*
    - Interim trustee appointed immediately after the order for relief
- *11 U.S.C. §702*
    - Election of trustee
        - A(1) Creditors are only allowed to vote if they hold an allowable, undisputed, fixed, liquidated, unsecured claim
        - A(2)- cannot have an interest materially adverse
        - A(3)- is not an insider
        - The majority of those voting and 20% of the claimants are needed to elect

11 U.S.C. §704. Duties of trustee

(a) The trustee shall—

(1) collect and reduce to money the property of the estate for which such trustee serves, and close such estate as expeditiously as is compatible with the best interests of parties in interest;

(2) be accountable for all property received;

(3) ensure that the debtor shall perform his intention as specified in section 521(2)(B) of this title;

(4) investigate the financial affairs of the debtor;

(5) if a purpose would be served, examine proofs of claims and object to the allowance of any claim that is improper;

(6) if advisable, oppose the discharge of the debtor;

(7) unless the court orders otherwise, furnish such information concerning the estate and the estate's administration as is requested by a party in interest;

(8) if the business of the debtor is authorized to be operated, file with the court, with the United States trustee, and with any governmental unit charged with responsibility for collection or determination of any tax arising out of such operation, periodic reports and summaries of the operation of such business, including a statement of receipts and disbursements, and such other information as the United States trustee or the court requires;

(9) make a final report and file a final account of the administration of the estate with the court and with the United States trustee.;

(10) if with respect to the debtor there is a claim for a domestic support obligation, provide the applicable notice specified in subsection (c);

(11) if, at the time of the commencement of the case, the debtor (or any entity designated by the debtor) served as the administrator (as defined in section 3 of the Employee Retirement Income Security Act of 1974) of an employee benefit plan, continue to perform the obligations required of the administrator; and

(12) use all reasonable and best efforts to transfer patients from a health care business that is in the process of being closed to an appropriate health care business that—

(A) is in the vicinity of the health care business that is closing;

(B) provides the patient with services that are substantially similar to those provided by the health care business that is in the process of being closed; and

(C) maintains a reasonable quality of care.

(b) (1) With respect to a debtor who is an individual in a case under this chapter—

(A) the United States trustee (or the bankruptcy administrator, if any) shall review all materials filed by the debtor and, not later than 10 days after the date of the first meeting of creditors, file with the court a statement as to whether the debtor's case would be presumed to be an abuse under section 707(b); and

(B) not later than 5 days after receiving a statement under subparagraph (A), the court shall provide a copy of the statement to all creditors.

(2) The United States trustee (or bankruptcy administrator, if any) shall, not later than 30 days after the date of filing a statement under paragraph (1), either

file a motion to dismiss or convert under section 707(b) or file a statement setting forth the reasons the United States trustee (or the bankruptcy administrator, if any) does not consider such a motion to be appropriate, if the United States trustee (or the bankruptcy administrator, if any) determines that the debtor's case should be presumed to be an abuse under section 707(b) and the product of the debtor's current monthly income, multiplied by 12 is not less than—

(A) in the case of a debtor in a household of 1 person, the median family income of the applicable State for 1 earner; or

(B) in the case of a debtor in a household of 2 or more individuals, the highest median family income of the applicable State for a family of the same number or fewer individuals.

(c) (1) In a case described in subsection (a)(10) to which subsection (a)(10) applies, the trustee shall—

(A) (i) provide written notice to the holder of the claim described in subsection (a)(10) of such claim and of the right of such holder to use the services of the State child support enforcement agency established under sections 464 and 466 of the Social Security Act for the State in which such holder resides, for assistance in collecting child support during and after the case under this title;

(ii) include in the notice provided under clause (i) the address and telephone number of such State child support enforcement agency; and

(iii) include in the notice provided under clause (i) an explanation of the rights of such holder to payment of such claim under this chapter;

(B) (i) provide written notice to such State child support enforcement agency of such claim; and

(ii) include in the notice provided under clause (i) the name, address, and telephone number of such holder; and

(C) at such time as the debtor is granted a discharge under section 727, provide written notice to such holder and to such State child support enforcement agency of—

(i) the granting of the discharge;

(ii) the last recent known address of the debtor;

(iii) the last recent known name and address of the debtor's employer; and

(iv) the name of each creditor that holds a claim that—

(I) is not discharged under paragraph (2), (4), or (14A) of section 523(a); or

(II) was reaffirmed by the debtor under section 524(c).

(2) (A) The holder of a claim described in subsection (a)(10) or the State child support enforcement agency of the State in which such holder resides may request from a creditor described in paragraph (1)(C)(iv) the last known address of the debtor.

(B) Notwithstanding any other provision of law, a creditor that makes a disclosure of a last known address of a debtor in connection with a request made under subparagraph (A) shall not be liable by reason of making such disclosure.

11 U.S.C. §1104(b). Appointment of trustee or examiner

(a) At any time after the commencement of the case but before confirmation of a plan, on request of a party in interest or the United States trustee, and after notice and a hearing, the court shall order the appointment of a trustee—

(1) for cause, including fraud, dishonesty, incompetence, or gross mismanagement of the affairs of the debtor by current management, either before or after the commencement of the case, or similar cause, but not including the number of holders of securities of the debtor or the amount of assets or liabilities of the debtor;

(2) if such appointment is in the interests of creditors, any equity security holders, and other interests of the estate, without regard to the number of holders of securities of the debtor or the amount of assets or liabilities of the debtor.; or

(3) if grounds exist to convert or dismiss the case under section 1112, but the court determines that the appointment of a trustee or an examiner is in the best interests of creditors and the estate.

(b) (1) Except as provided in section 1163 of this title, on the request of a party in interest made not later than 30 days after the court orders the appointment of a trustee under subsection (a), the United States trustee shall convene a meeting of creditors for the purpose of electing one disinterested person to serve as trustee in the case. The election of a trustee shall be conducted in the manner provided in subsections (a), (b), and (c) of section 702 of this title.

(2) (A) If an eligible, disinterested trustee is elected at a meeting of creditors under paragraph (1), the United States trustee shall file a report certifying that election.

(B) Upon the filing of a report under subparagraph (A)--

(i) the trustee elected under paragraph (1) shall be considered to have been selected and appointed for purposes of this section; and

(ii) the service of any trustee appointed under subsection (d) shall terminate.

(C) The court shall resolve any dispute arising out of an election described in subparagraph (A).

(c) If the court does not order the appointment of a trustee under this section, then at any time before the confirmation of a plan, on request of a party in interest or the United States trustee, and after notice and a hearing, the court shall order the appointment of an examiner to conduct such an investigation of the debtor as is appropriate, including an investigation of any allegations of fraud, dishonesty, incompetence, misconduct, mismanagement, or irregularity in the management of the affairs of the debtor of or by current or former management of the debtor, if—

(1) such appointment is in the interests of creditors, any equity security holders, and other interests of the estate; or

(2) the debtor's fixed, liquidated, unsecured debts, other than debts for goods, services, or taxes, or owing to an insider, exceed $5,000,000.

(d) If the court orders the appointment of a trustee or an examiner, if a trustee or an examiner dies or resigns during the case or is removed under section 324 of this title, or if a trustee fails to qualify under section 322 of this title, then the United States trustee, after consultation with parties in interest, shall appoint, subject to the court's approval, one disinterested person other than the United States trustee to serve as trustee or examiner, as the case may be, in the case.

(e) The United States trustee shall move for the appointment of a trustee under subsection (a) if there are reasonable grounds to suspect that current members of the governing body of the debtor, the debtor's chief executive or chief financial officer, or members of the governing body who selected the debtor's chief executive or chief financial officer, participated in actual fraud, dishonesty, or criminal conduct in the management of the debtor or the debtor's public financial reporting.[21]

[21] Effective as of the date of enactment of the Act; applicable to any case under the Bankruptcy Code commenced on or after such date. Pub. L. No. 109-8, 119 Stat. 23, Sec. 1406.

Fed. R. Bankr. P. 2015(a). Trustee's Avoiding Powers: Fraudulent Transfers/Conveyances

(a) The trustee shall have, as of the commencement of the case, and without regard to any knowledge of the trustee or of any creditor, the rights and powers of, or may avoid any transfer of property of the debtor or any obligation incurred by the debtor that is voidable by—

(1) a creditor that extends credit to the debtor at the time of the commencement of the case, and that obtains, at such time and with respect to such credit, a judicial lien on all property on which a creditor on a simple contract could have obtained such a judicial lien, whether or not such a creditor exists;

(2) a creditor that extends credit to the debtor at the time of the commencement of the case, and obtains, at such time and with respect to such credit, an execution against the debtor that is returned unsatisfied at such time, whether or not such a creditor exists; or

(3) a bona fide purchaser of real property, other than fixtures, from the debtor, against whom applicable law permits such transfer to be perfected, that obtains the status of a bona fide purchaser and has perfected such transfer at the time of the commencement of the case, whether or not such a purchaser exists.

(b) (1) Except as provided in paragraph (2), the trustee may avoid any transfer of an interest of the debtor in property or any obligation incurred by the debtor that is voidable under applicable law by a creditor holding an unsecured claim that is allowable under section 502 of this title or that is not allowable only under section 502(e) of this title.

(2) Paragraph (1) shall not apply to a transfer of a charitable contribution (as that term is defined in section 548(d)(3)) that is not covered under section 548(a)(1)(B), by reason of section 548(a)(2). Any claim by any person to recover a transferred contribution described in the preceding sentence under Federal or State law in a Federal or State court shall be preempted by the commencement of the case.

- *11 U.S.C. §541(d)*

(d) Property in which the debtor holds, as of the commencement of the case, only legal title and not an equitable interest, such as a mortgage secured by real property, or an interest in such a mortgage, sold by the debtor but as to which the debtor retains legal title to service or supervise the servicing of such mortgage or interest, becomes property of the estate under subsection (a)(1) or (2) of this section only to the extent of the debtor's legal title to such property, but not to the extent of any equitable interest in such property that the debtor does not hold.

11 U.S.C. § 544. Preferences

(2) For the purposes of this section, except as provided in paragraph (3) of this subsection, a transfer is made—

(A) at the time such transfer takes effect between the transferor and the transferee, if such transfer is perfected at, or within 30 days after, such time, except as provided in subsection (c)(3)(B);

(B) at the time such transfer is perfected, if such transfer is perfected after such 30 days; or

(C) immediately before the date of the filing of the petition, if such transfer is not perfected at the later of—

(i) the commencement of the case; or

(ii) 30 days after such transfer takes effect between the transferor and the transferee.

- *11 U.S.C. §547(e)(2)*

(2) For the purposes of this section, except as provided in paragraph (3) of this subsection, a transfer is made—

(A) at the time such transfer takes effect between the transferor and the transferee, if such transfer is perfected at, or within 30 days after, such time, except as provided in subsection (c)(3)(B);

(B) at the time such transfer is perfected, if such transfer is perfected after such 30 days; or

(C) immediately before the date of the filing of the petition, if such transfer is not perfected at the later of—

(i) the commencement of the case; or

(ii) 30 days after such transfer takes effect between the transferor and the transferee.

11 U.S.C. §548. Fraudulent transfers and obligations

(a) (1) The trustee may avoid any transfer (including any transfer to or for the benefit of an insider under an employment contract) of an interest of the debtor in property, or any obligation (including any obligation to or for the benefit of an insider under an employment contract) incurred by the debtor,[22] that was made or incurred on or within 2 years[23] before the date of the filing of the petition, if the debtor voluntarily or involuntarily—

(A) made such transfer or incurred such obligation with actual intent to hinder, delay, or defraud any entity to which the debtor was or became, on or after the date that such transfer was made or such obligation was incurred, indebted; or

(B) (i) received less than a reasonably equivalent value in exchange for such transfer or obligation; and

(ii) (I) was insolvent on the date that such transfer was made or such obligation was incurred, or became insolvent as a result of such transfer or obligation;

(II) was engaged in business or a transaction, or was about to engage in business or a transaction, for which any property remaining with the debtor was an unreasonably small capital;

(III) intended to incur, or believed that the debtor would incur, debts that would be beyond the debtor's ability to pay as such debts matured; or

(IV) made such transfer to or for the benefit of an insider, or incurred such obligation to or for the benefit of an insider, under an employment contract and not in the ordinary course of business.[24]

(2) A transfer of a charitable contribution to a qualified religious or charitable entity or organization shall not be considered to be a transfer covered under paragraph (1)(B) in any case in which—

(A) the amount of that contribution does not exceed 15 percent of the gross annual income of the debtor for the year in which the transfer of the contribution is made; or

---

[22] Effective as of the date of enactment of the Act; applicable to any case under the Bankruptcy Code commenced on or after such date. Pub. L. No. 109-8, 119 Stat. 23, Sec. 1406.

[23] Effective as of the date of enactment of the Act; applicable only to cases under the Bankruptcy Code commenced more than one year after such date. Pub. L. No. 109-8, 119 Stat. 23, Sec. 1406.

[24] Effective as of the date of enactment of the Act; applicable to any case under the Bankruptcy Code commenced on or after such date. Pub. L. No. 109-8, 119 Stat. 23, Sec. 1406.

(B) the contribution made by a debtor exceeded the percentage amount of gross annual income specified in subparagraph (A), if the transfer was consistent with the practices of the debtor in making charitable contributions.

(b) The trustee of a partnership debtor may avoid any transfer of an interest of the debtor in property, or any obligation incurred by the debtor, that was made or incurred on or within 2 years before the date of the filing of the petition, to a general partner in the debtor, if the debtor was insolvent on the date such transfer was made or such obligation was incurred, or became insolvent as a result of such transfer or obligation.[25]

(c) Except to the extent that a transfer or obligation voidable under this section is voidable under section 544, 545, or 547 of this title, a transferee or obligee of such a transfer or obligation that takes for value and in good faith has a lien on or may retain any interest transferred or may enforce any obligation incurred, as the case may be, to the extent that such transferee or obligee gave value to the debtor in exchange for such transfer or obligation.

(d) (1) For the purposes of this section, a transfer is made when such transfer is so perfected that a bona fide purchaser from the debtor against whom applicable law permits such transfer to be perfected cannot acquire an interest in the property transferred that is superior to the interest in such property of the transferee, but if such transfer is not so perfected before the commencement of the case, such transfer is made immediately before the date of the filing of the petition.

(2) In this section—

(A) "value" means property, or satisfaction or securing of a present or antecedent debt of the debtor, but does not include an unperformed promise to furnish support to the debtor or to a relative of the debtor;

(B) a commodity broker, forward contract merchant, stockbroker, financial institution, financial participant, or securities clearing agency that receives a margin payment, as defined in section 101, 741, or 761 of this title, or settlement payment, as defined in section 101 or 741 of this title, takes for value to the extent of such payment;

(C) a repo participant or financial participant that receives a margin payment, as defined in section 741 or 761 of this title, or settlement payment, as defined in section 741 of this title, in connection with a repurchase agreement, takes for value to the extent of such payment;

[25] Effective as of the date of enactment of the Act; applicable only to cases under the Bankruptcy Code commenced more than one year after such date. Pub. L. No. 109-8, 119 Stat. 23, Sec. 1406.

(D) a swap participant or financial participant that receives a transfer in connection with a swap agreement takes for value to the extent of such transfer; and

(E) a master netting agreement participant that receives a transfer in connection with a master netting agreement or any individual contract covered thereby takes for value to the extent of such transfer, except that, with respect to a transfer under any individual contract covered thereby, to the extent that such master netting agreement participant otherwise did not take (or is otherwise not deemed to have taken) such transfer for value.

(3) In this section, the term "charitable contribution" means a charitable contribution, as that term is defined in section 170(c) of the Internal Revenue Code of 1986, if that contribution—

(A) is made by a natural person; and

(B) consists of—

(i) a financial instrument (as that term is defined in section 731(c)(2)(c) of the Internal Revenue Code of 1986); or

(ii) cash.

(4) In this section, the term "qualified religious or charitable entity or organization" means—

(A) an entity described in section 170(c)(1) of the Internal Revenue Code of 1986; or

(B) an entity or organization described in section 170(c)(2) of the Internal Revenue Code of 1986.

(e) (1) In addition to any transfer that the trustee may otherwise avoid, the trustee may avoid any transfer of an interest of the debtor in property that was made on or within 10 years before the date of the filing of the petition, if—

(A) such transfer was made to a self-settled trust or similar device;

(B) such transfer was by the debtor;

(C) the debtor is a beneficiary of such trust or similar device; and

(D) the debtor made such transfer with actual intent to hinder, delay, or defraud any entity to which the debtor was or became, on or after the date that such transfer was made, indebted.

(2) For the purposes of this subsection, a transfer includes a transfer made in anticipation of any money judgment, settlement, civil penalty, equitable order, or criminal fine incurred by, or which the debtor believed would be incurred by—

(A) any violation of the securities laws (as defined in section 3(a)(47) of the Securities Exchange Act of 1934(15 U.S.C. 78c(a)(47))), any State securities laws, or any regulation or order issued under Federal securities laws or State securities laws; or

(B) fraud, deceit, or manipulation in a fiduciary capacity or in connection with the purchase or sale of any security registered under section 12 or 15(d) of the Securities Exchange Act of 1934(15 U.S.C. 781 and 78o(d)) or under section 6 of the Securities Act of 1933(15 U.S.C. 77f).[26]

11 U.S.C. § 549. Postpetition transactions

(a) Except as provided in subsection (b) or (c) of this section, the trustee may avoid a transfer of property of the estate—

(1) that occurs after the commencement of the case; and

(2) (A) that is authorized only under section 303(f) or 542(c) of this title; or

(B) that is not authorized under this title or by the court.

(b) In an involuntary case, the trustee may not avoid under subsection (a) of this section a transfer made after the commencement of such case but before the order for relief to the extent any value, including services, but not including satisfaction or securing of a debt that arose before the commencement of the case, is given after the commencement of the case in exchange for such transfer, notwithstanding any notice or knowledge of the case that the transferee has.

(c) The trustee may not avoid under subsection (a) of this section a transfer of an interest in real property to a good faith purchaser without knowledge of the commencement of the case and for present fair equivalent value unless a copy or notice of the petition was filed, where a transfer of an interest in such real property may be recorded to perfect such transfer, before such transfer is so perfected that a bona fide purchaser of such real property, against whom applicable law permits such transfer to be perfected, could not acquire an interest that is superior to such interest of such good faith purchaser. A good faith purchaser without knowledge of the commencement of the case and for less than present fair equivalent value has a lien on the property transferred to the extent of any present value given, unless a copy or notice of the petition was so filed before such transfer was so perfected.

(d) An action or proceeding under this section may not be commenced after the earlier of—

(1) two years after the date of the transfer sought to be avoided; or

[26] Effective as of the date of enactment of the Act; applicable to any case under the Bankruptcy Code commenced on or after such date. Pub. L. No. 109-8, 119 Stat. 23, Sec. 1406.

(2) the time the case is closed or dismissed.

- Uniform Fraudulent Transfer Act – see p. 1149
    - H- there are two kinds of fraud under the UFTA or 548:
- 1) intentional fraud- 548(a)(1)(a)- trustee may avoid any transfer of interest of the debtor in property if the debtor... did this with the intent to hinder, delay, or defraud someone to whome they were indebted
    - Bad intent- actual intent
        - Can be to future creditors as well as present creditors
        - H- almost never see actual intent
        - Mrs. Obrien testified on the stand about she made him put it in her name because she was concerned about the bank taking the house
        - No solvency test
- 2) constructive fraud transfers- 548(a)(1)(b)
    - H- 6 elements to a constructive fraud transfer (7 in the new code)
        - 1) transfer
        - 2) w/in statutory period
        - 3) for less than a reasonably equivalent value
        - 4) transferor was insolvent when the transfer was made or
        - 5) became insolvent as a result of the transfer, or
        - 6) engaged in a business with unreasonably small capital or
        - 7) intended to incur debt's beyond the debtors ability to pay or
        - 8) made the transfer for the benefit of an insider under an employment contract not in the ordinary course of business
    -
- *In re Messia* (172) (Declaration of homestead is not a fraudulent transfer
    - Transfer must go to a third party, and because homestead does not go to a third party there can be no transfer. Transfer includes the acquisition of an interest by a third party.
        - So court does not need to look as to whether it is fraudulent or not.
- *In re DVI, Inc.* (175) (State law determines whether it is a constructive trust)
    - 541(d) is subject to the rights of the debtor

11 U.S.C. §547. Trustee's Avoiding Powers: Preferences

- *11 U.S.C. §547-*
  - (c)(1)- intended to be for new value- not for an antecedent (substantially contemporaneous)
  - (c)(2)- payments made in the ordinary course of business
  - (c)(3)-
    - Enabling Loan "that creates a security interest in property acquired by the debtor (loans to the debtor to acquire something)
      (A) to the extent such security interest secures new value that was—
        (i) given at or after the signing of a security agreement that contains a description of such property as collateral;
        (ii) given by or on behalf of the secured party under such agreement;
        (iii) given to enable the debtor to acquire such property; and
        (iv) in fact used by the debtor to acquire such property; and
      (B) it was perfected on or before 30 days after debtor receives possession of such property
  - (c)(4)-
  - (c)(5)- Improvements in position during the preference period- if collateral increase in value
  - (c)(6)- non-avoidable statutory liens
  - (c)(7)- domestic support obligations
  - (c)(8)- can't sue to collect a consumer preference of less than 600
  - (c)(9)- can't sue to collect a non-consumer preference of less than 5,000
- Elements to a preference
  - 1) transfer
  - 2) of an interest in property of the debtor (pre-filing)
  - 3) to or for the benefit of a creditor
  - 4) for or on the account of an antecedent debt owed by the debtor before such an interest was made
  - 5) made while the debtor was insolvent (balance sheet test for insolvency)

        - 6) made within the preference period (either 90 days or one year for insiders)
        - In chapter 7- creditor received more than it otherwise would have been able to
    - In re Tolona Pizza Prods Corp. (181) (Pizza guy paid the sausage guy prior to filing bankruptcy)
        - New Test- now the test is the debt in the ordinary course of business, **and** either payment made in the ordinary course of business, **or** payment made according to ordinary business terms
    - In re Toyota of Jefferson, Inc (185) (547(c)(4)- woman's payments to car dealership)

11 U.S.C. §101(5). Claims

- The term "claim" means-
- (A) right to payment, whether or not such right is reduced to judgment, liquidated, unliquidated, fixed, contingent, matured, unmatured, disputed, undisputed, legal, equitable, secured, or unsecured; or
- (B) right to an equitable remedy for breach of performance if such breach gives rise to a right to payment, whether or not such right to an equitable remedy is reduced to judgment, fixed, contingent, matured, unmatured, disputed, undisputed, secured, or unsecured;.

§101(12)

(12) The term "debt" means liability on a claim.

(12A) The term "debt relief agency" means any person who provides any bankruptcy assistance to an assisted person in return for the payment of money or other valuable consideration, or who is a bankruptcy petition preparer under section 110, but does not include—

(A) any person who is an officer, director, employee, or agent of a person who provides such assistance or of the bankruptcy petition preparer;

(B) a nonprofit organization that is exempt from taxation under section 501(c)(3) of the Internal Revenue Code of 1986;

(C) a creditor of such assisted person, to the extent that the creditor is assisting such assisted person to restructure any debt owed by such assisted person to the creditor;

(D) a depository institution (as defined in section 3 of the Federal Deposit Insurance Act) or any Federal credit union or State credit union (as those terms are defined in section 101 of the Federal Credit Union Act), or any affiliate or subsidiary of such depository institution or credit union; or

(E) an author, publisher, distributor, or seller of works subject to copyright protection under title 17, when acting in such capacity.

§502. Allowance of claims or interests

(a) A claim or interest, proof of which is filed under section 501 of this title, is deemed allowed, unless a party in interest, including a creditor of a general partner in a partnership that is a debtor in a case under chapter 7 of this title, objects.

(b) Except as provided in subsections (e)(2), (f), (g), (h) and (i) of this section, if such objection to a claim is made, the court, after notice and a hearing, shall determine the amount of such claim in lawful currency of the United States as of the date of the filing of the petition, and shall allow such claim in such amount, except to the extent that—

(1) such claim is unenforceable against the debtor and property of the debtor, under any agreement or applicable law for a reason other than because such claim is contingent or unmatured;

(2) such claim is for unmatured interest;

(3) if such claim is for a tax assessed against property of the estate, such claim exceeds the value of the interest of the estate in such property;

(4) if such claim is for services of an insider or attorney of the debtor, such claim exceeds the reasonable value of such services;

(5) such claim is for a debt that is unmatured on the date of the filing of the petition and that is excepted from discharge under section 523(a)(5) of this title;

(6) if such claim is the claim of a lessor for damages resulting from the termination of a lease of real property, such claim exceeds—

(A) the rent reserved by such lease, without acceleration, for the greater of one year, or 15 percent, not to exceed three years, of the remaining term of such lease, following the earlier of

(i) the date of the filing of the petition; and

(ii) the date on which such lessor repossessed, or the lessee surrendered, the leased property; plus

(B) any unpaid rent due under such lease, without acceleration, on the earlier of such dates;

(7) if such claim is the claim of an employee for damages resulting from the termination of an employment contract, such claim exceeds—

(A) the compensation provided by such contract, without acceleration, for one year following the earlier of—

(i) the date of the filing of the petition; or

(ii) the date on which the employer directed the employee to terminate, or such employee terminated, performance under such contract; plus

(B) any unpaid compensation due under such contract, without acceleration, on the earlier of such dates;

(8) such claim results from a reduction, due to late payment, in the amount of an otherwise applicable credit available to the debtor in connection with an employment tax on wages, salaries, or commissions earned from the debtor; or

(9) proof of such claim is not timely filed, except to the extent tardily filed as permitted under paragraph (1), (2), or (3) of section 726(a) of this title or under the Federal Rules of Bankruptcy Procedure, except that a claim of a governmental unit shall be timely filed if it is filed before 180 days after the date of the order for relief or such later time as the Federal Rules of Bankruptcy Procedure may provide, and except that in a case under chapter 13, a claim of a governmental unit for a tax with respect to a return filed under section 1308 shall be timely if the claim is filed on or before the date that is 60 days after the date on which such return was filed as required.

(c) There shall be estimated for purpose of allowance under this section—

(1) any contingent or unliquidated claim, the fixing or liquidation of which, as the case may be, would unduly delay the administration of the case; or

(2) any right to payment arising from a right to an equitable remedy for breach of performance.

(d) Notwithstanding subsections (a) and (b) of this section, the court shall disallow any claim of any entity from which property is recoverable under section 542, 543, 550, or 553 of this title or that is a transferee of a transfer avoidable under section 522(f), 522(h), 544, 545, 547, 548, 549, or 724(a) of this title, unless such entity or transferee has paid the amount, or turned over any such property, for which such entity or transferee is liable under section 522(i), 542, 543, 550, or 553 of this title.

(e) (1) Notwithstanding subsections (a), (b), and (c) of this section and paragraph (2) of this subsection, the court shall disallow any claim for reimbursement or contribution of an entity that is liable with the debtor on or has secured, the claim of a creditor, to the extent that—

(A) such creditor's claim against the estate is disallowed;

(B) such claim for reimbursement or contribution is contingent as of the time of allowance or disallowance of such claim for reimbursement or contribution; or

(C) such entity asserts a right of subrogation to the rights of such creditor under section 509 of this title.

(2) A claim for reimbursement or contribution of such an entity that becomes fixed after the commencement of the case shall be determined, and shall be allowed under subsection (a), (b), or (c) of this section, or disallowed under subsection (d) of this section, the same as if such claim had become fixed before the date of the filing of the petition.

(f) In an involuntary case, a claim arising in the ordinary course of the debtor's business or financial affairs after the commencement of the case but before the earlier of the appointment of a trustee and the order for relief shall be determined as of the date such claim arises, and shall be allowed under subsection (a), (b), or (c) of this section or disallowed under subsection (d) or (e) of this section, the same as if such claim had arisen before the date of the filing of the petition.

(g) (1) A claim arising from the rejection, under section 365 of this title or under a plan under chapter 9, 11, 12, or 13 of this title, of an executory contract or unexpired lease of the debtor that has not been assumed shall be determined, and shall be allowed under subsection (a), (b), or (c) of this section or disallowed under subsection (d) or (e) of this section, the same as if such claim had arisen before the date of the filing of the petition.

(2) A claim for damages calculated in accordance with section 562 shall be allowed under subsection (a), (b), or (c), or disallowed under subsection (d) or (e), as if such claim had arisen before the date of the filing of the petition.

(h) A claim arising from the recovery of property under section 522, 550, or 553 of this title shall be determined, and shall be allowed under subsection (a), (b), or (c) of this section, or disallowed under subsection (d) or (e) of this section, the same as if such claim had arisen before the date of the filing of the petition.

(i) A claim that does not arise until after the commencement of the case for a tax entitled to priority under section 507(a)(8) of this title shall be determined, and shall be allowed under subsection (a), (b), or (c) of this section, or disallowed under subsection (d) or (e) of this section, the same as if such claim had arisen before the date of the filing of the petition.

(j) A claim that has been allowed or disallowed may be reconsidered for cause. A reconsidered claim may be allowed or disallowed according to the equities of the case. Reconsideration of a claim under this subsection does not affect the validity of any payment or transfer from the estate made to a holder of an allowed claim on account of such allowed claim that is not reconsidered, but if a reconsidered claim is allowed and is of the same class as such holder's claim, such holder may not receive any additional payment or transfer from the estate on account of such holder's allowed claim until the holder of such reconsidered and allowed claim receives payment on account of such claim proportionate in value to that already received by such other holder. This subsection does not alter or modify the trustee's right to recover from a creditor any excess payment or transfer made to such creditor.

(k) (1) The court, on the motion of the debtor and after a hearing, may reduce a claim filed under this section based in whole on an unsecured consumer debt by not more than 20 percent of the claim, if—

(A) the claim was filed by a creditor who unreasonably refused to negotiate a reasonable alternative repayment schedule proposed on behalf of the debtor by an approved nonprofit budget and credit counseling agency described in section 111;

(B) the offer of the debtor under subparagraph (A)--

(i) was made at least 60 days before the date of the filing of the petition; and

(ii) provided for payment of at least 60 percent of the amount of the debt over a period not to exceed the repayment period of the loan, or a reasonable extension thereof; and

(C) no part of the debt under the alternative repayment schedule is nondischargeable.

(2) The debtor shall have the burden of proving, by clear and convincing evidence, that—

(A) the creditor unreasonably refused to consider the debtor's proposal; and

(B) the proposed alternative repayment schedule was made prior to expiration of the 60-day period specified in paragraph (1)(B)(i).

- *§727(b)*

(b) Except as provided in section 523 of this title, a discharge under subsection (a) of this section discharges the debtor from all debts that arose before the date of the order for relief under this chapter, and any liability on a claim that is determined under section 502 of this title as if such claim had arisen before the commencement of the case, whether or not a proof of claim based on any such debt or liability is filed under section 501 of this title, and whether or not a claim based on any such debt or liability is allowed under section 502 of this title.

- In re Roxse Homes (191) (defaulted on HUD Loan)
  - Court held it was not a clai, under 101(5)(B) and therefore it is not within the bankruptcy court's power
- In re Ward (Maids International)

    - Maids has a right to obtain either damages for the debtors future competition or the right to an injunction against it (contract right)
      - So because there is a right to payment for the breach, then it is a claim
- Sir Speedy (121)
  - H- Go to the language of the contract. If there isn't money damage language then the case is like Roxse. If solely an equitable remedy then it is not for the bankruptcy court.
- When you file a claim?
  - P of Claim should be filed with 90 days of the first date set for the 341 meeting
    - Rule 3002(c)
    - Rule 2003(A)- between 20 and 40 days
  - H- claims by governmental units can be filed within 180 days
    - H- IRS is so inefficient that they could not filed with 90 days, so an amendment for the governmental unit to get their act together and stop losing my tax money
  - Rule 2002(e)
    - If it appears that it is a no asset case, then the courts notice will say that this appears to be a no asset case. Therefore there is no need to file a proof of claim. If assets surface then they will give you notice and then you can file
      - Once new notice goes out a new 90 days
      - 3002(C)(6)- have 90 days from the mailing of that notice

11 U.S.C. § 507. Priorities

- (1)First:
  - (a) domestic support obligations- owing to the spouse and children due at the date of filing- first priority
  - (b) domestic support obligations that have been assigned to a government agency, subject to (A)
  - (c) H- to take care of the trustees, the trustees fee comes before A,
- (2) administrative expenses
- (3) unsecured claims under 502(f)- gap claims

- (4) wage claims- number and time have been dramatically increased, under the revision it is 10,000 of the wages earned with 180 days of the filing
    - (a) Wages, salaries or commissions, including vacation, severance, and sick leave pay earned by an individual
    - (b) sales commissions earned by an individual or a corporation with one employee acting as an individual contractor
- (5) employee benefit plans
    - (a) arising from services rendered within 180 days of filing of the cessation of the business
- (6) agricultural shit- don't worry about it
- (7) unsecured claims of individuals up to 1,800 arising from the deposit of property or money that you never got the property
    - Ex.- gift certificates- are deposit within this context
    - Credit memos- 1 yes and 1 no
- Old 7th is gone it was the alimony provision, now it is one, from 8 on they are the same numbers as before
- (8) tax claims
- (9) depository institutions
- (10) <u>Tenth, allowed claims for death or personal injury resulting from the operation of a motor vehicle or vessel if such operation was unlawful because the debtor was intoxicated from using alcohol, a drug, or another substance</u>
    - these kinds of debts are not dischargeable, now they remain non-dischargeable and are the 10th priority

▪ § 726(a) if you are past priority and there is still money left then it is distributed to the remaining entities
- Everybody who is unsecured who filed on time is the next priority
- Unsecured who filed late

▪ Burden of Proof on claims:
- 502(a)- a claim for interest proof of which is filed under 501 is deemed allowed unless a party in interest objects

- The burden does not shift to the IRS- as to tax claims the Supreme court says that the burden of proof works the same as if the tax payer had not been in bankruptcy, the taxpayer has the burden of proving that they were correct

- 510(c)- equitable subordination of claims- concept is that if there has been some improper conduct that gave someone a leg up on a proceeding then it may be appropriate to subordinate that person to another claimant who is "good folk"

11 U.S.C. § 506. Setoff and Recoupment

- (a) (1) An allowed claim of a creditor secured by a lien on property in which the estate has an interest, or that is subject to setoff under section 553 of this title, is a secured claim to the extent of the value of such creditor's interest in the estate's interest in such property, or to the extent of the amount subject to setoff, as the case may be, and is an unsecured claim to the extent that the value of such creditor's interest or the amount so subject to setoff is less than the amount of such allowed claim. Such value shall be determined in light of the purpose of the valuation and of the proposed disposition or use of such property, and in conjunction with any hearing on such disposition or use or on a plan affecting such creditor's interest.
- (2) If the debtor is an individual in a case under chapter 7 or 13, such value with respect to personal property securing an allowed claim shall be determined based on the replacement value of such property as of the date of the filing of the petition without deduction for costs of sale or marketing. With respect to property acquired for personal, family, or household purposes, replacement value shall mean the price a retail merchant would charge for property of that kind considering the age and condition of the property at the time value is determined.

- §553(a)

Setoff

(a) Except as otherwise provided in this section and in sections 362 and 363 of this title, this title does not affect any right of a creditor to offset a mutual debt owing by such creditor to the debtor that arose before the commencement of the case under this title against a claim of such creditor against the debtor that arose before the commencement of the case, except to the extent that—

(1) the claim of such creditor against the debtor is disallowed;

(2) such claim was transferred, by an entity other than the debtor, to such creditor—

(A) after the commencement of the case; or

(B) (i) after 90 days before the date of the filing of the petition; and

(ii) while the debtor was insolvent (except for a setoff of a kind described in section 362(b)(6), 362(b)(7), 362(b)(17), 362(b)(27), 555, 556, 559, 560, or 561); or

(3) the debt owed to the debtor by such creditor was incurred by such creditor—

(A) after 90 days before the date of the filing of the petition;

(B) while the debtor was insolvent; and

(C) for the purpose of obtaining a right of setoff against the debtor (except for a setoff of a kind described in section 362(b)(6), 362(b)(7), 362(b)(17), 362(b)(27), 555, 556, 559, 560, or 561).

- Setoff- arising out of independent transactions
- Recoupment- arising out of the same transaction
- *In re Holyoke Nursing Home, Inc* (210) (Medicare overpayment to nursing home)
    - reimbursements from Medicaid
    - CT - this is not a setoff but a recoupment
    - Distinction is whether the debt owed by the creditor arose out of the same transaction; recoupment - same transaction / setoff – different

11 U.S.C. §523. Dischargeability

- *Fed. R. Bank. P. 4007 (b), (c)*
- *11 U.S.C. §523*

Exceptions to discharge

(a) A discharge under section 727, 1141, 1228(a), 1228(b), or 1328(b) of this title does not discharge an individual debtor from any debt—

(1) for a tax or a customs duty—

(A) of the kind and for the periods specified in section 507(a)(~~2~~3) or 507(a)(8) of this title, whether or not a claim for such tax was filed or allowed;

(B) with respect to which a return, or equivalent report or notice, if required—

(i) was not filed or given; or

(ii) was filed or given after the date on which such return, report, or notice was last due, under applicable law or under any extension, and after two years before the date of the filing of the petition; or

(C) with respect to which the debtor made a fraudulent return or willfully attempted in any manner to evade or defeat such tax;

- 523(a)(1)- assume that it will not be discharged
- Includes three types of taxes:
- 1) second and 8th priority taxes under 807-
- 8th priority- income and gross receipt taxes, property, withholding, and excise taxes
- Income tax priority generally includes only those taxes where a required return was due within three years of the filing 503(a)(8)???????
- Taxes assessed with 280 days of the filing will not only be priorities but will not be dischargeable
- H- tax debt older than the period is dischargeable- can discharge a tax debt older then 3 years
- H- SOL was tolled during the time when they were in bankruptcy and the IRS was limited by the automatic stay
- Supreme Court- look back period is tolled during the pendency of the prior bankruptcy case
- **H - good thing to do is go for this is a tax and is not dischargeable and go from there**
- *Young v. U.S. (syllabus)*
    - Held: Lookback period is tolled during the pendency of a prior bankruptcy petition
        - SOL was tolled during the time when they were in bankruptcy and the IRS was limited by the automatic stay
        - In this case, the prior tax debt is not dischargeable

- *523(a)(2)* - for money, property, services, or an extension, renewal, or refinancing of credit, to the extent obtained by—

(A) false pretenses, a false representation, or actual fraud, other than a statement respecting the debtor's or an insider's financial condition;

(B) use of a statement in writing—

(i) that is materially false;

(ii) respecting the debtor's or an insider's financial condition;

(iii) on which the creditor to whom the debtor is liable for such money, property, services, or credit reasonably relied; and

(iv) that the debtor caused to be made or published with intent to deceive; or

(C) (i) for purposes of subparagraph (A)

(I) consumer debts owed to a single creditor and aggregating more than $500 for luxury goods or services incurred by an individual debtor on or within 90 days before the order for relief under this title are presumed to be nondischargeable; and

(II) cash advances aggregating more than $750 that are extensions of consumer credit under an open end credit plan obtained by an individual debtor on or within 70 days before the order for relief under this title, are presumed to be nondischargeable; and

(ii) for purposes of this subparagraph—

(I) the terms "consumer", "credit", and "open end credit plan" have the same meanings as in section 103 of the Truth in Lending Act; and

(II) the term "luxury goods or services" does not include goods or services reasonably necessary for the support or maintenance of the debtor or a dependent of the debtor.

- *Field v. Mans (syllabus)*
  - Burden of proving 523(a)(2) claim
  - Held: the standard for excepting a debt from discharge as a fraudulent representation within the meaning of §523(a)(2)(a) is not reasonable reliance but the less demanding one of justifiable reliance on the representation
- *Palmacci v. Umpierrez* **(leading case)**
  - court goes through elements of fraud
  - 1) false representation as to one's intentions when the representation was made- so if you meant it to be true and then later decided not to do it later, then it would not be fraud
  - 2) made with the intent to manipulate, deceive, or defraud
  - If the maker of the statement knows it is not true or doesn't know whether it is true or not, but presents it as true, or knows he has no basis

for presenting what he is intending as true- then all are sufficient for a false representation

- 3) speaker intends to induce action from the person to whom the statement is made
- 4) person to whom the statement is made does in fact rely on the statement being made
- 5) reliance is justifiable (Field and Mans)
- 6) reliance caused damage to someone
- The above are the elements for 523(a)(2)(a)
- If you have all of them (need all) then the debt will not be dischargeable in bankruptcy- need to bring an adversary proceeding for it
- Facts of case
    - Palmacci invest 75,000 in a project with U and his brother
    - Said they would each invest 75,000 and would form a trust
    - P got only 80% of his investment back
    - U filed for bankruptcy
    - Court determined debt was dischargeable because P did not show that U intended to defraud him at the time of the representations

- *In re Pickett*
    - Debts were fraud and therefore were not dischargeable
    - "It is this Court's belief that, by using a credit card, the debtor is making a representation to the credit card issuer that he or she has both the intent and the ability to repay the debt in accordance with the requirements of the credit card agreement. At the very least, the debtor, by using his credit card to obtain a cash advance or make a purchase, is expressly telling the credit card issuer that he or she intends to repay the amount borrowed and has the ability to repay the amounts on the terms required by the issuer, whether that repayment is in the form of minimum monthly payments required by the credit care agreement or in different or larger amounts."
- *AT&T Universal Card v. Searle*
    - Each transaction- each use of the credit card is a unilateral contract where the cardholder promises to repay the debt plus to periodically

  - make partial payments along with accrued interest.... (242)
  - Young found that when Searle took the cash advances he had the intent to make the payments,
  - It was not a false representation when made
  - Dicta- even when if it were a false representation the creditor would still have to prove each of the elements by a preponderance of the evidence, making a false representation is insufficient
- *Sanford Institution for Savings v. Gallo*
  - Well respected business man who pledged the house even though his wife owned it and forged his signature
  - Issue was whether this was justifiable reliance?
  - Court said that because of the history the bank was justified in relying on Gallo
  - Bank's policy is doing a title check on all property loans
- *Zimmerman v. Soderlund (In re Soderlund)*
  - Debtor had entered into an agreement to pay legal fees to Bingham Dana
  - Ran up fees of 163,612.16. Had paid 46,712.35
  - Had made statements to the firm
  - Court held that those statements did not qualify as financial statements under 2(B)
  - H- issue here is what is a financial statement?
  - A(2)(A) deals with false statements other than a statement about the debtors financial condition
  - Trial judge had that it was not a statement of financial condition
  - "If I were to hold that a statement which reflected any aspect of a debtor's financial condition is the basis for a non-dischargability action only if in writing, egregious frauds could be perpetrated... (259
- *Fleming Cos. V. Eckert (In re Eckert)*
  - H- two points:
  - 1) was the statement materially false?- Yes, listing of the assets was not materially false, but because it greatly overstated its income then it was materuially false

        - 2) fleming did not even do a cursory investigation- Eckert is relying on Gallo below, and not Gallo above
        - Reliance case- also by the judge in Eckert
        - Bank is relying on borrowers who present financial information including income returns from two previous years showing good income
        - Borrower never told the bank that they owed the money due on those returns
        - Owed over 120,000 in taxes
        - Not justifiable to rely on the income tax return without asking whether they were paid or not
    - § 523(a)(2)(C)- loading up
    - People who run up a lot of bills knowing that they will never pay these debts back
    - Was added twenty years ago Non-dischargebale purchase of luxury goods and services and cash advances prior to bankruptcy
    - Numbers were indexed-
    - In the new statute the days went up and the numbers went down
    - The triggers are lower and the applicable time periods are longer
    - Also, reasonably necessary, not reasonably acquired

- *§523(a)(3)*

(3) neither listed nor scheduled under section 521(1) of this title, with the name, if known to the debtor, of the creditor to whom such debt is owed, in time to permit—

(A) if such debt is not of a kind specified in paragraph (2), (4), or (6) of this subsection, timely filing of a proof of claim, unless such creditor had notice or actual knowledge of the case in time for such timely filing; or

(B) if such debt is of a kind specified in paragraph (2), (4), or (6) of this subsection, timely filing of a proof of claim and timely request for a determination of dischargeability of such debt under one of such paragraphs, unless such creditor had notice or actual knowledge of the case in time for such timely filing and request;

    - *Fed. R. Bankr. P. 1007 (a), (b), 2002(e)*
        - See pages 754 and 795
    - *Chart* – see page 265 in packet
    - *In re Jones*
        - creditor was omitted from a list of schedules

- Court decided that reopening would give relief to the debtor
- What happens in a no asset case
- Time never runs because you get the notice saying don't worrying about the proof of claim
- You are in time to file the claim because the time never runs
- Unlisted creditors are discharged
- H- state court judges have a tendency to enforce these discharge debts in these circumstances
- Which is why he reopened it because some state court judge may well have enforced that claim even though it was discharged
- What happened in Cali
- H- goes into the record and there is a holding to that effect
- Reopening is not automatic
- Hillman found for Debtor b/c there were no assets
- Seems like no due process
- Why he reopened b/c state ct would have been overruled, really more of a formality b/c just gets the name in the record and then it is closed again

- *§523(a)(4)*

(4) for fraud or defalcation while acting in a fiduciary capacity, embezzlement, or larceny;

- fraud or defalcation while acting in a fiduciary capacity, embezzlement, or larceny;
- H- four different things:
- Larceny is when you steal
- Embezzlement is fraudulently appropriating property of another when you have been entrusted with protecting it
- H- look to the state statute to determine what they are
- Fraud
- Defalcation while acting in a fiduciary capacity- H- things that are not constructive but are real
- Ex- lawyer client, clergyman client, broker client, the kind of things where there is some responsibility take where there is a relationship
- H- if there is a fiduciary capacity between two people and money disappears, is that the kind of thing that this is directed at?

- For many years every court relied on a 2nd circuit case- Central Hanover Bank v. Burst (???) Learned Hand said you get this if you are a fiduciary who
- for any reason is short in his accounts
- A fiduciary is a guarantor of the assets entrusted to the fiduciary
- *Rutanen v. Baylis (In re Baylis)*
    - Probate Court held that he was negligent and under the state law it made him responsible
    - Filed for bankruptcy- judge Lynch said that inherent in defalcation is the requirement that there be a breach of fiduciary duty, must mean something other than fraud and other than willful and malicious injury
    - It is to be measured objectively. Leaves the question of the standard to use to measure when it is
    - Her conclusion was that not every breach of a fiduciary duty is a defalcation
    - 3 schools of thought:
    - 1) innocent mistake can be defalcation
    - 2) negligence is required, but don't need anything more
    - 3) negligence is not enough, you need at least recklessness
    - Defalcation is the 1st circuit requires some degree of fault closer to fraud without the necessity of meeting a strict fraud test
    - What over Bayliss had done as a co-trustee
    - In most cases his best judgment about how to handle his cotrustee was negligent but not so much as to rise to fraud or defalcation with one exception (in the exception it was defalcation)

§523(a)(5), (15)

(5) for a domestic support obligation;

(15) to a spouse, former spouse, or child of the debtor and not of the kind described in paragraph (5) that is incurred by the debtor in the course of a divorce or separation or in connection with a separation agreement, divorce decree or other order of a court of record, or a determination made in accordance with State or territorial law by a governmental unit;

- A)(5)- have to look at 5 and 15 at the same time

        - Under the old A(5) property settlements were dischargeable
        - Savy attorneys would call everything a property settlement
        - Obvious to the judges what was going on. Were framing things to get out of marital obligation
        - Judges said don't care about the label, will look at the economic realities
        - Old 15- determining whether a property settlement was or was not dischargeable
        - Weighing shit
        - New statute elminated all of the mikey mouse shit
        - Now that all the stuff that used to be 5 and 15 and now it is all together in one big lump ad it is non-dischargeable
        - The only reason 15 is left

    - *§523(a)(6)*
        - (6) for willful and malicious injury by the debtor to another entity or to the property of another entity;
        - *Kawaauhau v. Geiger*
            - Supreme court dealt with what is willful and malicious
            - Doctor cut off the wrong leg. Question was whether that was willful and malicious?
            - Court said it was not because intentional torts generally require the actor to intend the conseeuqnces. Because he didn't intend to do something wrong it was not willful and malicious
        - Hillman - I shot and arrow and knew not where. If out there and I not know not willful and malicious, but if did know then it is

    - *§523(a)(8)*

(8) unless excepting such debt from discharge under this paragraph would impose an undue hardship on the debtor and the debtor's dependents, for—

(A) (i) an educational benefit overpayment or loan made, insured, or guaranteed by a governmental unit, or made under any program funded in whole or in part by a governmental unit or nonprofit institution; or

(ii) an obligation to repay funds received as an educational benefit, scholarship or stipend; or

(B) any other educational loan that is a qualified education loan, as defined in section 221(d)(1) of the Internal Revenue Code of 1986, incurred by a debtor who is an individual;

- *Kopf v. U.S. Dept. of Ed. (In re Kopf)*
  - In re Kopf 285
  - To discharge student loans must show undue burden.
  - There are many tests In re Johnson
  - Checklist of factors:
  - Look at rate of pay, Wages, Skill, Sec, Ability to retain employment, Current status, Record, Education, Health, Access to transportation, Dependents
  - Also need good faith probe and a policy inquiry under Johnson
  - In re Brunner Test:
    - This is minimal standard of living test
    - And state of affairs will not continue
  - Totality of the circumstances test
    - Seldom spoken it is generally what they are doing
    - Most courts quote Brunner
  - Not undue burden
  - For heal loans which are med school not undue hardship
  - Undue burden to pay it all but can pay a half or quarter.
  - So student loans can be partially dischargeable
  - If not consolidated is it ok to say some are dischargeable and some are not then it is ok
  - ICP income contingent plans
  - Rather than saying yes or no to dischargable. Come to an agreement where use disposable income, Goes 25 yrs and after it is forgiven
  - Not bad faith to refuse to take because of tax like have to pay tax on whatever is forgiven
  - So now an idea courts have instead of forgiven it is discharged and then no tax
  - 523 most action
  - 523=dischargability of a debt
  - 727 is the discharge in general
  - 727 a is a list that prevents a discharge
  - for 727 a2 have to prove intent and it goes back to twines badges of fraud
- *42 U.S.C. §292f(g)*
  - Conditions for discharge of debt in bankruptcy - See page 300 in packet

- *§523(a)(13)*

(13) for any payment of an order of restitution issued under title 18, United States Code;

11 U.S.C. §727. Discharge

727. Discharge

(a) The court shall grant the debtor a discharge, unless—

(1) the debtor is not an individual;

(2) the debtor, with intent to hinder, delay, or defraud a creditor or an officer of the estate charged with custody of property under this title, has transferred, removed, destroyed, mutilated, or concealed, or has permitted to be transferred, removed, destroyed, mutilated, or concealed—

(A) property of the debtor, within one year before the date of the filing of the petition; or

(B) property of the estate, after the date of the filing of the petition;

(3) the debtor has concealed, destroyed, mutilated, falsified, or failed to keep or preserve any recorded information, including books, documents, records, and papers, from which the debtor's financial condition or business transactions might be ascertained, unless such act or failure to act was justified under all of the circumstances of the case;

(4) the debtor knowingly and fraudulently, in or in connection with the case—

(A) made a false oath or account;

(B) presented or used a false claim;

(C) gave, offered, received, or attempted to obtain money, property, or advantage, or a promise of money, property, or advantage, for acting or forbearing to act; or

(D) withheld from an officer of the estate entitled to possession under this title, any recorded information, including books, documents, records, and papers, relating to the debtor's property or financial affairs;

(5) the debtor has failed to explain satisfactorily, before determination of denial of discharge under this paragraph, any loss of assets or deficiency of assets to meet the debtor's liabilities;

(6) the debtor has refused, in the case—

(A) to obey any lawful order of the court, other than an order to respond to a material question or to testify;

(B) on the ground of privilege against self-incrimination, to respond to a material question approved by the court or to testify, after the debtor has been granted immunity with respect to the matter concerning which such privilege was invoked; or

(C) on a ground other than the properly invoked privilege against self-incrimination, to respond to a material question approved by the court or to testify;

(7) the debtor has committed any act specified in paragraph (2), (3), (4), (5), or (6) of this subsection, on or within one year before the date of the filing of the petition, or during the case, in connection with another case, under this title or under the Bankruptcy Act, concerning an insider;

(8) the debtor has been granted a discharge under this section, under section 1141 of this title, or under section 14, 371, or 476 of the Bankruptcy Act, in a case commenced within 8 years before the date of the filing of the petition;

(9) the debtor has been granted a discharge under section 1228 or 1328 of this title, or under section 660 or 661 of the Bankruptcy Act, in a case commenced within six years before the date of the filing of the petition, unless payments under the plan in such case totaled at least—

(A) 100 percent of the allowed unsecured claims in such case; or

(B) (i) 70 percent of such claims; and

(ii) the plan was proposed by the debtor in good faith, and was the debtor's best effort;

(10) the court approves a written waiver of discharge executed by the debtor after the order for relief under this chapter;

(11) after filing the petition, the debtor failed to complete an instructional course concerning personal financial management described in section 111, except that this paragraph shall not apply with respect to a debtor who is a person described in section 109(h)(4) or who resides in a district for which the United States trustee (or the bankruptcy administrator, if any) determines that the approved instructional courses are not adequate to service the additional individuals who would otherwise be required to complete such instructional courses under this section, or if the court finds that exigent circumstances merit a waiver of the requirements of this paragraph (The United States trustee (or the bankruptcy administrator, if any) who makes a determination described in this paragraph shall review such determination not later than 1 year after the date of such determination, and not less frequently than annually thereafter.); or

(12) the court after notice and a hearing held not more than 10 days before the date of the entry of the order granting the discharge finds that there is reasonable cause to believe that—

(A) section 522(q)(1) may be applicable to the debtor; and

(B) there is pending any proceeding in which the debtor may be found guilty of a felony of the kind described in section 522(q)(1)(A) or liable for a debt of the kind described in section 522(q)(1)(B).[27]

(b) Except as provided in section 523 of this title, a discharge under subsection (a) of this section discharges the debtor from all debts that arose before the date of the order for relief under this chapter, and any liability on a claim that is determined under section 502 of this title as if such claim had arisen before the commencement of the case, whether or not a proof of claim based on any such debt or liability is filed under section 501 of this title, and whether or not a claim based on any such debt or liability is allowed under section 502 of this title.

(c) (1) The trustee, a creditor, or the United States trustee may object to the granting of a discharge under subsection (a) of this section.

(2) On request of a party in interest, the court may order the trustee to examine the acts and conduct of the debtor to determine whether a ground exists for denial of discharge.

(d) On request of the trustee, a creditor, or the United States trustee, and after notice and a hearing, the court shall revoke a discharge granted under subsection (a) of this section if—

(1) such discharge was obtained through the fraud of the debtor, and the requesting party did not know of such fraud until after the granting of such discharge;

(2) the debtor acquired property that is property of the estate, or became entitled to acquire property that would be property of the estate, and knowingly and fraudulently failed to report the acquisition of or entitlement to such property, or to deliver or surrender such property to the trustee;

(3) the debtor committed an act specified in subsection (a)(6) of this section.; or

(4) the debtor has failed to explain satisfactorily—

(A) a material misstatement in an audit referred to in section 586(f) of title 28; or

(B) a failure to make available for inspection all necessary accounts, papers, documents, financial records, files, and all other papers, things, or

[27] Effective 180 days after date of enactment of the Act; applicable to any case under the Bankruptcy Code commenced on or after date of enactment. Pub. L. No. 109-8, 119 Stat. 23, Sec. 1501(2).

property belonging to the debtor that are requested for an audit referred to in section 586(f) of title 28.[28]

(e) The trustee, a creditor, or the United States trustee may request a revocation of a discharge—

(1) under subsection (d)(1) of this section within one year after such discharge is granted; or

(2) under subsection (d)(2) or (d)(3) of this section before the later of—

(A) one year after the granting of such discharge; and

(B) the date the case is closed.

- *Martin v. Gajgar (In re Bajgar)*
  - Issue is discharge with respect to prop that fradulantly transferred within one yr before the filing of his voluntary petition for relief
  - So here were gonna transfer intrest in house back so that not violate 727a2A. Did as trustee said
  - Disgruntle creditor said violated A2c
  - Hillman got reversed on Appeals
  - Said statute said transferred not stay transferred so he had violated and lost discharge
  - 727a2A Cannot discharge if transfer property within 1 yr
  - So need to remand
  - 727 a12 goes to 527q this is securities fraud RICO and willful negligent shit cap homestead at 125k.
  - 727a12 if possible that there is a hearing about this bad stuff then the discharge cant enter
  - H-bothers him b/c must hold a hearing no more then 10 days to determine if it exists
- *Fogal Legware v. Wills (In re Wills)*
  - got a judgment
  - And there was some bad faith
  - 727a4A
  - If made a false oath
  - Any asset can be material whether it is of little value or not
  - List every asset b/c everything is material whether it has value or not
  - If you fail on one of the elements of 727 you lose whole discharge
  - Case remanded
  - Secured Loans

[28] Effective 18 months after the date of enactment of the Act. Pub. L. No. 109-8, 119 Stat. 23, Sec. 603(e).

- Start with 506d but then go to 522f
- Judicial liens 101(36) means a lien obtained by judgment levy sequestration or other equitable ct or proceeding, need to go to ct.
- Statutory lien = real estate taxes
- Cannot use 522f with anything but a judicial lien
- 522f2a works out this complication

11 U.S.C. §101(36). Lien Avoidance

(36) The term "judicial lien" means lien obtained by judgment, levy, sequestration, or other legal or equitable process or proceeding;.

- *§101(37)*

(37) The term "lien" means charge against or interest in property to secure payment of a debt or performance of an obligation;.

- *§101(53)*

(53) The term "statutory lien" means lien arising solely by force of a statute on specified circumstances or conditions, or lien of distress for rent, whether or not statutory, but does not include security interest or judicial lien, whether or not such interest or lien is provided by or is dependent on a statute and whether or not such interest or lien is made fully effective by statute;.

(53A) The term "stockbroker" means person—

(A) with respect to which there is a customer, as defined in section 741 of this title; and

(B) that is engaged in the business of effecting transactions in securities—

(i) for the account of others; or

(ii) with members of the general public, from or for such person's own account.

(53B) The term "swap agreement"

(A) means—

(i) any agreement, including the terms and conditions incorporated by reference in such agreement, which is—

(I) an interest rate swap, option, future, or forward agreement, including a rate floor, rate cap, rate collar, cross-currency rate swap, and basis swap;

(II) a spot, same day-tomorrow, tomorrow-next, forward, or other foreign exchange or precious metals agreement;

(III) a currency swap, option, future, or forward agreement;

(IV) an equity index or equity swap, option, future, or forward agreement;

(V) a debt index or debt swap, option, future, or forward agreement;

(VI) a total return, credit spread or credit swap, option, future, or forward agreement;

(VII) a commodity index or a commodity swap, option, future, or forward agreement; or

(VIII) a weather swap, weather derivative, or weather option;

(ii) any agreement or transaction that is similar to any other agreement or transaction referred to in this paragraph and that—

(I) is of a type that has been, is presently, or in the future becomes, the subject of recurrent dealings in the swap markets (including terms and conditions incorporated by reference therein; and

(II) is a forward, swap, future, or option on one or more rates, currencies, commodities, equity securities, or other equity instruments, debt securities or other debt instruments, quantitative measures associated with an occurrence, extent of an occurrence, or contingency associated with a financial, commercial, or economic consequence, or economic or financial indices or measures of economic or financial risk or value;

(iii) any combination of agreements or transactions referred to in this subparagraph;

(iv) any option to enter into an agreement or transaction referred to in this subparagraph;

(v) a master agreement that provides for an agreement or transaction referred to in clause (i), (ii), (iii), or (iv), together with all supplements to any such master agreement, and without regard to whether the master agreement contains an agreement or transaction that is not a swap agreement under this paragraph, except that the master agreement shall be considered to be a swap agreement under this paragraph only with respect to each agreement or transaction under the master agreement that is referred to in clause (i), (ii), (iii), or (iv); or

(vi) any security agreement or arrangement or other credit enhancement related to any agreements or transactions referred to in clause (i) through (v), including any guarantee or reimbursement obligation by or to a swap participant or financial participant in connection with any agreement or transaction referred to in any such clause, but not to exceed the damages in connection with any such agreement or transaction, measured in accordance with section 562; and

(B) is applicable for purposes of this title only, and shall not be construed or applied so as to challenge or affect the characterization, definition, or treatment of any swap agreement under any other statute, regulation, or rule, including the Securities Act of 1933, the Securities Exchange Act of 1934, the Public Utility Holding Company Act of 1935, the Trust Indenture Act of 1939, the Investment Company Act of 1940, the Investment Advisers Act of 1940, the Securities Investor Protection Act of 1970, the Commodity Exchange Act, the Gramm-Leach-Bliley Act, and the Legal Certainty for Bank Products Act of 2000.

(53C) The term "swap participant" means an entity that, at any time before the filing of the petition, has an outstanding swap agreement with the debtor;.

(56A) The term "term overriding royalty" means an interest in liquid or gaseous hydrocarbons in place or to be produced from particular real property that entitles the owner thereof to a share of production, or the value thereof, for a term limited by time, quantity, or value realized;

(53D) The term "timeshare plan" means and shall include that interest purchased in any arrangement, plan, scheme, or similar device, but not including exchange programs, whether by membership, agreement, tenancy in common, sale, lease, deed, rental agreement, license, right to use agreement, or by any other means, whereby a purchaser, in exchange for consideration, receives a right to use accommodations, facilities, or recreational sites, whether improved or unimproved, for a specific period of time less than a full year during any given year, but not necessarily for consecutive years, and which extends for a period of more than three years. A "timeshare interest" is that interest purchased in a timeshare plan which grants the purchaser the right to use and occupy accommodations, facilities, or recreational sites, whether improved or unimproved, pursuant to a timeshare plan;.

11 U.S.C. §506. Determination of secured status

(a) (1) An allowed claim of a creditor secured by a lien on property in which the estate has an interest, or that is subject to setoff under section 553 of this title, is a secured claim to the extent of the value of such creditor's interest in the estate's interest in such property, or to the extent of the amount subject to setoff, as the case may be, and is an unsecured claim to the extent that the value of such creditor's interest or the amount so subject to setoff is less than the amount of such allowed claim. Such value shall be determined in light of the purpose of the valuation and of the proposed disposition or use of such property, and in conjunction with any hearing on such disposition or use or on a plan affecting such creditor's interest.

(2) If the debtor is an individual in a case under chapter 7 or 13, such value with respect to personal property securing an allowed claim shall be determined based on the replacement value of such property as of the date of the filing of the petition without deduction for costs of sale or marketing. With respect to property acquired for personal, family, or household purposes, replacement value shall mean the price a retail merchant would charge for property of that kind considering the age and condition of the property at the time value is determined.

(b) To the extent that an allowed secured claim is secured by property the value of which, after any recovery under subsection (c) of this section, is greater than the amount of such claim, there shall be allowed to the holder of such claim, interest on such claim, and any reasonable fees, costs, or charges provided for under the agreement or State statute under which such claim arose.

(c) The trustee may recover from property securing an allowed secured claim the reasonable, necessary costs and expenses of preserving, or disposing of, such property to the extent of any benefit to the holder of such claim, including the payment of all ad valorem property taxes with respect to the property.

(d) To the extent that a lien secures a claim against the debtor that is not an allowed secured claim, such lien is void, unless—

(1) such claim was disallowed only under section 502(b)(5) or 502(e) of this title; or

(2) such claim is not an allowed secured claim due only to the failure of any entity to file a proof of such claim under section 501 of this title.

- *§522(f)*

(f) (1) Notwithstanding any waiver of exemptions but subject to paragraph (3), the debtor may avoid the fixing of a lien on an interest of the debtor in property to the extent that such lien impairs an exemption to which the debtor would have been entitled under subsection (b) of this section, if such lien is—

(A) a judicial lien, other than a judicial lien that secures a debt <u>of a kind that is specified in section 523(a)(5); or</u>

(B) a nonpossessory, nonpurchase-money security interest in any—

(i) household furnishings, household goods, wearing apparel, appliances, books, animals, crops, musical instruments, or jewelry that are held primarily for the personal, family, or household use of the debtor or a dependent of the debtor;

(ii) implements, professional books, or tools, of the trade of the debtor or the trade of a dependent of the debtor; or

(iii) professionally prescribed health aids for the debtor or a dependent of the debtor.

(2) (A) For the purposes of this subsection, a lien shall be considered to impair an exemption to the extent that the sum of—

(i) the lien;

(ii) all other liens on the property; and

(iii) the amount of the exemption that the debtor could claim if there were no liens on the property; exceeds the value that the debtor's interest in the property would have in the absence of any liens.

(B) In the case of a property subject to more than 1 lien, a lien that has been avoided shall not be considered in making the calculation under subparagraph (A) with respect to other liens.

(C) This paragraph shall not apply with respect to a judgment arising out of a mortgage foreclosure.

(3) In a case in which State law that is applicable to the debtor—

(A) permits a person to voluntarily waive a right to claim exemptions under subsection (d) or prohibits a debtor from claiming exemptions under subsection (d); and

(B) either permits the debtor to claim exemptions under State law without limitation in amount, except to the extent that the debtor has permitted the fixing of a consensual lien on any property or prohibits avoidance of a consensual lien on property otherwise eligible to be claimed as exempt property; the debtor may not avoid the fixing of a lien on an interest of the debtor or a dependent of the debtor in property if the lien is a nonpossessory, nonpurchase-money security interest in implements, professional books, or tools of the trade of the debtor or a dependent of the debtor or farm animals or crops of the debtor or a dependent of the debtor to the extent the value of such implements, professional books, tools of the trade, animals, and crops exceeds $5,000.

(4) (A) Subject to subparagraph (B), for purposes of paragraph (1)(B), the term 'household goods' means—

(i) clothing;

(ii) furniture;

(iii) appliances;

(iv) 1 radio;

(v) 1 television;

(vi) 1 VCR;

(vii) linens;

(viii) china;

(ix) crockery;

(x) kitchenware;

(xi) educational materials and educational equipment primarily for the use of minor dependent children of the debtor;

(xii) medical equipment and supplies;

(xiii) furniture exclusively for the use of minor children, or elderly or disabled dependents of the debtor;

(xiv) personal effects (including the toys and hobby equipment of minor dependent children and wedding rings) of the debtor and the dependents of the debtor; and

(xv) 1 personal computer and related equipment.

(B) The term "household goods" does not include—

(i) works of art (unless by or of the debtor, or any relative of the debtor);

(ii) electronic entertainment equipment with a fair market value of more than $500 in the aggregate (except 1 television, 1 radio, and 1 VCR);

(iii) items acquired as antiques with a fair market value of more than $500 in the aggregate;

(iv) jewelry with a fair market value of more than $500 in the aggregate (except wedding rings); and

(v) a computer (except as otherwise provided for in this section), motor vehicle (including a tractor or lawn tractor), boat, or a motorized recreational device, conveyance, vehicle, watercraft, or aircraft.

- *In re Virello*
  - Loan by money store
  - And they could not get house because no value past first motgage
  - Issue is Money Store Inventory
  - Debtors get a hearing
  - 506d does not operate alone to void a deed need another statute
  - Under 506d a debtor cannot void a lein on which it was had
- *East Cambridge Savings Bank v. Silveira (In re Sileira)*
  - It explains it simply
  - In this case avoid lien by all but 24k
- *Nelson v. Scala*
  - 2 owners but one bankrupt

11 U.S.C. §101(30). Eligibility

(30) "individual with regular income" means individual whose income is sufficiently stable and regular to enable such individual to make payments under a plan under chapter 13 of this title, other than a stockbroker or a commodity broker.

- *§109(e)*

(e) Only an individual with regular income that owes, on the date of the filing of the petition, noncontingent, liquidated, unsecured debts of less than $307,675 and noncontingent, liquidated, secured debts of less than $922,975, or an individual with regular income and such individual's spouse, except a stockbroker or a commodity broker, that owe, on the date of the filing of the petition, noncontingent, liquidated, unsecured debts that aggregate less than $307,675 and noncontingent, liquidated, secured debts of less than $922,975 may be a debtor under chapter 13 of this title.

- *§706(a)*

§ 706. Conversion

(a) The debtor may convert a case under this chapter to a case under chapter 11, 12, or 13 of this title at any time, if the case has not been converted under section 1112, 1208, or 1307 of this title. Any waiver of the right to convert a case under this subsection is unenforceable.

- **Plan Issues**

- *11 U.S.C. §§1301 – 1308*

§ 1301. Stay of action against codebtor

(a) Except as provided in subsections (b) and (c) of this section, after the order for relief under this chapter, a creditor may not act, or commence or continue any civil action, to collect all or any part of a consumer debt of the debtor from any individual that is liable on such debt with the debtor, or that secured such debt, unless—

(1) such individual became liable on or secured such debt in the ordinary course of such individual's business; or

(2) the case is closed, dismissed, or converted to a case under chapter 7 or 11 of this title.

(b) A creditor may present a negotiable instrument, and may give notice of dishonor of such an instrument.

(c) On request of a party in interest and after notice and a hearing, the court shall grant relief from the stay provided by subsection (a) of this section with respect to a creditor, to the extent that—

(1) as between the debtor and the individual protected under subsection (a) of this section, such individual received the consideration for the claim held by such creditor;

(2) the plan filed by the debtor proposes not to pay such claim; or

(3) such creditor's interest would be irreparably harmed by continuation of such stay.

(d) Twenty days after the filing of a request under subsection (c)(2) of this section for relief from the stay provided by subsection (a) of this section, such stay is terminated with respect to the party in interest making such request, unless the debtor or any individual that is liable on such debt with the debtor files and serves upon such party in interest a written objection to the taking of the proposed action.

§ 1302. Trustee

(a) If the United States trustee appoints an individual under section 586(b) of title 28 to serve as standing trustee in cases under this chapter and if such individual qualifies under section 322 of this title, then such individual shall serve as trustee in the case. Otherwise, the United States trustee shall appoint one disinterested person to serve as trustee in the case or the United States trustee may serve as a trustee in the case.

(b) The trustee shall—

(1) perform the duties specified in sections 704(2), 704(3), 704(4), 704(5), 704(6), 704(7), and 704(9) of this title;

(2) appear and be heard at any hearing that concerns—

(A) the value of property subject to a lien;

(B) confirmation of a plan; or

(C) modification of the plan after confirmation;

(3) dispose of, under regulations issued by the Director of the Administrative Office of the United States Courts, moneys received or to be received in a case under chapter XIII of the Bankruptcy Act;

(4) advise, other than on legal matters, and assist the debtor in performance under the plan;

(5) ensure that the debtor commences making timely payments under section 1326 of this title~~.~~; and

(6) if with respect to the debtor there is a claim for a domestic support obligation, provide the applicable notice specified in subsection (d).

(c) If the debtor is engaged in business, then in addition to the duties specified in subsection (b) of this section, the trustee shall perform the duties specified in sections 1106(a)(3) and 1106(a)(4) of this title.

(d) (1) In a case described in subsection (b)(6) to which subsection (b)(6) applies, the trustee shall—

(A) (i) provide written notice to the holder of the claim described in subsection (b)(6) of such claim and of the right of such holder to use the services of the State child support enforcement agency established under sections 464 and 466 of the Social Security Act for the State in which such holder resides, for assistance in collecting child support during and after the case under this title; and

(ii) include in the notice provided under clause (i) the address and telephone number of such State child support enforcement agency;

(B) (i) provide written notice to such State child support enforcement agency of such claim; and

(ii) include in the notice provided under clause (i) the name, address, and telephone number of such holder; and

(C) at such time as the debtor is granted a discharge under section 1328, provide written notice to such holder and to such State child support enforcement agency of—

(i) the granting of the discharge;

(ii) the last recent known address of the debtor;

(iii) the last recent known name and address of the debtor's employer; and

(iv) the name of each creditor that holds a claim that—

(I) is not discharged under paragraph (2) or (4) of section 523(a); or

(II) was reaffirmed by the debtor under section 524(c).

(2) (A) The holder of a claim described in subsection (b)(6) or the State child support enforcement agency of the State in which such holder resides may request from a creditor described in paragraph (1)(C)(iv) the last known address of the debtor.

(B) Notwithstanding any other provision of law, a creditor that makes a disclosure of a last known address of a debtor in connection with a request made under subparagraph (A) shall not be liable by reason of making that disclosure.

§ 1303. Rights and powers of debtor

Subject to any limitations on a trustee under this chapter, the debtor shall have, exclusive of the trustee, the rights and powers of a trustee under sections 363(b), 363(d), 363(e), 363(f), and 363(l), of this title.

§ 1304. Debtor engaged in business

(a) A debtor that is self-employed and incurs trade credit in the production of income from such employment is engaged in business.

(b) Unless the court orders otherwise, a debtor engaged in business may operate the business of the debtor and, subject to any limitations on a trustee under sections 363(c) and 364 of this title and to such limitations or conditions as the court prescribes, shall have, exclusive of the trustee, the rights and powers of the trustee under such sections.

(c) A debtor engaged in business shall perform the duties of the trustee specified in section 704(8) of this title.

§ 1305. Filing and allowance of postpetition claims

(a) A proof of claim may be filed by any entity that holds a claim against the debtor—

(1) for taxes that become payable to a governmental unit while the case is pending; or

(2) that is a consumer debt, that arises after the date of the order for relief under this chapter, and that is for property or services necessary for the debtor's performance under the plan.

(b) Except as provided in subsection (c) of this section, a claim filed under subsection (a) of this section shall be allowed or disallowed under section 502 of this title, but shall be determined as of the date such claim arises, and shall be allowed under section 502(a), 502(b), or 502(c) of this title, or disallowed under section 502(d) or 502(e) of this title, the same as if such claim had arisen before the date of the filing of the petition.

(c) A claim filed under subsection (a)(2) of this section shall be disallowed if the holder of such claim knew or should have known that prior approval by the trustee of the debtor's incurring the obligation was practicable and was not obtained.

§ 1306. Property of the estate

(a) Property of the estate includes, in addition to the property specified in section 541 of this title—

(1) all property of the kind specified in such section that the debtor acquires after the commencement of the case but before the case is closed, dismissed, or converted to a case under chapter 7, 11, or 12 of this title, whichever occurs first; and

(2) earnings from services performed by the debtor after the commencement of the case but before the case is closed, dismissed, or converted to a case under chapter 7, 11, or 12 of this title, whichever occurs first.

(b) Except as provided in a confirmed plan or order confirming a plan, the debtor shall remain in possession of all property of the estate.

§ 1307. Conversion or dismissal

(a) The debtor may convert a case under this chapter to a case under chapter 7 of this title at any time. Any waiver of the right to convert under this subsection is unenforceable.

(b) On request of the debtor at any time, if the case has not been converted under section 706, 1112, or 1208 of this title, the court shall dismiss a case under this chapter. Any waiver of the right to dismiss under this subsection is unenforceable.

(c) Except as provided in subsection (e) of this section, on request of a party in interest or the United States trustee and after notice and a hearing, the court may convert a case under this chapter to a case under chapter 7 of this title, or may dismiss a case under this chapter, whichever is in the best interests of creditors and the estate, for cause, including—

(1) unreasonable delay by the debtor that is prejudicial to creditors;

(2) nonpayment of any fees and charges required under chapter 123 of title 28;

(3) failure to file a plan timely under section 1321 of this title;

(4) failure to commence making timely payments under section 1326 of this title;

(5) denial of confirmation of a plan under section 1325 of this title and denial of a request made for additional time for filing another plan or a modification of a plan;

(6) material default by the debtor with respect to a term of a confirmed plan;

(7) revocation of the order of confirmation under section 1330 of this title, and denial of confirmation of a modified plan under section 1329 of this title;

(8) termination of a confirmed plan by reason of the occurrence of a condition specified in the plan other than completion of payments under the plan;

(9) only on request of the United States trustee, failure of the debtor to file, within fifteen days, or such additional time as the court may allow, after the filing of the petition commencing such case, the information required by paragraph (1) of section 521;

(10) only on request of the United States trustee, failure to timely file the information required by paragraph (2) of section 521; or

(11) failure of the debtor to pay any domestic support obligation that first becomes payable after the date of the filing of the petition.

(d) Except as provided in subsection (e) of this section, at any time before the confirmation of a plan under section 1325 of this title, on request of a party in interest or the United States trustee and after notice and a hearing, the court may convert a case under this chapter to a case under chapter 11 or 12 of this title.

(e) Upon the failure of the debtor to file a tax return under section 1308, on request of a party in interest or the United States trustee and after notice and a hearing, the court shall dismiss a case or convert a case under this chapter to a case under chapter 7 of this title, whichever is in the best interest of the creditors and the estate.

(f) The court may not convert a case under this chapter to a case under chapter 7, 11, or 12 of this title if the debtor is a farmer, unless the debtor requests such conversion.

(g) Notwithstanding any other provision of this section, a case may not be converted to a case under another chapter of this title unless the debtor may be a debtor under such chapter.

§ 1308. Filing of prepetition tax returns

(a) Not later than the day before the date on which the meeting of the creditors is first scheduled to be held under section 341(a), if the debtor was required to file a tax return under applicable nonbankruptcy law, the debtor shall file with appropriate tax authorities all tax returns for all taxable periods ending during the 4-year period ending on the date of the filing of the petition.

(b) (1) Subject to paragraph (2), if the tax returns required by subsection (a) have not been filed by the date on which the meeting of creditors is first scheduled to be held under section 341(a), the trustee may hold open that meeting for a reasonable period of time to allow the debtor an additional period of time to file any unfiled returns, but such additional period of time shall not extend beyond—

(A) for any return that is past due as of the date of the filing of the petition, the date that is 120 days after the date of that meeting; or

(B) for any return that is not past due as of the date of the filing of the petition, the later of—

(i) the date that is 120 days after the date of that meeting; or

(ii) the date on which the return is due under the last automatic extension of time for filing that return to which the debtor is entitled, and for which request is timely made, in accordance with applicable nonbankruptcy law.

(2) After notice and a hearing, and order entered before the tolling of any applicable filing period determined under this subsection, if the debtor demonstrates by a preponderance of the evidence that the failure to file a return as required under this subsection is attributable to circumstances beyond the control of the debtor, the court may extend the filing period established by the trustee under this subsection for—

(A) a period of not more than 30 days for returns described in paragraph (1); and

(B) a period not to extend after the applicable extended due date for a return described in paragraph (2).

(c) For purposes of this section, the term "return" includes a return prepared pursuant to subsection (a) or (b) of section 6020 of the Internal Revenue Code of 1986, or a similar State or local law, or a written stipulation to a judgment or a final order entered by a nonbankruptcy tribunal.

§ 1321. Filing of plan

The debtor shall file a plan.

§ 1322. Contents of plan

(a) The plan shall—

(1) provide for the submission of all or such portion of future earnings or other future income of the debtor to the supervision and control of the trustee as is necessary for the execution of the plan;

(2) provide for the full payment, in deferred cash payments, of all claims entitled to priority under section 507 of this title, unless the holder of a particular claim agrees to a different treatment of such claim;

(3) if the plan classifies claims, provide the same treatment for each claim within a particular class.; and

(4) notwithstanding any other provision of this section, a plan may provide for less than full payment of all amounts owed for a claim entitled to priority under section 507(a)(1)(B) only if the plan provides that all of the debtor's projected disposable income for a 5-year period beginning on the date that the first payment is due under the plan will be applied to make payments under the plan.

(b) Subject to subsections (a) and (c) of this section, the plan may—

(1) designate a class or classes of unsecured claims, as provided in section 1122 of this title, but may not discriminate unfairly against any class so designated; however, such plan may treat claims for a consumer debt of the debtor if an individual is liable on such consumer debt with the debtor differently than other unsecured claims;

(2) modify the rights of holders of secured claims, other than a claim secured only by a security interest in real property that is the debtor's principal residence, or of holders of unsecured claims, or leave unaffected the rights of holders of any class of claims;

(3) provide for the curing or waiving of any default;

(4) provide for payments on any unsecured claim to be made concurrently with payments on any secured claim or any other unsecured claim;

(5) notwithstanding paragraph (2) of this subsection, provide for the curing of any default within a reasonable time and maintenance of payments while the case is pending on any unsecured claim or secured claim on which the last payment is due after the date on which the final payment under the plan is due;

(6) provide for the payment of all or any part of any claim allowed under section 1305 of this title;

(7) subject to section 365 of this title, provide for the assumption, rejection, or assignment of any executory contract or unexpired lease of the debtor not previously rejected under such section;

(8) provide for the payment of all or part of a claim against the debtor from property of the estate or property of the debtor;

(9) provide for the vesting of property of the estate, on confirmation of the plan or at a later time, in the debtor or in any other entity;

(10) provide for the payment of interest accruing after the date of the filing of the petition on unsecured claims that are nondischargeable under section 1328(a), except that such interest may be paid only to the extent that the debtor has disposable income available to pay such interest after making provision for full payment of all allowed claims; and

(11) include any other appropriate provision not inconsistent with this title.

(c) Notwithstanding subsection (b)(2) and applicable nonbankruptcy law—

(1) a default with respect to, or that gave rise to, a lien on the debtor's principal residence may be cured under paragraph (3) or (5) of subsection (b) until such residence is sold at a foreclosure sale that is conducted in accordance with applicable nonbankruptcy law; and

(2) in a case in which the last payment on the original payment schedule for a claim secured only by a security interest in real property that is the debtor's principal residence is due before the date on which the final payment under the plan is due, the plan may provide for the payment of the claim as modified pursuant to section 1325(a)(5) of this title.

(d) (1) If the current monthly income of the debtor and the debtor's spouse combined, when multiplied by 12, is not less than—

(A) in the case of a debtor in a household of 1 person, the median family income of the applicable State for 1 earner;

(B) in the case of a debtor in a household of 2, 3, or 4 individuals, the highest median family income of the applicable State for a family of the same number or fewer individuals; or

(C) in the case of a debtor in a household exceeding 4 individuals, the highest median family income of the applicable State for a family of 4 or fewer individuals, plus $525 per month for each individual in excess of 4,

the plan may not provide for payments over a period that is longer than 5 years.

(2) If the current monthly income of the debtor and the debtor's spouse combined, when multiplied by 12, is less than—

(A) in the case of a debtor in a household of 1 person, the median family income of the applicable State for 1 earner;

(B) in the case of a debtor in a household of 2, 3, or 4 individuals, the highest median family income of the applicable State for a family of the same number or fewer individuals; or

(C) in the case of a debtor in a household exceeding 4 individuals, the highest median family income of the applicable State for a family of 4 or fewer individuals, plus $525 per month for each individual in excess of 4,

the plan may not provide for payments over a period that is longer than 3 years, unless the court, for cause, approves a longer period, but the court may not approve a period that is longer than 5 years.

(e) Notwithstanding subsection (b)(2) of this section and sections 506(b) and 1325(a)(5) of this title, if it is proposed in a plan to cure a default, the amount necessary to cure the default, shall be determined in accordance with the underlying agreement and applicable nonbankruptcy law.

(f) A plan may not materially alter the terms of a loan described in section 362(b)(19) and any amounts required to repay such loan shall not constitute "disposable income" under section 1325.

§ 1323. Modification of plan before confirmation

(a) The debtor may modify the plan at any time before confirmation, but may not modify the plan so that the plan as modified fails to meet the requirements of section 1322 of this title.

(b) After the debtor files a modification under this section, the plan as modified becomes the plan.

(c) Any holder of a secured claim that has accepted or rejected the plan is deemed to have accepted or rejected, as the case may be, the plan as modified, unless the modification provides for a change in the rights of such holder from what such rights were under the plan before modification, and such holder changes such holder's previous acceptance or rejection.

§ 1324. Confirmation hearing

(a) Except as provided in subsection (b) and after notice, the court shall hold a hearing on confirmation of the plan. A party in interest may object to confirmation of the plan.

(b) The hearing on confirmation of the plan may be held not earlier than 20 days and not later than 45 days after the date of the meeting of creditors under section 341(a), unless the court determines that it would be in the best interests of the creditors and the estate to hold such hearing at an earlier date and there is no objection to such earlier date.

§ 1325. Confirmation of plan

(a) Except as provided in subsection (b), the court shall confirm a plan if—

(1) the plan complies with the provisions of this chapter and with the other applicable provisions of this title;

(2) any fee, charge, or amount required under chapter 123 of title 28, or by the plan, to be paid before confirmation, has been paid;

(3) the plan has been proposed in good faith and not by any means forbidden by law;

(4) the value, as of the effective date of the plan, of property to be distributed under the plan on account of each allowed unsecured claim is not less than the amount that would be paid on such claim if the estate of the debtor were liquidated under chapter 7 of this title on such date;

(5) with respect to each allowed secured claim provided for by the plan—

(A) the holder of such claim has accepted the plan;

(B) (i) the plan provides that—

(I) the holder of such claim retain the lien securing such claim until the earlier of—

(aa) the payment of the underlying debt determined under nonbankruptcy law; or

(bb) discharge under section 1328; and

(II) if the case under this chapter is dismissed or converted without completion of the plan, such lien shall also be retained by such holder to the extent recognized by applicable nonbankruptcy law;

(ii) the value, as of the effective date of the plan, of property to be distributed under the plan on account of such claim is not less than the allowed amount of such claim; and

(iii) if—

(I) property to be distributed pursuant to this subsection is in the form of periodic payments, such payments shall be in equal monthly amounts; and

(II) the holder of the claim is secured by personal property, the amount of such payments shall not be less than an amount sufficient to provide to the holder of such claim adequate protection during the period of the plan; or

(C) the debtor surrenders the property securing such claim to such holder;

(6) the debtor will be able to make all payments under the plan and to comply with the plan.;

(7) the action of the debtor in filing the petition was in good faith;

(8) the debtor has paid all amounts that are required to be paid under a domestic support obligation and that first become payable after the date of the filing of the petition if the debtor is required by a judicial or administrative order, or by statute, to pay such domestic support obligation; and

(9) the debtor has filed all applicable Federal, State, and local tax returns as required by section 1308.

For purposes of paragraph (5), section 506 shall not apply to a claim described in that paragraph if the creditor has a purchase money security interest securing the debt that is the subject of the claim, the debt was incurred within the 910-day preceding the date of the filing of the petition, and the collateral for that debt consists of a motor vehicle (as defined in section 30102 of title 49) acquired for the personal use of the debtor, or if collateral for that debt consists of any other thing of value, if the debt was incurred during the 1-year period preceding that filing.

(b) (1) If the trustee or the holder of an allowed unsecured claim objects to the confirmation of the plan, then the court may not approve the plan unless, as of the effective date of the plan—

(A) the value of the property to be distributed under the plan on account of such claim is not less than the amount of such claim; or

(B) the plan provides that all of the debtor's projected disposable income to be received in the applicable commitment period beginning on the date that the first payment is due under the plan will be applied to make payments to unsecured creditors under the plan.

(2) For purposes of this subsection, the term 'disposable income"' means current monthly income received by the debtor (other than child support payments, foster care payments, or disability payments for a dependent child made in accordance with applicable nonbankruptcy law to the extent reasonably necessary to be expended for such child) less amounts reasonably necessary to be expended—

(A) (i) for the maintenance or support of the debtor or a dependent of the debtor, or for a domestic support obligation, that first becomes payable after the date the petition is filed; and

(ii) for charitable contributions (that meet the definition of 'charitable contribution' under section 548(d)(3) to a qualified religious or charitable entity or organization (as defined in section 548(d)(4)) in an amount not to exceed 15 percent of gross income of the debtor for the year in which the contributions are made; and

(B) if the debtor is engaged in business, for the payment of expenditures necessary for the continuation, preservation, and operation of such business.

(3) Amounts reasonably necessary to be expended under paragraph (2) shall be determined in accordance with subparagraphs (A) and (B) of section 707(b)(2), if the debtor has current monthly income, when multiplied by 12, greater than—

(A) in the case of a debtor in a household of 1 person, the median family income of the applicable State for 1 earner;

(B) in the case of a debtor in a household of 2, 3, or 4 individuals, the highest median family income of the applicable State for a family of the same number or fewer individuals; or

(C) in the case of a debtor in a household exceeding 4 individuals, the highest median family income of the applicable State for a family of 4 or fewer individuals, plus $525 per month for each individual in excess of 4.

(4) For purposes of this subsection, the "applicable commitment period"—

(A) subject to subparagraph (B), shall be—

(i) 3 years; or

(ii) not less than 5 years, if the current monthly income of the debtor and the debtor's spouse combined, when multiplied by 12, is not less than—

(I) in the case of a debtor in a household of 1 person, the median family income of the applicable State for 1 earner;

(II) in the case of a debtor in a household of 2, 3, or 4 individuals, the highest median family income of the applicable State for a family of the same number or fewer individuals; or

(III) in the case of a debtor in a household exceeding 4 individuals, the highest median family income of the applicable State for a family of 4 or fewer individuals, plus $525 per month for each individual in excess of 4; and

(B) may be less than 3 or 5 years, whichever is applicable under subparagraph (A), but only if the plan provides for payment in full of all allowed unsecured claims over a shorter period.

(c) After confirmation of a plan, the court may order any entity from whom the debtor receives income to pay all or any part of such income to the trustee.

§ 1326. Payments

(a) (1) Unless the court orders otherwise, the debtor shall commence making payments not later than 30 days after the date of the filing of the plan or the order for relief, whichever is earlier, in the amount—

(A) proposed by the plan to the trustee;

(B) scheduled in a lease of personal property directly to the lessor for that portion of the obligation that becomes due after the order for relief, reducing the payments under subparagraph (A) by the amount so paid and providing the trustee with evidence of such payment, including the amount and date of payment; and

(C) that provides adequate protection directly to a creditor holding an allowed claim secured by personal property to the extent the claim is attributable to the purchase of such property by the debtor for that portion of the obligation that becomes due after the order for relief, reducing the payments under subparagraph (A) by the amount so paid and providing the trustee with evidence of such payment, including the amount and date of payment.

(2) A payment made under paragraph (1)(A) shall be retained by the trustee until confirmation or denial of confirmation. If a plan is confirmed, the trustee shall distribute any such payment in accordance with the plan as soon as is practicable. If a plan is not confirmed, the trustee shall return any such payments not previously paid and not yet due and owing to creditors pursuant to paragraph (3) to the debtor, after deducting any unpaid claim allowed under section 503(b).

(3) Subject to section 363, the court may, upon notice and a hearing, modify, increase, or reduce the payments required under this subsection pending confirmation of a plan.

(4) Not later than 60 days after the date of filing of a case under this chapter, a debtor retaining possession of personal property subject to a lease or securing a claim attributable in whole or in part to the purchase price of such property shall provide the lessor or secured creditor reasonable evidence of the maintenance of any required insurance coverage with respect to the use or ownership of such property and continue to do so for so long as the debtor retains possession of such property.

(b) Before or at the time of each payment to creditors under the plan, there shall be paid—

(1) any unpaid claim of the kind specified in section 507(a)(2) of this title;

(2) if a standing trustee appointed under section 586(b) of title 28 is serving in the case, the percentage fee fixed for such standing trustee under section 586(e)(1)(B) of title 28; and

(3) if a chapter 7 trustee has been allowed compensation due to the conversion or dismissal of the debtor's prior case pursuant to section 707(b), and some portion of that compensation remains unpaid in a case converted to this chapter or in the case dismissed under section 707(b) and refiled under this chapter, the amount of any such unpaid compensation, which shall be paid monthly—

(A) by prorating such amount over the remaining duration of the plan; and

(B) by monthly payments not to exceed the greater of—

(i) $25; or

(ii) the amount payable to unsecured nonpriority creditors, as provided by the plan, multiplied by 5 percent, and the result divided by the number of months in the plan.

(c) Except as otherwise provided in the plan or in the order confirming the plan, the trustee shall make payments to creditors under the plan.

(d) Notwithstanding any other provision of this title—

(1) compensation referred to in subsection (b)(3) is payable and may be collected by the trustee under that paragraph, even if such amount has been discharged in a prior case under this title; and

(2) such compensation is payable in a case under this chapter only to the extent permitted by subsection (b)(3).

§ 1327. Effect of confirmation

(a) The provisions of a confirmed plan bind the debtor and each creditor, whether or not the claim of such creditor is provided for by the plan, and whether or not such creditor has objected to, has accepted, or has rejected the plan.

(b) Except as otherwise provided in the plan or the order confirming the plan, the confirmation of a plan vests all of the property of the estate in the debtor.

(c) Except as otherwise provided in the plan or in the order confirming the plan, the property vesting in the debtor under subsection (b) of this section is free and clear of any claim or interest of any creditor provided for by the plan.

§ 1328. Discharge

(a) Subject to subsection (d),[29] as soon as practicable after completion by the debtor of all payments under the plan, and in the case of a debtor who is required by a judicial or administrative order, or by statute, to pay a domestic support obligation, after such debtor certifies that all amounts payable under such order or such statute that are due on or before the date of the certification (including amounts due before the petition was filed, but only to the extent provided for by the plan) have been paid, unless the court approves a written waiver of discharge executed by the debtor after the order for relief under this chapter, the court shall grant the debtor a discharge of all debts provided for by the plan or disallowed under section 502 of this title, except any debt—

(1) provided for under section 1322(b)(5);

(2) of the kind specified in section 507(a)(8)(C) or in paragraph (1)(B), (1)(C), (2), (3), (4), (5), (8), or (9) of section 523(a);

(3) for restitution, or a criminal fine, included in a sentence on the debtor's conviction of a crime; or

(4) for restitution, or damages, awarded in a civil action against the debtor as a result of willful or malicious injury by the debtor that caused personal injury to an individual or the death of an individual.

[29] Effective 180 days after the date of enactment of the Act; applicable to any case under the Bankruptcy Code commenced on or after the date of enactment. Pub. L. No. 109-8, 119 Stat. 23, Sec. 1501(2).

(b) Subject to subsection (d),[30] at any time after the confirmation of the plan and after notice and a hearing, the court may grant a discharge to a debtor that has not completed payments under the plan only if—

  (1) the debtor's failure to complete such payments is due to circumstances for which the debtor should not justly be held accountable;

  (2) the value, as of the effective date of the plan, of property actually distributed under the plan on account of each allowed unsecured claim is not less than the amount that would have been paid on such claim if the estate of the debtor had been liquidated under chapter 7 of this title on such date; and

  (3) modification of the plan under section 1329 of this title is not practicable.

(c) A discharge granted under subsection (b) of this section discharges the debtor from all unsecured debts provided for by the plan or disallowed under section 502 of this title, except any debt—

  (1) provided for under section 1322(b)(5) of this title; or

  (2) of a kind specified in section 523(a) of this title.

(d) Notwithstanding any other provision of this section, a discharge granted under this section does not discharge the debtor from any debt based on an allowed claim filed under section 1305(a)(2) of this title if prior approval by the trustee of the debtor's incurring such debt was practicable and was not obtained.

(e) On request of a party in interest before one year after a discharge under this section is granted, and after notice and a hearing, the court may revoke such discharge only if—

  (1) such discharge was obtained by the debtor through fraud; and

  (2) the requesting party did not know of such fraud until after such discharge was granted.

(f) Notwithstanding subsections (a) and (b), the court shall not grant a discharge of all debts provided for in the plan or disallowed under section 502, if the debtor has received a discharge—

  (1) in a case filed under chapter 7, 11, or 12 of this title during the 4-year period preceding the date of the order for relief under this chapter, or

  (2) in a case filed under chapter 13 of this title during the 2-year period preceding the date of such order.

---

[30] Effective 180 days after the date of enactment of the Act; applicable to any case under the Bankruptcy Code commenced on or after the date of enactment. Pub. L. No. 109-8, 119 Stat. 23, Sec. 1501(2).

(g) (1) The court shall not grant a discharge under this section to a debtor unless after filing a petition the debtor has completed an instructional course concerning personal financial management described in section 111.

(2) Paragraph (1) shall not apply with respect to a debtor who is a person described in section 109(h)(4) or who resides in a district for which the United States trustee (or the bankruptcy administrator, if any) determines that the approved instructional courses are not adequate to service the additional individuals who would otherwise be required to complete such instructional course by reason of the requirements of paragraph (1), or if the court finds that exigent circumstances merit a waiver of the requirements of this paragraph.

(3) The United States trustee (or the bankruptcy administrator, if any) who makes a determination described in paragraph (2) shall review such determination not later than 1 year after the date of such determination, and not less frequently than annually thereafter.

(h) The court may not grant a discharge under this chapter unless the court after notice and a hearing held not more than 10 days before the date of the entry of the order granting the discharge finds that there is no reasonable cause to believe that—[31]

(1) section 522(q)(1) may be applicable to the debtor; and

(2) there is pending any proceeding in which the debtor may be found guilty of a felony of the kind described in section 522(q)(1)(A) or liable for a debt of the kind described in section 522(q)(1)(B).

§ 1329. Modification of plan after confirmation

(a) At any time after confirmation of the plan but before the completion of payments under such plan, the plan may be modified, upon request of the debtor, the trustee, or the holder of an allowed unsecured claim, to—

(1) increase or reduce the amount of payments on claims of a particular class provided for by the plan;

(2) extend or reduce the time for such payments;

(3) alter the amount of the distribution to a creditor whose claim is provided for by the plan to the extent necessary to take account of any payment of such claim other than under the plan.; or

[31] Effective 180 days after the date of enactment of the Act; applicable to any case under the Bankruptcy Code commenced on or after the date of enactment. Pub. L. No. 109-8, 119 Stat. 23, Sec. 1501(2).

(4) reduce amounts to be paid under the plan by the actual amount expended by the debtor to purchase health insurance for the debtor (and for any dependent of the debtor if such dependent does not otherwise have health insurance coverage) if the debtor documents the cost of such insurance and demonstrates that—

(A) such expenses are reasonable and necessary;

(B) (i) if the debtor previously paid for health insurance, the amount is not materially larger than the cost the debtor previously paid or the cost necessary to maintain the lapsed policy; or

(ii) if the debtor did not have health insurance, the amount is not materially larger than the reasonable cost that would be incurred by a debtor who purchases health insurance, who has similar income, expenses, age, and health status, and who lives in the same geographical location with the same number of dependents who do not otherwise have health insurance coverage; and

(C) the amount is not otherwise allowed for purposes of determining disposable income under section 1325(b) of this title;

and upon request of any party in interest, files proof that a health insurance policy was purchased.

(b) (1) Sections 1322(a), 1322(b), and 1323(c) of this title and the requirements of section 1325(a) of this title apply to any modification under subsection (a) of this section.

(2) The plan as modified becomes the plan unless, after notice and a hearing, such modification is disapproved.

(c) A plan modified under this section may not provide for payments over a period that expires after the applicable commitment period under section 1325(b)(1)(B) after the time that the first payment under the original confirmed plan was due, unless the court, for cause, approves a longer period, but the court may not approve a period that expires after five years after such time.

§ 1330. Revocation of an order of confirmation

(a) On request of a party in interest at any time within 180 days after the date of the entry of an order of confirmation under section 1325 of this title, and after notice and a hearing, the court may revoke such order if such order was procured by fraud.

i. (b) If the court revokes an order of confirmation under subsection (a) of this section, the court shall dispose of the case under section 1307 of this title, unless, within the time fixed by the court, the debtor proposes and the court confirms a modification of the plan under section 1329 of this title.

Secret Weapon Outline

MD – Maryland; SI – Security Interest; SC – secured creditor; SP – secured party; T/E – tenancy by the entirety; DIP – Debtor in Possession; TIB – trustee in bankruptcy; FMV – Fair Market Value; Ct, ct – court; MD – Maryland; GUSC – General Unsecured Creditors; DSO – domestic support obligations (including child support, alimony, etc.)

I. **INTRODUCTION**
   a. Focus on the code and structure of the rules
   b. More than 1 million file bankruptcy historically in US per year
      i. MD has its fair share → 35K+ in 2005
         1. half were husband-wife joint cases, so more people involved than you think
   c. ***Key statutory changes by Congress in 2005
      i. in response to spikes in bankruptcy cases in recent years
      ii. after new 2005 law, saw sharp dropoff in bankruptcy filings and numbers have stayed low
         1. Congress made it more difficult to file
   d. Bankruptcy tends to be very cyclical
      i. Highest numbers in March-April due to post-holiday bump
      ii. Numbers drop in the summer and December is traditionally a slow year
   e. Why do people file for bankruptcy?
      i. Lots of dischargeable unsecured debt
      ii. In this day and age, credit is very easy to get and can lead to bankruptcy
         1. interest rates also affect credit and bankruptcy
         2. credit scores are very important these days → making payments in a timely fashion
      iii. unemployment and related factors
      iv. other theories → attorney advertising on TV and the Yellow Pages; also, lessening of the stigma associated with filing bankruptcy (even rich people with lots of debt file)
   f. **Players in the Bankruptcy System:**
      i. The Bankruptcy Court → the Judge!!
      ii. Debtors
         1. as well as DIPs – debtor in possession, in essence they act as a Trustee
      iii. Creditors
      iv. Trustees
         1. the US trustees
            a. representative of the DOJ
            b. they appoint the case trustees
         2. Case Trustees → usually lawyers and accountants

a. Different types for different bankruptcy Chapters, i.e. 7, 11, 13, etc.
b. They actually administer the cases and deal with the assets
c. Get paid from assets they get from the creditors
d. Commission-based

v. Finally, have creditors' committees, e.g. in Ch. 11

g. NOTE: Bankruptcy involves many areas of law → the bankruptcy code overlays other systems of law
   i. IP, Torts, Family, Property, Employment, Criminal, **Tax, Contract, Ethics Law, etc...

h. **Bankruptcy also relies heavily on State Law**
   i. Bankruptcy looks to state law for many of the substantive rights of the parties
      1. e.g., definition of property is based upon state statutes and case law
      2. T/E exemption is based on state law
   ii. Exemptions is a bankruptcy issue but it can incorporate state property law
   iii. Leases are also important in many bankruptcies
   iv. Bankruptcy is federal law, no doubt about that
      1. it is supreme over state law through the supremacy clause

i. **Basic Secured Transaction Concepts (based on state law/UCC)**
   i. All debts can generally be divided into two categories: secured and unsecured
   ii. <u>Unsecured Transactions and Debt</u>
      1. Defined → any transaction involving an advance of value (usually money) made against some future promise or performance that are not guaranteed or secured by any collateral
         a. e.g. a demand note → payable on demand
         b. without collateral, the debt is unsecured
         c. you can sue and get a judgment and take it to the sheriff → post-judgment collection
            i. but if the debtor is judgment-proof, then creditor is screwed and judgment is worth nothing

2. what alternatives does an unsecured creditor when he or she can recover nothing, or when it is hard to recover something from the debtor?
    a. Sell the debt to someone who specializes in collection possibly (?)
    b. You can wait
    c. Make a notation on the debtors credit report
    d. **BUT YOU CAN'T GET THE MONEY NOW

iii. <u>Secured Transactions and Debt</u>
1. Defined → any transaction involving an advance of value (usually money) made against some future promise or performance that is guaranteed or secured by collateral
    a. E.g., a promissory note, on demand, with a security agreement (a contract) that secures the loan with a printing press as collateral; thus a security interest is created in the printing press to secure repayment of the demand note
2. governed by Art. 9 of the UCC for personal property collateral (MD version is in Title IX of the Maryland Commercial Law Article)
3. UCC → set of scholarly texts to bring uniformity to state laws and foster interstate commerce
    a. Each individual state must adopt thru its legislature before it takes effect
    b. Not entirely uniform → state legislatures made adjustments
4. **Default** → UCC is silent on this; parties bargain for what constitutes default in the security agreement contract (i.e. list events of default)
    a. Almost certainly, failure to make payment constitutes default
    b. Assuming financing statement was filed, what can SC do?
        i. SC can repossess the printing press from above example → Self-Help without prior notice unless:
            1. the parties agree to notice in the sec agreement (but

lenders never agree to this)

2. or if there is a breach of the peace
    a. i.e. a verbal confrontation will likely constitute a breach of the peace
    b. essentially, any protest by any person there present, but if protest is after creditor has already repossessed, then it's too late for debtor
3. Note, that SCs can be very clever with repossession, many tricks

ii. Another option is for SC to enter into a forbearance agreement that states that SC will not repossess if debtor pays

iii. SC can also sue for the money, and SC has to do this if they can't repossess without a breach of the peace
    1. In personam rights → the money owed
    2. In rem rights → the SI in the printing press

5. Under UCC Art. 9, only personal property can be collateral
    a. i.e. tangible property, like goods and machinery

   b. and also intangible property, like accounts receivables (A/R)
   c. **does not include real estate or cars!!**
6. After repossession, SC can do several things:
   a. Sell the collateral so long as the creditor does so in a commercially reasonable manner
      i. Depends on the type of collateral and the market for it
      ii. There are other requirements in the sale process, but it's beyond the purview of this course
   b. Strict foreclosures → SC can keep the collateral and forget the rest of the debt
      i. This is rare!
      ii. Exception for consumer goods
7. if you sell the collateral, the proceeds are distributed in a certain priority:
   a. first, pay off expenses of repossession and the sale
   b. second, pay the debt owed to the SC
   c. third, any debts owed to subordinate SCs with subordinate liens
   d. after any other creditors, what's leftover goes to the debtor
   e. if there is a deficiency, i.e. SC does get full debt back, then the SC can sue debtor for that deficiency
8. **Perfection**
   a. Purpose of perfection → lien is never secret between debtor and creditor
   b. Generally, perfection does not affect the rights of the original parties, i.e. the debtor and creditor
   c. Definition → process the parties must go through to make sure that the creditor's SI in the collateral is good again most of the rest of the world (most b/c there are some exceptions including a trustee in bankruptcy)

- i. Gives the SC more rights than prior to perfection

d. Adding to above hypo: if debtor sells printing press to someone else, then:
   - i. If no financing statement, SC is in big trouble unless the buyer has actual knowledge of the original SI in the printing press
     1. if no knowledge on the part of the buyer, then can take title to printing press free and clear of SC's lien as long as the buyer paid something for the collateral
        a. i.e. a 3rd part purchaser for value without notice takes the collateral free and clear of the unperfected SI
   - ii. If there is financing statement, then SC can repossess or seek other remedies from buyer/debtor

e. So SCs are further bifurcated into perfected or unperfected SCs
   - i. In many cases, being an unperfected SC is like being an unsecured

f. <u>Perfection is accomplished in 3 main ways:</u>
   - i. Usually, you file a financing statement to perfect and put the world on notice → refer to state law (in MD, at SDAT)
   - ii. By possession

iii. Automatic perfection → See § 9-309, occurs in special instances
    1. most commonly, a PMSI in consumer goods
    2. a PMSI → the debtor borrows the money and purchases the collateral from the same entity (like at Sears)
    3. Non-PMSI → when money is used from someone else to purchase a good/collateral from another seller (i.e. use the bank's money to purchase a good from someone else)

iv. For real estate, you will file in the land records office in that county

II. LEVERAGE & COLLECTION METHODS & POST-JUDGMENT REMEDIES (STATE LAW)

a. **Leverage** basically refers to the type of pressure that a creditor can place on a debtor to pay
    i. The better position the creditor is in, the more leverage they have
    ii. In most situations, creditors avoid courts in debt collection process because of the high cost of litigation → place pressure on the debtor in other ways
    iii. Indirect leverage in the legal system
        1. sometimes state statutes help especially in the context of employment and family law

b. **Restrictions on Nonjudicial Collection (the statutes)**
    i. Usury Laws
        1. basically controls certain types of predatory or extremely high interest rates → if determined to be usurious, debt would be deemed uncollectible
        2. today, not much impact because of Supreme Court decision *Omaha Bank* in which the court concluded that the bank charge whatever rate is legal in the bank's home state (and not where the debtor is located)

- ii. Fair Credit Reporting Act
  1. well-established credit reporting agencies help creditors report bad debtors to everyone
     - a. helps create leverage upon debtors to pay
  2. statute was passed to prevent abuses
     - a. two principal themes → giving the debtor access to the credit report information and prescribing procedures to assure the accuracy of the information in the file
     - b. if a user of credit information takes adverse action based on the info in the consumer reports, then they must notify the debtor of this (i.e. of the bad debt that lead to their decision/action)
     - c. plus the act provides for grievance procedures for consumers → dispute info
     - d. imposes liability for noncompliance of the statute
- iii. Fair Debt Collection Practices Act
  1. **3 main forms of compliance:**
     - a. when collecting, must identify that you are the debt collector
     - b. advise a debtor that he/she has a right to verify and dispute the debt
     - c. avoid harassment, false representations, misrepresentations, unfair practices
  2. plus, a requirement that collection agencies verify the accuracy of debt information and limitation on collection agencies bringing lawsuits in forums far from the debtor
  3. Act provides for both FTC and private enforcement actions with the recovery of actual damages, costs, and $1000 statutory damages for violations (1 yr SOL though)
  4. *Heintz v. Jenkins*: applied FDCPA to attorneys
     - a. Facts – attorney sent letter to debtor asking for loan repayment as well as an insurance payment to keep the car insured; yet the insurance not only covered loss/damages but it also insured the bank for the debtor's

failure to pay the loan itself and the P/debtor argued that this amount was not authorized by the original loan agreement, thus violating the Act (amount of debt was false)

b. Ct looks to plain language of statute and congressional intent in repealing an exemption for lawyers

5. **Note that this statute applies to debt collectors, i.e. someone removed from the debt; debt owners are not covered by the statute (law only applies to debts that are due to ANOTHER)**
    a. Thus a bank is a debt owner of its own debt and they are not a debt collector
    b. Congressional policy to encourage people to sue on their own debt as owners rather than farming it out to a collection agency
        i. Plus, collectors are paid by the percentage and the more they "stiff-arm" and recover in debts, the more they get paid, thus it makes sense to regulate them

iv. <u>Maryland Fair Debt Collection Practices Act</u>
1. attorneys are subject to this also
2. definition of "debt collector" here
    a. means a person trying to collect an alleged debt arising out of a consumer transaction
        i. **this includes everyone including debt owners themselves!**
        ii. **But only for consumer not business debts**
3. Damages, see 14-203
    a. A lot more mush than the federal version → involves "mental and emotional distress," i.e. tort terms

v. As an attorney, you must give notice on the least sophisticated consumer standard → has to be understandable by the least sophisticated consumer

c. **Post-Judgment Collection/Remedies (State Law)**
i. Judgment → an order entered by a court (a mere direction to pay is insufficient)

ii. <u>The Law in the Context of the Relevant Maryland Provisions</u>

1. **Md. Cts. & Jud. Proc. § 11-402(b) → Judgment Constitutes Lien, original entry judgment**
   a. Judgment is automatically indexed and recorded in that county
   b. "a money judgment of a court constitutes a lien to the amount and from the date of the judgment on the **judgment debtor's interest in land located in the county in which the judgment was rendered** except a lease . . ."
   c. HYPO: e.g., house worth 700K with a first lien on it of 400K leaving 300K in equity
      i. Judgment of 500K attached second lien to the house
      ii. If house is sold, first lien creditor gets 400K, judgment lien creditor gets 300K and is left with a 200K deficiency → so judgment creditor can go after other property of judgment debtor to cover deficiency
   d. SUPPOSE property is leased then it is still "interest in land," but there are exceptions in the statute:
      i. **"a lease**
         1. **from year to year OR**
         2. **for a term of not more than five years and not renewable."**
      ii. E.g. a 99-year ground rent is not exempted from the statute
   e. IF house is not in the judgment debtor's name, then the judgment lien does not attach
   f. IF prior to entry of judgment, judgment debtor sells interest in land to

someone else, then judgment lien doesn't attach

2. **§ 11-402(c) → Judgment of Another Court**
    a. just index and record the judgment in the other county and it constitutes a lien in land in that other county just like a 11-402(b) court of original entry judgment
3. **§ 11-802(b) → Foreign Judgment** (i.e. federal or another state) can be brought to Maryland and recorded and enforced in Maryland
4. **§ 11-403 → Personal Property, NOT LAND**
    a. no automatic attachment, must levy on the property
        i. Implementing document is called a WRIT OF EXECUTION → this is what sheriff gets from the court
        ii. Fi. Fa. → personal property levy, writ of execution
    b. Md. Rule 2-642(b) → done through the sheriff by levy pursuant to a writ of execution
        i. Must have description of property entered on a schedule
        ii. Then must remove the property, OR
        iii. Affix copy of the writ and schedule to the property, OR
        iv. Post notices of writ of execution and schedule with labels affixed to each item of property, OR
        v. Post without labels if not practical
    c. Judgment creditor's lien attaches to the property when the sheriff levies on the property according to 2-642(b)
    d. 2-642(c) → sheriff can also levy and leave the property where found if property is possession of some other third party
    e. 2-643 → Release of Property from Levy

i. (a) → when judgment is satisfied
ii. (b) → by positing a bond in amount to satisfy the judgment and costs
iii. 2-643(c) → judgment debtor can file motion to release property from levy based on 6 grounds:
    1. judgment vacated, expired, satisfied
    2. exempt property
    3. creditor failed to comply with the rules
    4. other property sufficient in value will remain under levy
    5. undue hardship and debtor makes other property available for levy
    6. levy exists for 120 days without sale, unless court extends time for good cause
iv. 2-643(d) → election of exemptions by judgment debtor
v. 2-643(e) → third parties can file motions if property was wrongfully taken
vi. (f) → provides for a hearing

f. 2-642(e) → requires sheriff to file a RETURN, together with the schedule, listing what was captured by the sheriff's levy
    i. 2-641(b) → must file the return in the other county also

g. 2-632(b) → stay of enforcement of money judgment for 10 days

- i. **for attorneys, breaking this will lead to malpractice claims**
- ii. gives some time to debtors to pay judgment and allows for post trial motions and other motions (appeal will stay enforcement with posting of a bond)

5. **GARNISHMENT (and attachment of bank accounts, wages, etc.)**
   - a. This deals with the non-tangible forms of property that creditors go after
     - i. Wages → creditors will look at credit report to see where you work; they will also ask you in your application for credit
     - ii. Stocks, bonds, royalties, etc.
     - iii. **Bank Accounts**
       1. sometimes found in credit report
       2. or if the lender is a bank, they can look at their own accounts to see if debtor has one
       3. these will also be listed in an application for credit
       4. asset searches and geographic searches where they live/work
   - b. Writ of Garnishment (or Attachment)
     - i. Typically used to "attach" debts owed to the debtor for the benefit of the debtor's judgment creditor
     - ii. **RULE: A judgment creditor cannot obtain rights against a garnishee which are superior to those rights which the judgment debtor**

held at the moment of the garnishment

1. garnishing creditor stands in the shoes of the debtor

iii. The court will issue such writs for you to serve on the bank

c. Md. Rule 2-645(d): can't just mail the writ it to the bank, you must send it to a special recipient

i. For corporations, see 2-124(d): must serve process upon its resident agent (see State Dep't of Tax/Assessments for resident agents)

d. 2-645(e): Garnishee must file an answer

i. Note, garnishment is essentially a separate lawsuit after the initial judgment is rendered

1. Writ/complaint; service of writ/complaint; answer; then another judgment if trial is needed for garnish.

e. 2-645(j): Judgment against garnishee

f. 2-645(i): Judgment debtor is allowed to contest garnishment if he/she feels as if there are improprieties under 2-643

g. **Wage Garnishment**

i. Service of process is again necessary, just like bank accounts

ii. Same Md. Rules apply, see 2-645

iii. Collection and payment is somewhat different

1. Md. Comm. Law. § 15-603(a):

employer will have to withhold debtor's wages and remit them to the creditor

2. if employer fails to pay, then ER can be liable for full amount of garnishment to the creditor

iv. What about two garnishments at the same time? Pro rata?
    1. § 15-603(b): first, pay the one that was received first, i.e. the one served on employer first; pay the next one once the first one is satisfied

v. Exemptions, see § 15-601.1: exemption from attachment for wages
    1. usually about 75% is exempt, if not more
    2. this is after paying for other deductions withheld by law, such as taxes, Medicare, FICA etc. (and even alimony and child support)

vi. § 15-606: employer cannot fire employee because attachment/garnish.
    1. but if the EE has 2 in the same year, then can be fired

vii. *Webb v. Erickson*
    1. Judgment creditor gets default

judgment against garnishee for full amount owed against judgment debtor

a. Garnishee had ignored garnishment, but now doesn't want to pay after default judgment b/c judgment creditor had started collection proceeding against garnishee
b. special facts here: garnishee has serious medical condition, divorced, lost kids, and he didn't understand the writ/summons plus language of summons didn't make sense

2. Draconian result was averted by Arizona high court

a. Garnishee wants default judgment overturned and this court did so → took a liberal view and looking at all the facts overturned the lower ct b/c concluded that garnishee didn't understand what was required of him (excusable neglect)

b. It was the many factors together that lead to this result

c. Plus, garnishee didn't even know that he owed money to the judgment debtor in the first place

iii. <u>ASIDE: Joint Tenants, Tenants in Common, and Tenants by the Entirety Properties</u>

1. **Tenants in Common Property →** e.g. 50/50 interest between 2 people, divisible
    a. If there is judgment against one of them, then judgment lien is against 50% of the property
    b. If property was transferred after liens attach, the lien goes with the property
2. **Joint Tenants Property →** the tenants own the property jointly together, i.e. each has an undivided interest in the whole
    a. Prof cited case, *Eastern Shore Corp. v. Bank of Somerset*, 253 Md. 525
        i. Basic fact: joint tenants property sold after judgment but before sheriff's levy

ii. HOLDING: Basically judgment creditor must levy for judgment to attach to joint tenants property, but they must do so before a sale for the judgment to attach to joint tenants property
    1. in essence, the levy process severs the unities and then you can become a tenant in common
iii. a sale before levy results in the judgment creditor losing out → i.e. cannot enforce judgment against the property/new buyer

b. note #1: that if there is just a single tenant, then a properly indexed and recorded judgment results in a judgment lien
    i. as long as the date of judgment is before the sale, then the judgment lien attaches, and buyer takes property with the lien
c. note #2: if property is owned as tenants in common, then judgment creditor can attach lien on their debtor's interest as long as sale was not prior to entry of judgment (i.e. buyer takes property subject to a lien covering the judgment debtor's interest)

3. **Tenants by the Entirety** → property held jointly by husband and wife
    a. 5 unities established by common law → time, title interest, possession, and marriage
    b. this is discussed below in the outline in more detail

III. **EXEMPTIONS & JOINT PROPERTY (Tenants by the Entirety, T/E)**

a. **Exemptions**

i. Basically, money property that creditors can't reach because of state laws

- ii. POLICY → debtors need basics to live
    - 1. benevolence and allow debtors to get back on their feet
    - 2. and b/c we don't want them to become a complete burden on society/communities
- iii. These vary widely from state to state and between the federal and state laws
    - 1. in MD, the exemptions arise from the MD Constitution
        - a. protect from execution a reasonable amount of property of the debtor
    - 2. **on the other hand, MD has no homestead exemptions**
        - a. Texas and Florida have huge homestead exemptions
            - i. In FL, no limitation in value if you are below half an acre
    - 3. **Federal bankruptcy code sets uniform federal exemptions, but states can opt-out of these exemptions and thus deny bankruptcy filers federal exemptions (only state ones would then be available) → 35 states opt out, including Maryland, 11-504(g)**
- iv. Exemptions DO NOT apply to corporations, only flesh and blood humans
- v. Maryland Provisions
    - 1. Md. Cts. & Jud. Proc. § 11-507
        - a. exemptions do not apply to consensual, i.e. security, agreements → mortgages and SIs
    - 2. **§ 11-504 provides the MD Exemptions and only these can be used in bankruptcy**
        - a. Value is FMV on date of filing of bankruptcy petition, or on date of execution or some other judicial process
        - b. Unlimited vs. Capped Exemptions
            - i. Capped
                - 1. cash, or cash equivalents, is capped at 6K
                - 2. furniture up to 1K
                - 3. tools of the trade up to 5K
            - ii. Unlimited
                - 1. money payable in event of sickness,

accident, injury, death, etc. gets an unlimited exemption
   a. Note, this one has its limits in bankruptcy → equitable reasons not to exempt some stuff
2. home health aid for debtor and dependents of debtor
3. also see 11-504(h) → unlimited exemption for retirement accounts if set up and maintained in accordance with IRS regulations
   a. Note, there are some complexities, but this is usually true
   b. Mutual fund accounts are not exempt

c. (b)(2) → "death of any person"
   i. Prof calls this a glitch in the statute → very broad
d. Wage attachments are not exempted, 11-504(e)
e. **11-504(f) → gives an extra 5000 for a debtor in bankruptcy**

3. see chart for MD Exemptions Summary

EXEMPTIONS	MD State Law	Bankruptcy 11-504(f)
No Trade or Profession	7K/14K for dual couple	$12K/24K for dual couple
11-504(b)(1) Trade or Profession (very hard to get to get in MD)	12K/24K for 2 debtors	17K/34K for 2 debtors

vi. <u>Partially Exempt Property and Security Interests in Exempt Property</u>

1. If there is a dollar value limit on the exemption, then the property worth more is only partially exempt
    a. usually, property can still be levied on and sold, and the exemption attaches up to the dollar limit and this goes to the debtor
    b. note, if the dollar value of the property does not exceed the exemption limit, the debtor keeps it
2. SIs → exemptions do not apply to these
    a. The secured party moves ahead of the debtor and TIB
        i. Only when the value of the car exceeds the sum of the allowed secured claim and the debtor's exemption would the TIB be able reach any value from the property
    b. HYPO: Car has FMV of 10K
        i. If there is a lien of 11K on it, after default, SC can take the car without exemptions → voluntary lien

b. **Joint Property: Tenancy by the Entirety Property (T/E)**

i. Discussed in the context of 2 cases in Maryland

1. *In re Ford*
    a. Facts: only one debtor, husband, filed for bankruptcy; assets at issue are house, car
    b. Debtor argues that T/E property is exempt under MD nonbankruptcy law while trustee claims that MD common law inapplicable in bankruptcy
    c. <u>Ct holds three things:</u>

i. Filing of bankruptcy case does not sever T/E unities (IRS can do it, special)
ii. T/E property is property of the estate under § 541 of the Code
iii. But, T/E property may be exempted under § 522 by the debtor

d. Note, that with cars and other property, title is not determinative of who owns the property → have to look at joint bank accounts, etc. to see if it's T/E

2. *Sumy v. Schlossberg*
   a. Companion case to *Ford*, and here the individual debtor tries to extend *Ford* and block joint creditors from reaching T/E property
   b. **Ct says no way, sticks to state rule that joint creditors can reach T/E property**
      i. So the trustee can administer joint property for the benefit of joint creditors
      ii. If debtor and non debtor spouse are jointly indebted, then property cannot be exempted under § 522(b)(2)(B)

ii. **RULE: Property held by T/E is completely exempt from creditors who only have a claim against one spouse (i.e. a single creditor).**
   1. one exception: the IRS can pierce it to get to it, highly uncommon
   2. this is true both at state courts and in bankruptcy
   3. this is why lenders/banks make both the husband and wife sign on the mortgage → makes them a joint creditor and then they can go after the house
   4. POLICY → protects the nondebtor spouse from the debtor spouse
   5. ****in Maryland, T/E exemption is huge!!!**

6. Note, if nondebtor spouse dies, then property becomes available to the single creditors subject to the dollar exemptions in MD (but no homestead exemption in MD)

iii. Maryland Joint Property Garnishment Provision
   1. Md. Cts. Jud. & Proc. § 11-603: single creditors cannot go after joint husband and wife bank accounts → **joint bank account of husband and wife is safe from single creditors of 1 spouse**
   2. For joint savings account, banks must comply with c1, c2, and c3
      a. if 2 or more persons on the account, (doesn't matter if it's husband and wife) but less than all are judgment debtors, then "the garnishee shall hold the lesser of the amount of the judgment or the amount in the account" and answer to the garnishing creditor
      b. (c)(3) safe harbor: if bank complies, garnishee may not be held liable to judgment creditor or persons on the account for any claim relating to the garnishment
   3. Trust accounts, § 11-603(b)(1)
      a. Judgment is not valid against accounts held by one person or more persons in trust (for that person or another person(s))unless all of the persons are judgment debtors

IV. FRAUDULENT CONVEYANCES

a. **Basic Idea** → Such claims protect creditors against debtors who would obstruct collection efforts by conveying away all their property, usually with an intent to have it re-conveyed back to themselves at a future date
   i. In bankruptcy, § 548 allows the trustee to avoid fraudulent conveyances → only goes back 2 years
      1. Congress made an exception for conveyances to Churches, see § 548(a)(2), but it is subject to percentage limits of gross income and based on past patters of charitable contributions
   ii. § 544 of the Code allows the trustee to use relevant state fraudulent conveyance provisions to avoid transfers going back further

1. NOTE, state law is still all over the place on this issue

b. **Overview of the Law**
   i. When you owe two debts outside of bankruptcy, you can choose who to pay if not done with intent to defraud the actual conveyance is in the open (i.e. not in secret)
   ii. But when you owe one debt and then give someone else a gift then you might be in trouble if the comes after you with an actions
   iii. *Twyne's Case* → common law case from 1601 in England
      1. Facts: Pierce owed money to C and Twyne, 200 to C, 400 to Twyne; Pierce pays Twyne's debt in entirety by gifting him a bunch of goods; C sues Pierce on the other debt and there is an execution on property that is now in Twyne's possession; there is a dispute over the property...
      2. Ct agrees with C because ct finds conveyance to Twyne to be a fraudulent conveyance that can be undone; a number of factors here:
         a. Ct found actual fraudulent intent towards C and undoes the transaction
         b. Pierce kept the property even after supposedly "conveying" it to Twyne
         c. The gift was made in secret
         d. The gift was made pending the writ
         e. Trust used as cover
   iv. In *Twyne*, the ct found actual fraudulent intent; in modern day fraudulent conveyance law, actual intent is not necessary
      1. i.e. fraud doesn't matter and intent does not matter
      2. **constructive fraud** can be enough (term is misnomer b/c you don't really need fraud)
      3. New rule permitted a creditor to avoid (to set aside) a transfer even though the debtor was entirely innocent of any fraudulent intent
         a. Courts define circumstances in which the transfer is regarded as unfairly disadvantageous to the debtor's creditors, regardless of intent
         b. Casebook refers to new Uniform Fraudulent Transfer Act (UFTA) from 1984

- i. Allows creditor to avoid any transfer made in exchange for an unfairly low consideration or at a time when the debtor was insolvent
- ii. No fraudulent intent necessary

- c. Creditor could proceed under this or in the alternative show actual intent to defraud

- v. *ACLI Gov't Sec. v. Rhoades* → Modern case decided under an older version of the UFTA
  1. **1.** Facts: Brother had a huge judgment rendered against him; right after judgment he transfers his 3/5 interest in a home valued at 325K to his sister (~195K to sister)
  2. **2.** Creditor/AGS makes three specific allegations:
     - **a.** w/out fair consideration (note, no MD parallel to this)
     - **b.** w/out fair consideration rendered debtor insolvent
     - **c.** actual intent to defraud AGS
  3. **3.** AGS sues to have conveyance undone
     - **a.** D/sister allege that the conveyance was for an antecedent debt
     - **b.** Ct says NO, b/c their accounts were commingled and they never balanced them → could not separate their assets and liabilities
     - **c.** Ct also looks to "badges of fraud," i.e. secrecy
     - **d.** Ct also finds constructive fraud
       - **i.** Property in Carolina is important b/c it affects whether he is insolvent or not → ct finds it wasn't worth as much as he thought

c. **Maryland Provisions:**

- **i.** Maryland family law provisions
  - **1.** § 4-206: gives some rights to women
  - **2.** § 4-301: Protection from liability for spouse's obligations → important for fraudulent conveyances

a. (a) → individual is not liable for debts of spouse from before the marriage
b. (d)(2)(i) → **transfer of property between spouses is invalid if made in prejudice of the rights of present creditors**
    i. (d)(2)(ii) → such a claim must be assert within 3 years after transfer or be barred absolutely; thus such a transfer is *voidable*, not void
    ii. (d)(2)(iii) → all claims are considered due and mature for this section
    iii. thus, such a transfer is voidable if the creditor can get to no other assets

ii. <u>Maryland Fraudulent Conveyance Statute</u>
1. Md. Commercial Law § 15-207 → actual intent provision
    a. **Every conveyance with actual intent to defraud present and future creditors is fraudulent as to both present and future creditors**
    b. § 15-203(1) → Fair consideration defined as property given as fair equivalent and in good faith (i.e. paying correct value for it); can be satisfaction of antecedent debt
        i. § 15-203(2) prevents unfair secret liens
2. § 15-204 → conveyances by insolvent
    a. **every conveyance by <u>insolvent</u> (or will be rendered insolvent by conveyance) is fraudulent as to creditors (i.e. present creditors w/ matured claims), w/out regard to actual intent, if made w/out <u>fair consideration</u>**
        i. **NOTE, this only applies to PRESENT CREDITORS WITH MATURED CLAIMS!!!!**
    b. § 15-202(a) → defines insolvency as assets < liabilities

    c. § 15201(b)(1) → Assets means property of a debtor not exempt from liability for his debts

3. § 15-205 → conveyances by persons in business (i.e. conveyer is in business or ABOUT TO ENGAGE in business)
    a. **conveyance w/out fair consideration that results in only unreasonably small capital remaining with debtor is fraudulent as to creditors and *other persons who become creditors* (meaning unmatured claims, see § 15-210) w/out regard to actual intent**
4. § 15-206 → person about to incur debt
    a. fraud conveyance, w/out fair consideration, when conveyer believes she will incur debts beyond her ability to pay as they mature is fraudulent to both present and future creditors
5. § 15-209 → creditors with matured claims
    a. (a) gives exception for any purchaser for <u>fair consideration</u> without knowledge of the fraud at the time of the purchase
    b. (b) → creditor does not need a judgment
    c. (c) → if no fraudulent intent on part of purchaser, but less than fair consideration given, then purchaser can retain property as security for repayment
6. § 15-210 → unmatured claims
    a. where debt has not yet become due (i.e. payment date has not yet come), then the court can do a number of things – restrain debtor, appoint receiver, set it aside, and catch-all provision ("enter any order which the circumstances of the case require")
7. § 15-210.1 → Exempts certain conveyances (new provision)
    a. i.e. foreclosure sales, statutory lien sale, judicial sale, sale after levy

d. **Leveraged Buyouts**
   i. <u>Basic Idea</u> → Basically where you use other people's money to buy another corporation, but the bank loaning the money will want a security interest in the acquired corp's assets to secure future repayment (i.e. **assets of the corporation being acquired are used to secure the purchase price paid for those assets**)
      1. Fraudulent conveyance issues come in because creditors of acquired corp say that the bank jumps ahead of this creditor as a secured creditor so the original creditor is subordinate → **creditor tries to avoid that transfer of assets to a bank as a fraudulent conveyance b/c acquired corp is not getting back anything**
         a. In essence, the bank is getting the SI for less than reas equiv value and subject to a fraudulent conveyance
      2. lots of case law and discussion of underlying public policies of allowing such conveyances to be undone as a fraudulent conveyance

e. **ASIDE: State Alternatives to Bankruptcy**
   i. <u>UCC Art. 6 Bulk Sale for Business Organizations</u>
      1. Procedure for debtors to sell substantially all of their assets to one buyer at one time → notice procedure, required to tell creditors that they are going out of business and creditors can submit claims for payment of the debts
      2. Advantage: faster and less expensive than bankruptcy
      3. Disadvantage: no mechanism from stopping creditors' action against the debtor, i.e. no automatic stay
   ii. <u>Assignment for the Benefit of Creditors</u>
      1. Advantage: again, lesser time and lesser cost for creditors
      2. Some Big Disadvantages: if creditors not paid in full, can still sue debtor for balance of claims
         a. In addition, if a bankruptcy is filed after an assignment for the benefit of creditors and a distribution to the creditors has taken place, that distribution may be avoided by a trustee in bankruptcy as a **Preference.**
         b. An assignment for the benefit of creditors constitutes grounds for

entering an order for relief in an involuntary bankruptcy case.

- iii. State Receivership
    1. Non bankruptcy trustee person that the court appoints as guardian over the debtor's assets
    2. Advantage: can be used against certain organizations that cannot be forced into an involuntary bankruptcy case – churches, family farmers, nonprofit organizations, etc.
    3. Disadvantage: receiver doesn't have authority and control like bankruptcy trustee
        - a. Plus, receivership does not prevent debtor from filing bankruptcy
- iv. Composition Agreement
    1. Between the debtors and 2 OR MORE CREDITORS
    2. Advantage: may be cheaper and faster, depends on number of creditors involved
    3. Disadvantage: no way to force creditor to agree to enter into a composition agreement
        - a. If only one creditor doesn't want to play nice, it may crater the whole deal
    4. Done usually by bankruptcy lawyers

V. BANKRUPTCY OVERVIEW AND GENERALLY APPLICABLE PROVISIONS

- a. Bankruptcy should generally be the last choice for most clients
- b. **Historical and Statutory Review**
    - i. Bankruptcy authority arises from Art. I, § 8, cl. 4 → congress can make uniform bankruptcy law
    - ii. Bankruptcy Act of 1898 → just called "the Act"
        1. only a few cases still remaining under this today
    - iii. Modern day US Bankruptcy law comes from the 1978 Code
        1. there have been amendments made since 1978
        2. **2005 Amendments are very important for our discussion esp. for consumer bankruptcies → from the The Bankruptcy Abuse Prevention and Consumer Protection Act (BAPCPA)
            - a. many viewed these provisions as anti-judge, anti-debtor, and anti-attorney by increasing monitoring of judge/attorney work and making it harder to get a discharge
        3. Bankruptcy judges are Art. I judges appointed for 14 year terms

4. Jurisdiction, Venue, and Appeals are discussed in the last part of the outline
    a. Cases are termed "In re [name]" and adversary proceedings within the overarching cases are like a typical federal lawsuit, i.e. A v. B
5. Bankruptcy Rules and Procedure promulgated by the Supreme Court
    a. Incorporates Fed Rules of Civil Proc and Evidence
    b. LOCAL RULES in each jurisdiction that implement local rules
        i. Interim rules supplement local rules
        ii. Administrative Orders → describe local practices in each jurisdiction
        iii. In time, Interim Rules and Admin Orders are incorporated into the local rules

c. **Policy and Goals**
    i. Debtor Relief through the automatic stay (362), exemptions (522, Md comm law 11-504), discharge and confirmation plans (727, 1328, 1141)
    ii. Creditor Protection:
        1. similarly situation creditors are treated the same
        2. protect the substance of any bargain struck by a secured creditor
        3. protect creditors by accounting for all of the debtor's non-exempt assets through the schedules the debtor files and trustee oversight

d. **Structure of the Code**
    i. NOTE: Key distinction in the Code and Chapter Provisions → Chs. 1, 3, & 5 apply to all bankruptcy chapters unless otherwise noted specifically in one of the other chapters; on the other hand, Ch. 7 and subsequent chapter provisions are only applicable to those specific chapters
    ii. Ch. 1 → general definitions, rules of construction, etc.
        1. § 101 – definitions
        2. § 104 – dollar amounts adjusted by the CPI
    iii. Ch. 3 → case commencement, general professionals/officers, general administration, general trustee provisions
    iv. Ch. 5 → Debtor's duties and benefits, The Estate, and Creditors and Claims

- **v.** Ch. 7 → Liquidation Proceedings
  - **1.** for individuals and corporations
- **vi.** Ch. 9 → Municipalities [unrelated to this course]
- **vii.** Ch. 11 → Reorganization
  - **1.** for individuals and corporations
  - **2.** this chapter allows a corporation to file and later liquidate through this and not Ch. 7
- **viii.** Ch. 12 → Family Farmer and Fisherman Adjustments [we don't cover this]
- **ix.** Ch. 13 → Streamlined Individual Reorganization Proceeding
  - **1.** 3-5 year plan generally
- **x.** Ch. 15 → Ancillary and Other Cross-Border Cases [new chapter, very specialized, we don't cover]

e. Another key distinction in the Code: Consumer vs. Business bankruptcies

f. In general, the pre-bankruptcy period is crucial

- **i.** i.e. prior to petition or filing date → this petition date is of special significance in the Code
- **ii.** 90 days or 1 year prior to filing date
- **iii.** See §§ 547 (preferences), 548 (fraudulent conveyances) → under these sections the trustee can put creditors in the same position as other creditors [e.g. can undo perfection of an SI]

g. Getting Started

- **i.** Debtor files a petition in bankruptcy court to commence a case
  - **1.** once the clerk gets the fee and date stamps the petition, then an estate is automatically created and an automatic stay on all collection activities against debtor and debtor' property
- **ii.** Must file specific schedules along with petition
  - **1.** listing of all assets and liabilities (Sched A – Real Property, Sched B – Personal Property)
  - **2.** Exemptions listed in Sched C
  - **3.** List of all Sec Creditors in D
  - **4.** Unsecured priority claims in E
  - **5.** General Unsecured Debt in F (medical expenses, credit card debt, etc.)
  - **6.** Executory Ks and Unexpired Leases in G
  - **7.** Co-debtors in H
  - **8.** Current Income in I
  - **9.** Statement of Financial Affairs lists other pertinent information about the debtor
- **iii. What do attorneys need to ask clients before filing?**

1. Income (means test, etc.), assets, liabilities, expenses
    a. Income → Tax returns, payment stubs
    b. Assets → Titles, deeds of trust, autos, etc.
2. Divorce decrees
3. Maryland property settlements
4. Previous bankruptcy filing history
5. Plus other prior/ongoing litigation that may impact bankruptcy cases
6. Creditor collection activities from past
7. Residence history for venue purposes
    a. Plus for Exemptions etc.

iv. **Eligibility to File Bankruptcy, § 109**
1. (a) → ". . . only a person that resides or has domicile, a place of business, or property in the United States, or a municipality, may be a debtor under this title."
2. The subsequent provisions give limitations for filing under each chapter
    a. (e) → **debt limits for Ch. 13 filers, 300K for unsecured, 900K for secured
3. (h) → individual debtors need to go get credit counseling first before filing

v. **§ 101 contains definitions applicable throughout Title 11**
1. (41) person → includes an individual, partnership, and corporation

h. **Property of the Estate, § 541**

i. Trustee basically stands in the shoes of the debtor on date of bankruptcy
1. you can't expand the debtor's rights against others more than they exist on petition date
2. trustee can take no greater rights than the debtor had on petition date

ii. § 541(a): "estate is comprised of all the following property, wherever located and by whomever held," key ones the prof pointed out:
1. (a)(1) → "all legal or equitable interests of the debtor in property as of he commencement of the case"
    a. this includes T/E property, but you can exempt it under exemptions, see below
    b. **be careful with property belonging to debtor's business → if it is titled in**

the business's name, then not property of the estate in debtor's bankruptcy

i. obviously would be property of estate in the business's bankruptcy

2. (a)(5) → allows for postpetition date property that the debtor acquires to be part of the estate
    a. this clawback provision runs **180 days after petition date**
    b. includes a divorce settlement postpetition if it is within 180 days
    c. NOTE, that if spouse dies within 180 days of petition then all T/E property becomes severed and property of the estate (but it still could be exempt under MD exemptions, but there is no homestead exemption in MD)
3. (a)(6) → estate includes proceeds, products, offspring, rents, profits from property
    a. **no 180 day limit here**
    b. **Exception → wages/money earned by debtor after filing is not property (for services performed after filing)**, but prepetition wages are part of the estate (i.e. already earned and in the bank)
        i. *Sharp v. Dery* – bonus plan wages prepetition were at issue, but bonus was not paid until after petition date
            1. Ct held that because the employer still had discretion to approve or deny bonus then the debtor did not enforceable right to receive bonus on petition date, thus it is not part of estate
                a. To get this bonus, debtor

needed to be continued to be employed by employer postpetition

ii. NOTE: pay date is not controlling; the key inquiry is whether the debtor had an enforceable right to those wages/bonuses on petition date

iii. § 541(b): exclusions from property of the estate
1. (b)(1) → exempts debtor in possession/trustee from exerting control of property for another entity, i.e. the business; or for power of attorney; or mort companies holding property solely for others [see also §541(d)]
2. (b)(2) → interest of debtor in a nonresidential lease that is terminated prior to commencement of the case (i.e. commercial leases) are not property of estate

iv. § 541(c): special circumstances
1. (c)(1) → invalidates ipso facto clauses in contracts
   a. if you say in a K that "if you file bankruptcy, this property is not property of the estate," then this provision is invalid under bankruptcy law
   b. also preempts state law that restricts debtor's property
2. (c)(2) → basically makes spendthrift trusts exempt from property of the estate, i.e. one that is enforceable under applicable nonbankruptcy law
   a. in essence, helps debtor keep retirement accounts out of bankruptcy estates
   b. *In re Orkin*
      i. P could tried to exempt property as ERISA-qualified and as a spendthrift trust under Massachusetts law

            1. Ct failed to find ERISA qualification here
        ii. Spendthrift trust is basically money put away so someone doesn't spend it
            1. you can get income from it, but not all of it and you can't transfer it to someone else (i.e. anti-alienation provision)
                a. here ct found the plan to lack a real restriction on transfer of a beneficial interest so it was not enforceable under Mass spendthrift law
        iii. 541c2 protects such trusts → policy decision Congress made and creditors should never have relied on this to pay their claims anyways
        iv. key is whether the account is a spendthrift trust under state law
    c. Sup Ct has held that ERISA-qualified IRA and accounts are not part of estate
    d. NOTE: that even if some of these are part of estate, there still may be an exemption for them under state law or § 522

v. **Alimony, Child Support, and Maintenance Coming in to Debtor Postpetition**
    1. Child Support is excluded from the estate
        a. under either 541(b)(1) or 541(d)
    2. Alimony → cases have held that this is generally not property of the estate

vi. Pending lawsuits are still property of the estate under 541(a)(1), but there may be an exemption under 522 or state exemptions
   1. cause of action, even without money judg, is still property of estate
   2. if cause of action accrues after petition date, then it will be apportioned

vii. **NOTE: there is a big difference between what is and is not property of the estate and what is exempt**
   1. threshold question → is this part of the estate at all? Must look at § 541, and if it is not, then no need to exempt it
   2. on the other hand, something could be part of the estate, but exempt under the exemption provisions

viii. Three main issues arise with case law on 541 that above cases somewhat illustrate
   1. Like in *Sharp* above, some involve a situation where there is a legal interest that is not enforceable on date of bankruptcy but may be enforceable in the future
   2. Second, there are cases about entitlements, like nontransferable licenses and permits, like for taxicabs, being in the estate (is it property or a privilege?)
      a. Generally, liquor licenses are held to be property of the estate even though they are not transferable by law (see 541(c)(1)(A)), and they can be sold or assigned by trustees subject to some limitations
         i. Adds value to a business
         ii. *In re Burgess* → ct held that brothel license was property of the estate, i.e. again added value to the business
            1. adds enormous value to the estate; without the license to operate as a brothel, there would essentially be no business left to reorganize

2. results-driven approach and creditors would be harmed with the opposite conclusion

iii. Driver's lic is not property of the estate, just a privilege

b. The case law tends to all over the place on this and in conflict

i. E.g. season ticket holders → not transferable so not property of the estate by some courts, but others say these restrictions are unenforceable in bankruptcy

c. **ANALYSIS should focus on whether the trustee can get the license in the first place if the trustee holds all the attributes of the business?**

i. Differences if debtor is reorganizing or liquidating

ii. Public policy behind transfers that take place

iii.

3. third, cases discuss issues involving restrictions on transferability imposed by K or law → 541(c)(1) makes most of these unenforceable; but see *Orkin* above

i. **The Automatic Stay, § 362**

i. POLICY – Helps give the debtor some breathing room while he/she gets its affairs in order

ii. The stay stops ALL collection activities against debtor, debtor's property and property of the estate and it automatically comes into effect the minute the petition is filed by the clerk

iii. Structure and Key Provisions of § 362:

1. (a) → tells us what is stopped

a. **subsections 1, 2, 6, 7, & 8 applies to debtors**

i. 1 – any action against the debtor is stayed

ii. 2 – any enforcement against the debtor is stayed

- iii. 6 – stays collection activities against debtor
- iv. 7 – stays any setoff of any debt owing to the debtor that arose before the petition date against any claim against the debtor
- v. 8 – stays United States Tax Court proceedings against debtor

b. **subsections 2, 3, & 4 applies to property of the estate**
- i. 2 – any enforcement against the property of the estate is stayed
- ii. 3 – any act to obtain possession of the property of/from the estate or to exercise control over such property is stayed
- iii. 4 – stops lien perfection of property of the estate [subject to some limitations → PMSIs]

c. **subsection 5 applies to property of the debtor**
- i. 5 – stops lien perfection of property of the debtor

2. (b) → tells us what is not stayed, subsections:
   - a. 1 – no stay of criminal proceedings against debtor
   - b. 2 – no stay of domestic disputes or DSO
   - c. 3 – trustee can still perfect stuff
   - d. 4 – gov'tal organizations and agencies can still continue with civil proceedings
   - e. 9 – tax audits by the gov't can continue (i.e. IRS audits)
   - f. 18 – ad valorem property taxes and other special assessments on real property are not stayed
     - i. if you don't pay real estate taxes in MD, then they get a first lien on your house which takes priority over

everything else; this is why your mortgage company withholds and escrows your real estate taxes

ii.

3. (c) → tells us when stay ceases to exist [AUTOMATIC, no motion needed]
   a. different for property of the estate vs. the debtor
   b. 1 – stay against property of estate continues until such property is no longer part of the estate
   c. 2 – stay of any other act continues until case is closed, dismissed, or discharge
   d. some interesting **new provisions here with the 2005 amendments:**
      i. 3A – stay comes into effect but only for 30 days if you had 1 or more bankruptcy cases dismissed in the last year
         1. but this only applies to **"debt or property securing such debt or with respect to any lease"** → this is very narrow, only deals with secured creditors and landlords
         2. so the stay is in effect as against the debtor him/herself
      ii. 3C – gives a list that makes a case "presumptively filed not in good faith" → this "presumption may be rebutted by clear and convincing evidence to the contrary"
         1. you can rebut it by showing that you

now have a job and can reorganize, whereas before you couldn't

iii. 4 – stay doesn't go into effect at all if you had 2 or more cases dismissed in the previous year
   1. you need to go to court to get the stay in effect
   2. some surplusage language here - Congress messed up in new amendments

4. (d) → tells us how we can get relief from the stay [NEED MOTION, not automatic]
   a. creditor or a party in interest can motion the court to grant relief from stay
      i. ct can modify, terminate, annul, or condition such stay
   b. 1 – for cause, including **lack of adequate protection**
      i. this is basically for secured creditors → property dissipated underneath the amount of security that the SC has
         1. for when the debtor is essentially not paying mortgage or car payments
         2. HYPO: car FMV of 5K, debt is 10K → SC lacks adequate protection and has a right to 5K secured
            a. SC can file a motion for relief from the stay due to

lack of adequate protection for their 10K debt

b. Usually debtor will pay SC X amount per month to keep it adequate protected

c. 2 – if there is **no equity in the property and the "property is not necessary to an effective reorganization,"** then ct can lift stay as to that property

   i. if in Ch. 7, you don't have to worry about reorganization part

   ii. if in Ch. 11, if no equity in property like in HYPO and it is not needed for an effective reorganization, then creditor can win on such a motion

d. 3 – purpose is to get single asset real estate cases moving quickly

e. 4 – new provision → with respect to real property, stay is lifted for SC if the debtor filed bankruptcy petition in a scheme to "delay, hinder, and defraud creditors" that involved a transfer of all or part ownership in such real property (or with multiple bankruptcy filings

5. (e) → miscellaneous, deals with timing of hearings, subsections:

   a. 1 – within 30 days, need a preliminary determination on relief from the stay

   b. 2 – new anti-judge provision in 2005 amendments

      i. makes such a motion get to court faster → stay will terminate in 60 days after a request under section (d) unless ct makes a final decision before that time period ends or such period is extended by agreement of parties or by the ct for "good cause"

c. TERM OF ART here – **"after notice and a hearing," defined in § 102**
   i. Fallacy is that you think there must be a hearing, but this is not a requirement
   ii. 102 defines it as after such notice under particular circumstances and such hearing under particular circumstances, but authorizes such action without hearing if notice is given, and if hearing is not requested by party or court determines there is insufficient time for hearing

6. (f) → allows ct to "grant such relief from the stay . . . as is necessary to prevent irreparable damage to the interest of an entity in property, if such interest will suffer such damage before there is an opportunity for notice and a hearing . . ."
7. (g) → burden of proof is on party requesting relief on the issue of debtor's equity in the property
   a. but the party opposing such relief has the burden of proof on all other issues
8. (h) → new complex provision, only applies to individual debtors
   a. connects to § 521(a)(2) which is the provision dealing with statement of intention with request to property
      i. deals with personal property, secured in whole or in part
      ii. stay will be lifted if debtor does not file statement within a certain time or if the debtor fails to take timely action specified in the statement
   b. Prof says this provides conundrum for the trustees, HYPO: debtor has diamond ring and jewelry store has sec int in the ring

i. If debtor fails to do a statement of intention about it to surrender, retain, or redeem, then this ring may be lost to the estate if stay is lifted
ii. If diamond ring has FMV 10K, and debt is down to 2K, if stay terminates within 30 days, then trustee worries about it slipping out of the estate in 30 days without statement of intentions (so trustee must make quick decisions about such personal property)

9. (k) → broad damage relief if stay is violated, including attorneys' fees and costs and even punitive damages
10. (n) → special provision for small businesses
    a. automatic relief from stay
    b. § 101 defines small business → basically total debts of less than 2 million dollars

iv. Stay is very broad
1. *Andrews* → university can't even refuse to give a debtor-student his/her transcript
    a. Withholding transcript until student pays debt may be seen as a violation of 362(a)(6) → i.e. collect, assess, or recover prepetition debt
2. *Nissan Motor* → creditor can't act alone, must go through the court to lift the stay
    a. Sec cred violated the stay basically inadvertently and debtor gave notice of the bankruptcy case, but SC still kept the car
    b. SC made motion for relief from the stay but while it is pending, the SC sold the car
        i. Ct holds that they violated the stay and is furious with the SC
        ii. Nissan was on tenuous ground holding the car while bankruptcy case was going on

- iii. **Under § 542(a), certain property has to be turned over to the estate**
  1. **even if repossession happens before bankruptcy filing, if the property is property of the estate, then obligation is on creditor to give it back to debtor/to the estate**
     a. technically, some wiggle room here for creditor to motion ct, but it's very tricky

v. <u>§ 366 → Utility Service</u>
   1. special section for this basic it involves basic human needs
   2. (a) → "utility may not alter, refuse, or discontinue service to, or discriminate against, the trustee or debtor solely" on the basis of the bankruptcy case or overdue debt
   3. (b) → allows discontinuation of utilities if no adequate assurance of payment is made within 20 days of petition date
      a. in essence, debtor and trustee need to cough up a security deposit
      b. most cts find that a 3 month deposit is adequate
   4. this section also applies to business/corporate debtors and it can be a big deal, millions of dollars in utility bills
   5. this issue comes up very quickly after filing
   6. 'utility' is broad → electricity, telephone, water, internet, etc.

vi. NOTE: credit card companies and other financing companies are allowed to cut off access to future business by not extending anymore credit and this DOES NOT VIOLATE THE STAY

- vii. <u>More on the stay in context of new provisions/amendments from 2005:</u>
    1. **Where to send the notice of bankruptcy for creditors?**
        - a. Congress amended § 342 to deal with large conglomerate corporations and credit card companies → made it easier for creditors to have one place where debtors have to file notice
            - i. 342(f)(1) allows for creditors file such a notice of address with the bankruptcy court so all notices of bankruptcy must be sent to this address
        - b. 342(g) allows for creditor to designate a person or organizational subdivision to receive the notices
            - i. notice must be brought to the attention of the creditor in accordance with this
        - c. there is a whole body of case law from before these amendments dealing with ACTUAL NOTICE under 342 → not sure what will happen will all this now

j. **Exemptions under the Bankruptcy Code § 522**

- i. Note: Valid, unavoidable consensual security interest trump exemption claims, so that a debtor may claim only an exemption in the "equity," the value remaining after secured creditor is paid in full
- ii. <u>§ 522(b)(1):</u> allows for the taking of exemptions under (b)(2) or (3); if husband and wife fight over fed or state exemptions, then they get state exemptions
    1. (b)(2) → directs non opt-out state debtors to use the exemptions in subsection (d) and allows opt-out for states as discussed above [35 states do it, including MD, while other states leave the choice to debtors to choose b/t fed and state law]
    2. (b)(3)(A) → brings in other Federal and state law that is applicable
        - a. **this brings in Md. Cts. & Jud. Proc. § 11-504 exemptions*****
        - b. Domicile Requirement
            - i. Wherever the debtor lived for the 730 day preceding petition date

- **ii.** If not in a single state in this 730 day period, then look at the 180 day period before this 730 day period
  - **1.** if in one location during that 180 day period, that's it
  - **2.** if again split in the 180 day period, then wherever the debt was the longest in that period (i.e. a plurality)
    - a. if this is split exactly evenly leaving debtor ineligible for any exemption, then you basically get the federal exemptions in subsection (d) → see last hanging sentence in (b)(3)
      - i. so even though MD is opt-out, you could still get fed exemptions if you have been moving around and this domiciliary provision kicks in
- **iii.** leads to interesting exemption planning

3. (b)(3)(B) → federal acknowledgement of exempt T/E and joint tenant property under applicable nonbankruptcy law

- **a.** NOTE: joint tenants is not an issue in MD

4. (b)(3)(C) → new provision that also exempts retirement accounts at federal level; this is already exempt in MD through state exemptions

iii. § 522(d) → lists the federal exemptions and amounts

iv. § 522(e) → a contractual waiver of exemption is unenforceable with unsecured creditors and claims

v. **§ 522(f) → Lien Avoidance to the Extent they Impair Exemptions**

1. (1) → "the debtor may avoid the fixing of a lien on an interest of the debtor in property to the extent that such lien impairs an exemption to which the debtor would have been entitled ... if such lien is –
    a. <u>(A) a **judicial lien, other than one that secures a DSO debt (i.e. alimony, child support, etc.)**</u>
        i. i.e. protects debtor from all those state law judgments
    b. <u>(B) **nonpossessory, nonpurchase-money security interest** in</u>
        i. household goods, appliances, apparel, books, jewelry primarily for the personal, family, or household use of the debtor or a dependent; professional books and other tools of the trade; health aids, etc.
        ii. PMSI → if the lender/store gives the product and the money
        iii. We allow these to be avoided because these creditors have way too much leverage with an SI in these items, doesn't allow debtor to exempt anything
2. (2) → **Formula to determine whether an lien impairs an exemption**
    a. (Avoidable Lien + All other liens on the property + Exemptions) = SUBTOTAL – Value of the Property => Amount of the avoidable lien avoided
    b. <u>HYPO:</u> Property, FMV of 105K, Avoidable Lien of 16K, First mortgage of 94K, Exemption of 5K
        i. Subtotal of 115K – 105K => 10K is the amount of avoidable lien avoided

   ii. 6K of the lien remains, along with 94K and 5K exemption = 105K

c. HYPO 2: Husband and wife own single asset, a boat, as T/E and have a judgment creditor
   i. If judgment is against both husband and wife, then what?
      1. boat may or may not be personal property; if it is, this cred must have to execute and levy on the problem
   ii. assuming it gets that far, then 10K avoidable lien, 45K mortgage/lien, exemptions 24K (12K for each spouse) = 79K – 70K (value of property), leaves 9K, so 9K of lien is amount of avoidable lien avoided in bankruptcy
      1. 1K remains of the lien, even in bankruptcy; 9K unsecured in bankruptcy

d. HYPO 3: Another tricky problem, when avoidable lien is first lien, not 2nd lien
   i. Avoidable lien of 10K (judicial lien), 2nd mortgage of 60K, exemption of 24K = subtotal of 94K – 60K (value of property) = 34K, but this is greater than 10K → Answer is that the whole lien goes!!! (10K becomes unsecured)
      1. there is no equity in this property → 60K second mortgage and 60K value of the property
      2. the trustee and debtor are knocking out the lien in hopes of gaining some

equity in the property later one

3. unless trustee can avoid the 2nd mortgage, debtor will get property after bankruptcy subject to the 60K mortgage

e. **NOTE: remainder of liens avoided become unsecured claims in bankruptcy!!**

3. (4) → defines "household goods"
4. Debtor cannot avoid tax liens with this section

vi. § 522(m) → subject to paragraph (b), each debtor in a joint case gets separate exemptions

vii. new provisions from 2005 amendments to deal with Enron and corporate executives

1. § 522(o) → adds a 10 year lookback provision if debtor converts certain nonexempt property into exempt property with intent to hinder, delay, or defraud a creditor, then exemption is decreased by some dollar amount and the property is no longer exempt
2. § 522(p) → if property acquired within 1215 days (~3.32 yrs) preceding petition date is worth over 125K, then exemption is not allowed over this 125K amount
    a. no intent requirement here
    b. limitations to this section → does not apply to family farmers nor does it apply to value transferred from old house (acquired before 1215 day period) to new one if the residences are located in the same state
3. § 522(q) → deals with federal securities violators and other felons that are disallowed from exempting some property

viii. **Bankruptcy Rule 4003 implements § 522 on EXEMPTIONS**

1. list exemptions on the schedule of assets debtor files
2. allows dependent to file the exemption in the debtor's stead
3. MALPRACTICE DEADLINE → if creditor (and its lawyer) wants to object to an exemption, the party must do so within 30 days after § 341 meeting of the creditors or within 30 days after

whenever list or schedules are amended, whichever is later

a. Debtor gets whatever they list on the schedule, unless objected to by another party

ix. Exemption Planning case law → courts are all over the place on this

1. *In re Reed*: dealt with homestead exemption; 5th cir held that debtor who converts nonexempt assets to exempt homestead immediately before bankruptcy, with intent to defraud his creditors, must be denied discharge in bankruptcy (ct focused on the facts here)
   a. **intent to delay, hinder, or defraud creditors is key → if present, then you can be denied discharge and open yourself up to civil fraud/criminal charges (see below)
   b. can lose discharge completely under § 727, or with individual debts under § 523
2. Trio of conflicting 8th circuit cases that are all over the place with other exemptions:
   a. Basically, case law is all over the place on this, depends on how the judges view the debtors
      i. Farmers may get more lenient treatment as opposed to rich doctors
   b. Prof says, "pigs get fed, hogs get slaughtered," so don't ask for too much
   c. Prof says there is usually nothing wrong with telling client hide assets, even offshore, in state law judgment cases
      i. But transfers can lead to big problems
      ii. And in bankruptcy, be careful and disclose everything you have and did
   d. Some debtors and lawyers have been utilizing asset protection trusts of late
3. *In re Coplan*: debtors had just recently moved to Florida from Wisconsin and bankruptcy ct limited

the normally unlimited FL homestead exemption as applied to them

a. Ct considered all the circumstances, didn't like it, and limited them to Wisconsin exemption limit of 40K → testimony of debtors for reasons for move were not credible plus timing was so close, moved 1 yr before filing bankruptcy

b. **Congress fixed this problem, see § 522(b)(3)(A) domicile provision above**

k. **Claims Process and Procedures**

i. § 501 → basically allows filing of claims by creditors through a simple form

ii. Rule 3002 → time for filing proof of claim is no later than 90 days after the first date set for meeting of the creditors (does not matter if meeting actually happens or not), subject to certain exceptions

1. Rule 3001 → gives form and content for a claim

iii. **§ 502(a) → a claim is deemed allowed unless a party in interest objects (i.e. prepetition claims)**

1. *In re Lanza* → abysmal bookkeeping by the bank can lead to a reduction of it's claim

a. Claim can be challenged by the trustee

2. in today's age, banks sell off mortgages and investment companies further package them away → this can lead to a problem in finding a paper trail of the debt in bankruptcy

iv. **§ 502(b) → gives a list of when ct can reduce and deny claims (i.e. prepetition claims)**

1. (b)(2) one is if the claim is for unmatured interest

a. **no postpetition interest for unsecured claims**

i. policy is that you want to put all GUSC on an even plane to pay pro rata

2. (b)(6) another is for lease termination → lessor can get some damages, but not excessive one or ones going on for many years [see handout/wksheet for example]

3. (b)(5) deals with future domestic support claims, i.e. unmatured on date of filing

4. NOTE: debtor's postpetition bills will not share in distribution b/c these are not claims against the estate

v. § 502(c) → for unliquidated or contingent claims, ct can do an estimation to see how much they get

vi. § 503 → Postpetition Claims for Administrative Expenses
    1. these are made priority claims by § 507(a)(1) and (2) so they come before GUSC

vii. usually, no **postpetition attorneys' fees** awarded to unsecured creditors
    1. for oversecured sec creditors, attorneys' fees get in under 506(b)
    2. for undersecured sec creditors, no more attorneys' fees after bankruptcy filed
    3. if the attorneys' fees are from before bankruptcy, then it's prepetition and gets in for both unsecured and sec creditors

viii. but unsecured claims will be completely accelerated so debtor's debts can all be taken care of in one forum → i.e. need to mature all pre-bankruptcy claims

ix. **§ 506 → determination of secured status, SECURED CLAIMS**
    1. (a) defines secured claims as a claim that is secured up to the value of the property
        a. any excess is unsecured → BIFURCATION PROCESS
        b. NOTE: bifurcation only occurs if the property is ever sold, sec creditor does not bifurcate on their own when filing the claim
            i. **Also, undersecured property is usually not sold in bankruptcy, trustee can abandon the property b/c it has no value for GUSC, and sec cred will sit on their rights and wait until bankruptcy is over**
                1. **ONE EXCEPTION**: it can benefit the unsec creditors indirectly because if this secured creditor has liens on other pieces of property of the estate

and they sell this one and pay this down in hopes of creating equity in something else in the estate for the benefit of the unsecured creditors

2. (b) if a secured claim is oversecured, then SC can continue to get reasonable interest and fees in bankruptcy (including attorneys' fees)
    a. unlike 502(b), for fully secured creditors, unmatured interest is not capped
    b. reasonable → can only go up to the FMV of the property, then capped
3. (c) allows for trustees' expenses for costs associated with preserving and selling the property
    a. trustee can take this cost out of the sec creditor's interest/claim → i.e. ALL COSTS
4. (d) tells us what secured claims make it out of bankruptcy
    a. *Dewsnup v. Timm* → a ch. 7 case, prof says it may not apply to a 11 or 13
        i. Property had FMV of 39K, lien of 120K
            1. 81K deficiency in essence
        ii. debtors argued that bifurcation results in permanent unsec claim in bankruptcy and even outside of bankruptcy (post-bankruptcy)
            1. i.e. only lien after bankruptcy was for 39K and 81K should be discharged according to debtors
        iii. **SC says no → allowed secured claim does not have the same meaning in 506(a) and (d)**

1. holds that the bifurcation stays in bankruptcy and the full lien survives afterwards → combine it for a 120K secured claim after bankruptcy
2. 506(d) only voids liens that are not allowed secured claims and 506(a) bifurcates allowed sec claims, but it's still allowed

iv. if property is sold in bankruptcy, sec credit gets 39K, and 81K deficiency

v. if not sold (more likely outcome, b/c no equity in it), and it leaves bankruptcy, then creditor retains lien of 120K

1. can foreclose on it and sell it, but cannot sue debtor later for any deficiency

vi. MORAL → liens flow thru bankruptcy unaffected unless there is an exception

1. but with Ch. 7, personal liability is discharged → lender can foreclose on property, but can't deficiency.

x. **§ 507(a) → Priorities**

1. secured claims come before these subject to trustee expenses in 506(c)
2. if more than 1 creditor exists is any given priority group, they are paid pro rata

   a. **RULE: claims paid in full until insufficient funds to pay all claims in**

group, in which case claims are paid *pro-rata* by group

3. these are creditors who are entitled to priority above the GUSC, 10 subsections listing with who will be paid in what order!!
    a. First, DSO claims (Congress moved these straight to the top)
        i. Including third party claims under (a)(1)(B)
        ii. **NOTE: under (a)(1)(C), attorneys/trustees actually get paid first, even before DSO obligations, otherwise, the whole system would fail
    b. ****Second, other admin claims under 503(b)**
    c. Third, don't worry, some claim in an involuntary case
    d. Fourth, wages for corporations up to 10K
    e. Fifth, similar to (a)(4), employee benefit plans
    f. Sixth, don't worry about it
    g. Seventh, important, up to $2225 for each individual arising from the deposit (before the case) of money in connection with the purchase, lease, or rental of property, or services, for personal, family, or household use, that were not delivered or provided
    h. Eighth, allows for tax claims of federal and state gov'ts
        i. **Timeline for tax priority claims**
            1. tax timeline runs backward from date of petition
            2. examine when taxes are last due, must be in preceding 3 yrs before filing of the petition
            3. HYPO: debtors file on Feb. 2006

a. Look at 2001 and 2002 tax returns
   i. 2001 are out because they are due in April 2002 which is more than 3 yrs prior to filing
   ii. 2002 taxes are in b/c they are due in April 2003 and that is within 3 yrs preceding filing
   iii. also 2005 is included, but not 2006 b/c tax yr is not over

ii. NOTE: if taxes come in under this timeline, then they are also non-dischargeable under § 523(a)(1)

   1. very important to determine this before filing

iii. NOTE 2: even if past taxes are excluded, IRS has special power to go back and get a federal tax lien which will be secured in bankruptcy

   1. but the IRS must do this before filing

of bankruptcy, i.e. petition date

2. IRS also has power to seize property exempt under state law

iv. This section includes many other kinds of taxes also → Social security, property, etc.

1. pre-petition interest on these taxes enjoys same priority advantage
2. postpetition interest does not accrue on unsec tax claims, but does accrue for any unpaid, undischarged tax debts after bankruptcy

i. Ninth, don't worry about it, some FDIC

j. Tenth, new important, allows for claims arising from DWI incidents of debtor

VI. CH. 7 BANKRUPTCY (classic liquidation-style bankruptcy)

a. Most of the above provisions were discussed in the context of Ch. 7 cases

i. Debtor files case unless there is an involuntary filing by creditors under § 303

b. **No-Asset Cases:** 96-98% of Ch. 7 cases are no-asset cases, i.e. there are no non-exempt assets for the trustee to distribute to GUSC

i. so there may be some assets, but none that are available in bankruptcy → either the property is not property of the estate or it's exempt or it's encumbered by security interests

ii. Example → 1 million dollar condo is only asset, 1 million mortgage on it, so no asset case

1. Rule of thumb → it costs the trustee 10% of FMV of property to sell it

iii. Debtor sort of wants a no asset case, with the rest of their assets covered by exemptions, plus they get discharge from unsec debt

iv. **When house has a lot of equity (and no exemptions to cover it) or if debtor is really behind on house/car payments, then he/she will consider Ch. 13 because they don't want this property sold; or if you have a lot of priority claims and/or nondischargeable debt**

v. **Remember, under 109(h), individual debtor must get credit counseling before filing**

c. **Basic Ch. 7 Timeline**

i. Must get credit counseling within 180 days prepetition

ii. After filing, you have 15 days to get all your schedules and statements in

iii. § 341 meeting of creditors → debtor will testify with regard to assets and liabilities

1. happens 20-40 days postpetition

iv. 60 days after creditors meeting, debtor is entitled to discharge

1. deadline to filing objections to discharge

v. that's it for a ch. 7 case

1. realize that debtor can get a discharge, but the trustee will still be administering the assets for benefit of creditors

a. but be careful → debtor can't have done anything wrong

b. plus, if trustee needs to debtor to do certain things, deals can be worked out and times can be extended

vi. hard to get a discharge undone, so trustee may extend things

d. **§ 726 → Gives order for distribution of the property of the estate**

i. trustee expenses etc., then secured claims, then priority claims (including 503 admin/postpetition claims), then GUSC

1. i.e. trustee expenses in selling property of SC comes before secured claims, BUT trustee's compensation and other fees are after secured claims, they get priority under 507(a)(1)(C)

2. priority claims/creditors are not secured

3. some creditors claims are equitably subordinated b/c of wrongdoing

e. **Discharge → this is why most individual debtors file bankruptcy**

i. Losing discharge is the civil equivalent of death penalty in bankruptcy → once debts are declared nondischargeable then debtor keeps them forever (don't want that to happen)

ii. <u>Discharge § 727 vs. Dischargeability of a Debt § 523</u>
   1. **727 → allows for a complete discharge of all debts, global**
      a. only applies to Ch. 7 bankruptcies (except there is § 1141 corollary for Ch. 11)
      b. objection to discharge becomes an adversarial proceeding in the bankruptcy
      c. disaster if debtor loses discharge here b/c it's global
      d. only for individuals, not corporations
      e. personal liability on all debts is discharged, even ones that flow through
   2. **523 → one debt claim may not be dischargeable**
      a. this applies to all chapters of bankruptcy
      b. can lose discharge on individual debts here
   3. only a creditor can bring 523 proceeding, see 523(c)(1)
      a. 727 proceedings can be brought by creditor, trustee and other parties

iii. **§ 727 Discharge**
   1. (a)(1) → discharge for individuals only, not corporations (business go out of business, do not come out of bankruptcy with a discharge)
   2. (a)(2) – (a)(6) → bad acts by the debtor can result in loss of discharge
      a. intent to hinder, delay, or defraud a creditor through transfers, destruction, mutilation of property
      b. concealment, destruction, falsification, or failure to properly keep books, records, etc., "unless such act or failure to act was justified under all of the circumstances"
         i. better have a reasonable set of records, otherwise could lose discharge

c. making knowing and fraudulent false oaths, claims, etc.
d. withholding information, lying on schedules
e. failing to explain loss of assets satisfactorily
f. disobeying/refusing court orders

3. (a)(8) & (a)(9) → deals with prior discharges
    a. can only get a Ch. 7 bankruptcy discharge once every 8 yrs
    b. can only get at Ch. 13 discharge once every 6 yrs (but some exceptions here)
4. (b) → result of discharge "discharges the debtor from all debts that arose before the date of the order for relief under this chapter"
5. (c)(1) → allows for trustee, creditor or US trustee to object to discharge
6. (d) → allows for revocation of a prior discharge IF fraud on part of debtor and such fraud was not known until after discharge
    a. other reasons here also, such as failing to reveal property of the estate
7. (e) → puts 1 yr time limit on (d) after discharge was granted
    a. later times for other bad acts under (d)
8. bottom line is that these are all bad acts that make debtor unworthy of any bankruptcy relief, but these cases involve a great deal of judgment and discretion
    a. *In re McNamara* → global discharge case under 727(a)(5) & (a)(2)
        i. Ct held that the debtor losing 130K in a poker game did not satisfactorily explain the loss and was a fraudulent prepetition transfer of money
            1. there may have never been a poker game and debtor did not want wife getting money

iv. **§ 523 Exceptions to Discharge (and debtor remains personally obligated on such debts)**

1. Prof pointed out the important debt exceptions below from subsection (a)
2. (a)(1) → tax or customs duty, relates to 507(a)(3) & (a)(8) priority claims
    a. i.e. any unpaid portion of these taxes not paid through 507 are exempted from discharge
3. **(2) → false statements, both oral and in writing (i.e. when getting money or more credit)
    a. includes special provision for consumer debts owed to a single creditor for more than $500 of luxury goods/services obtained within 90 days of bankruptcy
    b. also other cash advances for consumer credit
4. (3) → for creditors and debts that were not part of the bankruptcy proceeding
5. **(4) → fraud and defalcation while acting in as a fiduciary, embezzlement, larceny
6. (5) → domestic support obligations, very broad
7. **(6) → intentional torts against person or entity ("willful and malicious injury" by debtor)
8. (7) → fines, penalties, forfeiture payable to a gov'tal unit (including penalties on taxes)
9. (8) → student loans are not dischargeable, unless there is an undue hardship
10. (9) → death or personal injury caused by DWIs on motor vehicle/boat/aircraft
11. (13) → federal (not state) criminal restitution orders are not dischargeable
12. (14) → any debt incurred to pay taxes to gov't or to pay fines under fed election law
13. (15) → not DSO, but a property settlement between debtor/family other than DSOs
14. **§ 523(c) → all these are automatic nondischargeable, except for 2, 4, & 6**
    a. 2, 4, & 6 require creditors to request and file motion/objection
    b. this is b/c 2, 4, 6 involve a lot of factual determinations
    c. student loans are automatically nondischargeable under (a)(8) unless the student comes to court and shows

the ct that forcing payment will cause undue hardship

- **i.** basically have to show that you are near or below the poverty line b/c it's very hard to do
- **ii.** case law provides the *Brunner* test for "undue hardship," must show:
  - **1.** debtor cannot maintain minimal standard of living
  - **2.** additional circumstances say this minimal standard will persist
  - **3.** debtor made good faith efforts to repay the loan
- **iii.** some courts use equitable powers under § 105(a) to grant partial discharge of student loan debt, but very unlikely that this will happen

v. **§ 524 Effect of Discharge**

- **1.** (a)(1) → voids judgments for personal liability (and not other judgment liens or other liens)
- **2.** (a)(2) → injunctions against recovery for against dischargeable personal debts
  - **a.** they are not wiped out, but legally the creditor is enjoined from continuing collection activity against the debtor
  - **b.** but there may be other supporting obligors/guarantors the creditor can still collect the debt from → this is why some debtors reaffirm the debt
- **3.** (c) → allows for **reaffirmation agreements**
  - **a.** must meet a number of requirements for it to be enforceable
- **4.** (f) → nothing prevents the debtor from still paying debts voluntarily
- **5.** NOTE: Liens are not discharged or affected here
- **6.** Plus, there is a debate about how much effect a discharge has on state gov'ts collecting debt

- vi. **§ 525 → prevents debtors in bankruptcy from receiving discriminatory treatment**
  1. (a) applies to governmental entities → cannot deny employment (or other services) SOLELY b/c person has filed bankruptcy
  2. (b)applies to private employers and individuals→again, no disc SOLELY b/c person is bankrupt
  3. (c) gov'tal unit may not deny student loans based on bankruptcy
     - a. but this does not apply to private creditor student loans

f. **Bankruptcy Crimes**

- i. Crimes dealing with debtor's concealment of assets, false oaths, false claims etc.
- ii. 18 U.S.C. § 157 → allows for imprisonment of up to 5 yrs and fines for bankruptcy fraud by the debtor

g. **Reaffirmation & Redemption/Prof gave list of ways that debtors try to keep property:**

- i. Redemption under § 722
  1. remember, only applicable to Ch. 7 cases and individual debtors, and applies regardless of whether there was a waiver
  2. redeem only tangible personal property intended primarily for personal/family/household use from a lien securing a DISCHARGEABLE CONSUMER DEBT, by paying the creditor it's allowed secured claim or FMV of the property (whichever is less) ONLY IF exempted under § 522 or abandoned under § 554
     - a. it may be forced over objections of the creditor
- ii. Reaffirmation under § 524(c) & (d)
  1. this is where the debtor and a creditor come to an agreement for the debtor to pay the debt, i.e. reaffirm the debt → becomes legally enforceable notwithstanding discharge
     - a. debtor does it b/c they want to have good credit to get future credit, or a creditor may threaten to object to discharge
     - b. plus, even with unsec debt, a relative may be a guarantor/obligor on the loan

- c. plus with secured creditors, allows for debtor to keep property and creditor won't repossess (debts are discharged under 524, but liens are not)

2. **524(c) → reaffirmation agreements must meet a number of requirements to be enforceable**
   - a. Congress added in an new form recently also to protect debtors
   - b. <u>Main requirements:</u>
     - i. Must happen before granting of discharge
     - ii. Disclosures must be made to debtor
     - iii. File agreement with the court and attorney must file affidavit that shows no undue hardship for debtor and debtor has been fully advised of legal consequences of agreement and any default
       1. makes the attorney almost become a financial advisor
     - iv. debtor has to have option to rescind within 60 days
     - v. if no attorney present for debtor during negotiation, then ct must advise of no undue hardship and in the best interest of the debtor
       1. this part does not apply to consumer debt secured by real property
   - c. courts deny these reaffirmations all the time
   - d. creditor must be very careful
     - i. reaff process must be started by the debtor
     - ii. any attempts to collect debt can violate the stay
   - e. large national retailers have created national programs to object to discharge in search of reaffirmation

agreements, plus some programs offer continued credit if debtor reaffirms; this has lead to litigation with judges getting angry

i. *Latanowich/Sears case*
   1. ct held that agreement that was not filed with or approved by bankruptcy ct was void and Sears' attempt to collect prepetition debt pursuant to agreement violated discharge injunction
   2. compensatory damages for debtor and pun damages against Sears!!!
   3. Sears was not filing these agreements and not giving debtors full disclosures, got them in a lot of trouble

3. some case law allows another method, **"ride-through" (retention)** where debtor keeps the collateral by continuing to make pre-bankruptcy payments without reaffirming or redemption
   a. allows debtor to keep collateral while discharging personal liability on the debt if they were up to date on payments on the debt
      i. in rem interest remains while in personam one is gone
   b. Congress may have dealt with this in the 521 statement of intentions with secured property
      i. 521(a)(6) → must redeem, reaffirm, or surrender the property
      ii. so this may do away with the retention doctrine from the case law

- iii. Abandonment of Property, § 554
  1. trustee can abandon property that is burdensome to the estate or of inconsequential value
- iv. Exemptions under § 522(b)
- v. Avoidance of Liens (judicial and other non-PMSI ones) to the Extent they Impair Exemptions 522(f)

h. **Ch. 7/Abuse/***Means Testing*****

- i. If doctor makes 300K/year, he is making too much money, can have case dismissed from the beginning
  1. different than denial of discharge under 727
  2. can have case dismissed under 707(b), but you could still conceivably come back later and get debts discharge, must first follow instructions of the ct
     - a. use to be substantial abuse std fleshed out by the courts, discretionary role
     - b. now changed, we have MEANS TESTING with the new 2005 amendments
- ii. Basic Idea → defines income and expenses and subtract the second from the first, if the difference (surplus of income over expenses) would pay at least X amount of debt, the debtor is presumptively abusive and barred from Ch. 7 bankruptcy, absent special circumstances
- iii. **new modified § 707, Dismissal of a case or conversion to Ch. 11 or 13**
  1. (a) → permits ct to dismiss case for "cause," such as for unreasonable delay, etc.
  2. (b)(1) → if court finds "abuse" with an individual debtor who primarily has consumer debts, then can dismiss the case or convert to 11 or 13
     - a. ct may not take into account charitable contributions here
  3. **(b)(2) → MEANS TESTING can create a PRESUMPTION OF "ABUSE" for (b)(1)
     - a. (A) presumption arising takes discretion away from judges
       - i. look at "current monthly income," defined in § 101(10A) → avg monthly income for 6 months income prior to petition date, includes all sources taxable

or not; this excludes benefits from Social Security

1. must start with last day of month previous to bankruptcy filing
2. so if Nov 1st filing, go back from Oct 31; if Nov 30 filing, back from Oct 31st

ii. take the CMI and subtract the allowed deductions, then multiply by 60 (for 5 years → CMI – deductions x 60 = #

1. **Presumption of Abuse if # is NOT lesser than the lesser of**
    a. **(1) 25% of debtor's nonpriority unsecured debt, or $6000, whichever is greater; OR**
    b. **(2) $10,000**

iii. RANGE for CMI minus Allowed Deductions

1. < 100, no presumption, you are in bankruptcy
2. over 166.67, presumptively abusive, you're out
3. in between the two, must compare to 25% of gen unsec debt

iv. Deductions, 2 types on the means test form

1. capped (based on IRS standards) vs. unlimited deductions

- b. (B) presumption of abuse can only be rebutted by certain special circumstances, such as a medical condition or being in the military, then it lists certain tests
- c. (C) requires the filing of means test form
- d. (D) safe harbor for vets – above sections not applicable under certain circumstances

4. (b)(3) → GENERAL GROUNDS FOR ABUSE, this brings back in the old law, i.e. "mushy" analysis; **even if debtor past means test, the ct shall consider:**
   - a. (A) whether the debtor filed petition in bad faith
   - b. (B) the totality of circumstances of debtor's finances demonstrates abuse
5. (b)(4) → deals with attorneys
   - a. (A) imposes penalties on attorneys to reimburse trustee if case gets dismissed , reasonable costs, etc. AND if attorney violates Rule 9011 of bankruptcy procedure
     - i. Rule 9011 is like Rule 11 in FRCP, so this probably won't happen much
   - b. (B) if attorney violated Rule 9011, ct can impose civil penalties here
   - c. (C) need attorney's signature certifying that there has been a "reasonable investigation" and ensure motions are "well grounded in fact"
   - d. (D) attorney's signature constitutes certification that nothing on the schedules is incorrect
   - e. **so, in essence, statement of financial affairs and schedules must be accurate**
6. (b)(5) → allows debtor to get cost and fees for creditor that brings 707 motion just to harass the debtor and violated Rule 9011, i.e. "solely to coerce the debtor to waive" other rights
7. (b)(6) → if debtor is below the median income test, then only the judge or US trustee can bring

a motion under 707(b) [probably will be 707(b)(3)]

a. but can bring a 707(b)(2) if combining non-filing spouse income puts them over applicable median

8. (b)(7) → Median Income Threshold Test, disallows anyone from bringing (b)(2) means testing motion if debtor is below median income threshold based on their family size
9. (c)(3) → no dismissal under (b)(2) if bankruptcy is necessary to satisfy a DSO claim

iv. **Enforcing the new standard**

1. 704(b)(1) → requires US Trustee to check for abuse in every case filed by an individual debtor
2. if debtor is above-median, the US Trustee must further file a motion to dismiss or convert if presumptively abusive, or file a statement explaining why it has not done so

v. **The Means Test Form**

1. file the form with the petition for bankruptcy
   a. only fill out if debts are primarily consumer debts
      i. consumer debt is incurred primarily for personal, family, or household purpose, § 101(8)
2. based on Census Bureau and other official numbers
3. dependents → includes those you would list on your taxes (they all need not live with you)
4. **Median Income Test in Part III of the form**
   a. If your CMI x 12 month is less than the applicable median income, no presumption, and you are done
   b. Majority of cases will be below median cases
   c. If couple files jointly, both incomes count
   d. If only one files, non-spouses income is included for the median income test
      i. But here, if you are above median and have to continue the form, then only the debtor's income (excluding spouse's) is used for doing

the rest of the means test and budget

- e. MD Median Incomes: 1-earner = 48929, 2-people = 63761, 3-people = 75764, etc.

5. **Otherwise, must do the deductions:**
   - a. Standard deductions → food, housing utilities, mortgage/rent, transportation, plus car ownership allowance
   - b. Unlimited deductions →
     - i. secured credit debt for car – can claim it all
     - ii. same thing for the mortgage – can claim it all
     - iii. **but double-dipping with standard deductions are not allowed**
       1. you get the greater of:
          - a. IRS standard; OR
          - b. Actual payment
     - iv. Car & mortgage can be unlimited
       1. raising mortgage payments can result in lower income and thus no presumption → seems unfair if you buy a bigger house and there is no presumption against you
       2. **but remember, motion under 707(b)(3) can still be brought for bad faith and totality of the circumstances test**
       3. for a debtor with a very small car payment, then you

can take the IRS deduction

a. but if you paid off your car completely and have no payment and it breaks down later, then too bad

v. If you rent or lease, you can only get the IRS standards, not unlimited

6. CMI is a historical 6 month analysis
   a. If debtor just lost job, US Trustee can file statement of declination even though she fails mean test → i.e. argue motion is not appropriate, special circumstances
   b. Such a historical analysis does not fit with someone who just lost their job

VII. CH. 13 BANKRUPTCY, PLANS OF REORGANIZATIONS FOR INDIVIDUALS

a. <u>Basic Idea/Overview</u> → rather than focus on liquidation, concerned with debtor's future earnings in order to pay creditors
   i. Streamlined reorganization process for individuals that is short and simple
   ii. Debtor keeps all assets, unlike Ch. 7
   iii. Debtor makes payments over a period of years that trustee distributes to creditors according to a court-approved plan; when debtor has completed payout, then debtor's remaining obligations are discharged
      1. plans range from 3 to 5 years; 5 yrs is max under 1322(d)
   iv. Creditors now get paid from debtor's future income rather than debtor's assets
   v. All the general provisions from Chs. 1, 3, & 5 still apply
   vi. Many Ch. 13 filings driven by default and acceleration on home mortgage and Ch. 13 is filed to stop foreclosure on the house
      1. in Ch. 7, you can still lose house after discharge b/c liens survive

b. <u>More differences between Ch. 13 & Ch. 7, and more Ch. 13 provisions:</u>
   i. No involuntary Ch. 13 proceedings

- ii. Under 1306(b), debtor can keep the property
    1. this section also provides for debtor's postpetition earnings to be part of the property of the estate, 1306(a)(2) → different than 541; this makes sense b/c it's needed to make plan pmts
- iii. No liquidation of assets, trustee just administers for the benefit of creditors
    1. § 1302 → rights and duties of the trustee
    2. § 1303 → rights and duties of the debtor
- iv. No redemption of property available under 722, that only applies to Ch. 7
- v. Discharge only after completion of plan, 1328(a)
- vi. Co-debtor stay found in 1301(a) for consumer debts → to the extent that another individual is liable with the debtor, then the automatic stay is actually extended to this co-debtor even though they are not in bankruptcy
    1. but this is not a codebtor discharge
    2. creditor can also move to have stay lifted, 1301(c), while the case is pending and the stay is in effect
- vii. § 1327(b) → confirmation of a plan vests all of the property of the estate in the debtor
- viii. in addition to filing a petition, debtor files a plan providing for repayment of claims

c. <u>Eligibility to File Ch. 13 is determined by § 109(e)</u>

- i. "Only an individual with **regular income** that owes, on the date of the filing of the petition, **noncontingent, liquidated**, unsecured debts of less than $307,675 and **noncontingent, liquidated** secured debts of less than $922,975 . . . "
    1. same for joint case with spouse
- ii. "noncontingent" refers to a claim that HAS to be paid, i.e. it is not contingent
    1. EX: a jury claim is contingent – depends on the jury
- iii. Unliquidated claims are those in which liability may have been admitted, but the amount of the debt is in dispute
    1. i.e. plaintiff vs. defendant, there is a claim, but don't know how much just yet
- iv. Note, that under § 104, the numbers here are adjusted for inflation every so often

d. **Basic Ch. 13 Timeline**
   - **i.** Ch.13 stays the same as Ch. 7, except you need a plan within 15 days (unless debtor gets an extension with the court)
   - **ii.** Ch. 13 plans are not complex
     - **1.** Shortly after filing, debtor must start making plan payments within 30 days (even though it hasn't been approved by the court)
       - **a.** These payments get escrowed until confirmation
   - **iii.** Deadline for a 341 meeting is 20-50 after petition date
   - **iv.** Confirmation hearing , § 1325
     - **1.** New amendments make this come quicker
     - **2.** Plan runs 3-5 years....
   - **v.** **Discharge is only after payment plan is complete, i.e. after 5 years**, see **1328**

e. **Elements of an Acceptable Confirmation Plan, § 1322**
   - **i.** <u>1322(a) → Mandatory Provisions, Plan must provide that:</u>
     - **1.** debtor will pay sufficient amount of money to the trustee sot he plan can be fully performed
     - **2.** all priority creditors, (i.e. claims entitled to priority under 507), will be paid in full, unless a priority claim holder agrees otherwise
     - **3.** if the plan classifies claims, that all claims within a given class are treated the same
       - **a.** for example, dischargeable vs. nondischargeable
     - **4.** notwithstanding (a)(2), a plan may provide for less than full payment of a 507(a)(1)(B) claim (DSOs assigned to or owed directly to a gov't unit) only if all disposable income for 5 years is devoted to plan
       - **a.** new provision that Congress added in → policy is that Congress did not want a giant DSO gov't claim to kill a Ch. 13 plan
       - **b.** but remember, portion not paid is non-dischargeable under 523(a)(5) so it will remain after bankruptcy
   - **ii.** <u>(b) → Selected Permissive Provisions:</u>
     - **1.** (b)(2) provide for the modification of rights of secured creditors **other than creditors whose only security is real property that is the debtor's residence,** or of holders of unsec claims

a. must be mortgage holders secured EXLUSIVELY by the house to fit exception
    i. so bifurcation allowed unless SC has lien on the house
    ii. remember *Dewsnup*, SI will survive bankruptcy
2. (b)(3) provide for the cure or waiving of any defaults (has to be reasonable time)
3. (b)(4) provide for payments on any unsec claim to be made concurrently with payments on any secured claim or any other unsec claim
4. (b)(5) notwithstanding paragraph (2), a Chap. 13 plan may provide for the cure of defaults on any claim even though final payment on the claim is not due until after the plan is completed
    a. NOTE: even though (b)(2) seems to imply that a debtor cannot modify mortgage debt on debtor's principal residence in any way, this subsection provides that a debtor can cure mortgage arrears in a Ch. 13 plan (i.e. can cure home mortgage)

iii. (d)(1) if the current monthly income of the debtor and the debtor's spouse is **above the state median income**, the plan may not provide for payments over a period that is longer than 5 years
    1. **median income test again**

iv. (d)(2) if the CMI of the debtor and spouse is **below the state median income**, the plan may not provide for payments over a period that is longer than 3 yrs, unless the court **for cause** approves a longer period (not to exceed 5 years), but ct cannot approve plan longer than 5 years

f. **Confirmation of the Plan, Required Findings under § 1325**

i. <u>1325(a) → Required Findings, need all of them according to prof (case law may vary):</u>
    1. the plan complies with provisions of Ch. 13
    2. all filing fees have been paid
    3. the plan has been proposed in **good faith**
    4. **the value, as of the effective date of the plan, of property to be distributed under the plan on account of each allowed unsecured claim is not less than the amount that would be paid on such

claim if the estate of the debtor were liquidated under Ch. 7

a. **"best interests of the creditors test"**
b. if, for example, GUSC were going to get 5K in Ch. 7 from equity in some asset, then they must get the same or more here in Ch. 13
    i. must do hypothetical liquidations to figure this out in your/their minds
c. remember, most Ch. 7 cases are **no asset**, so unless you are representing wealthy debtors, you don't have to worry about it when there is no equity in their assets and exemptions cover the rest

5. with respect to each allowed secured claim the court must find existence of at least one of the following three alternatives:
    a. the secured creditor has accepted the plan
    b. the SC retains the lien securing their claim AND the debtor will pay them the amount of their claim
        i. **SC has to be paid in full → see time value of money below, *Till***
    c. the debtor will surrender the SC's collateral
6. the debtor will be able to make all payments under the plan and be able to comply with the plan
    a. **"feasibility test"** → courts generally find the plan passes this test unless there is some overt evidence that the plan is not feasible (i.e. the debtor's own budget reflects that the debtor does not make enough money to support the proposed plan payments)
7. the action of the debtor in filing the petition was in **good faith**
8. all postpetition DSOs have been paid (new provision)
9. debtor has filed ALL applicable tax returns (new provision)

- ii. 1325(b) → the Disposable Income Test:
  - 1. (b)(1) If there is an objection to plan, court may not approve plan unless:
    - a. all claims are paid in full; OR
    - b. the plan provides that all of debtor's ***projected*** **disposable income** to be received in the **"applicable commitment period"** will be applied to make payments to unsecured creditors
      - i. note: in most jurisdictions, the Ch. 13 trustee will object to any proposed plan with a duration of less than 3 yrs unless the plan proposes to pay all creditors in full
      - ii. ***projected*** → means test is just a starting point (this is in litigation right now)
        - 1. these litigants argue means test is just a starting point and they have to show the ct what the real projected DI actually is, i.e. based on their income postpetition date
          - a. they want to pay less than what means test would make them pay
          - b. trustees say this is the right argument
      - iii. DI use to be a postpetition number, but now CMI and expenses is used from means test for above median debtors (schedules still used for below median)

1. and CMI is a historical, not postpetition, number

2. (b)(2) → "Disposable Income" means current monthly income (minus child or other support payments for a dependent), less amounts **"reasonably necessary to be expended"** for:
   a. (A)(i) the maintenance or support of the debtor or a dependent (or for a DSO); and
   b. (A)(ii) certain charitable contributions
   c. (B) if the debtor is engaged in business, the expenditures necessary for the continuation of the business
3. ***(b)(3) Amounts **"reasonably necessary to be expended"** shall be determined in accordance with § 707(b)(2)(A)&(B) if the debtor's CMI is greater than the median family income for the state [**this is the means test from 707**]
4. (b)(4) **"applicable commitment period"** shall be:
   a. (A) subject to (B):
      i. 3 years; or
      ii. not less than 5 yrs, if the CMI of the debtor and spouse combined is not less than the median family income for the state; and
   b. (B) may be less than 3 or 5 yrs, but only if the plan provides for payment in full of all allowed unsecured claims over a shorter period

iii. 1325(c) → ct can order any employer of debtor to pay debtor's income to the trustee

DISPOSABLE INCOME TEST

All Debtors Must Pass Best Interests of Creditors Test for Unsec Claims	Divided Into: Above Median and Below Median for ACP	Based on Division, figure out what to use for projected DI

Above Median	App Comm Period not less than 5 yrs	Use **means test** to figure out expenses and disposable income for payments **If surplus**, then pay this surplus to unsec nonpriority creditors **If no surplus under test**, then basically treated like below median and use disp inc/reas nec expenses and case law to figure it out
Below Median	App Comm Period is 3 yrs	Debtor's budget is used here to figure this out, i.e. use schedules I & J to figure out current monthly income, etc.

g. **Secured Debt/Creditors → 3 exceptions to bifurcation/cramdown, i.e. it is allowed by 1322(b)(2), but these are three situations where you can't (cramdown is bifurcation of the claim where you basically get rid of unsec part; it is mainly for cars, not real estate so much):**
   - **i.** 1) claims secured ONLY by a SI in real property that is the debtors principal residence (see 1322b2)
      - **1.** some courts have recently allowed the stripping off of a 2nd mortgage when the 1st mortgage completely encumbers the property → it's basically like an unsecured 2nd mortgage
      - **2.** but you are allowed to cure such claims under 1322a5
         - **a.** 1322(c) also allows for deacceleration of loan and procurement
         - **b.** 1322(e) → interest rate with curing home mortgage is determined by underlying agreement and applicable nonbankruptcy law
   - **ii.** 2) new provision at end of 1325(a) → cramdown use to be used a lot for cars, but now it is limited

1. **for vehicles purchase (with PMSI), acquired for personal use of the debtor, in 910 days (about 2.5 yrs) preceding petition date, you can't bifurcate or modify the claim**

iii. 3) new provision at end of 1325(a) → catchall for the previous 1 year

1. **for any other thing of value purchased 1 year before filing with that thing of value as collateral, can't bifurcate or modify the claim**

iv. How do you determine interest rates and FMVs for cramdowns? → 2 Sup Ct cases

1. remember, you can only have bifurcation if FMV of collateral < debt on collateral, § 506
2. *Rash* → **FMV is based on debtor's replacement value for cramdown purposes**
   a. Now codified in 506(a)(2)
   b. Replacement value is higher than foreclosure value, i.e. your cost to buy a like car of age, mileage, etc.; it is even higher than trade in value
   c. So these higher FMVs will result in higher bifurcated secured debt that must be paid
3. *Till* → discussing interest rates for 1325(a)(5) and present value of the SC's claim
   a. Secured debt has to be paid in full under 1325a5 unless something else happens
      i. Including interest
   b. **This case holds that interest is PRIME PLUS SOME NOMINAL RISK ASSESSMENT (like 1-3%, but it is undefined)**
      i. The latter covers the risk for the secured lender
   c. This interest will be paid over the time period of the plan

v. Remember, no redemption for Ch. 13 debtors, so they try to cramdown

1. you may be able to get retention under Ch. 7 and that is better than Ch. 13 cramdown b/c Ch. 7 discharges all personal liability
2. but while a Ch. 13 plan is in effect, the automatic stay prevents creditor from getting property, unless debtor stops making payments

vi. **don't forget the UNSECURED PORTION after Cramdown**
  1. still must do the best interests of creditors test here for this to make sure they get at least as much as they would in Ch. 7
  2. do disp inc test to figure out how much they will get, i.e. the payment

vii. **If you cramdown something, don't worry about the arrears → you are paying off as much as the debt as is covered by the FMV of the property**

h. **Unsecured Creditors in Ch. 13**

i. They can't vote on a Ch. 13 plan
  1. they get in a better position by filing an objection
    a. <u>2 main objections:</u>
      i. Best interests of Creditors Test → argue they would get more in Ch. 7, see 1325(a)(4)
      ii. if debtor fails to devote all of their projected disposable income to the plan for the applicable commitment period, see 1325(b)
        1. use means test/disposable income test
        2. means test used to figure out projected disposable income if you are above median debtor

ii. Can a Ch. 13 plan pay them zero dollars?
  1. Yes, if this would have been a no asset case in Ch. 7
  2. so in the past, these types of plans have been confirmed, but it is the exception not the rule
    a. plus there is still a good faith test courts use

iii. 1325(a)(3) **good faith** requirement requires debtors to usually pay something to the unsecured creditors
  1. **usually pay 10% to unsecured creditors → use this in calculation**
  2. MD jurisdiction have thumbnail test for good faith → ~11%, unless there are some very unusual circumstances

a. If you don't meet this, debtor is in big trouble and there will be litigation
3. case law shows haggling over reasonably necessary expenses, etc.
4. fairness requirement will be imposed upon debtor here with unsecured creditors → mushy analysis
5. new amendments encourage payments to sec creditors even more so now than unsecured creditors

iv. See table above also

i. **Priority Creditors** under 507 are still entitled to get paid in full in Ch. 13, 1322(a)(2)
j. **Trustee Compensation will be in calculation also**
k. § 1328 → discharge after completion of payments, and subject to other limits
   i. limits on how many discharges you can get over time → subsection (f)
l. **§ 1329** → allows trustees to revisit a plan if a debtor starts earning a lot more and the section allows for plan changes

VIII. INVOLUNTARY BANKRUPTCY CASES

a. **§ 303**
   i. available only for Ch. 7 or 11
      1. you can't force someone into an payment plan like in Ch. 13
         a. unconstitutional and code bars it
      2. no involuntary bankruptcy against family farmer or charitable organizations
   ii. (b)(1) → can be done by 3 or more creditors holding unsecured claims worth at least $12,300
   iii. (b)(2) → if fewer than 12 unsecured claims against debtor, then one or more of these may file involuntary bankruptcy against debtor if they are holding a claim(s) of at least $12,300
   iv. (b)(3) → special for partnerships, i.e. by fewer than all the general partners in a partnership

b. <u>Logistics</u>
   i. a 303 case starts a filing of a complaint, then there is period for debtor's answer, then discovery, then trial → basically like a normal lawsuit
      1. **if judge makes an order for relief under bankruptcy, then it runs like any other bankruptcy case under 301 (voluntary cases) or 302 (joint case)**

- a. all other provisions of the code become automatically applicable

2. **303(h) → gives what the creditors must prove**
    - a. if no answer by debtor, then automatic bankruptcy under the Code
    - b. if answer, then bankruptcy ONLY IF creditor can prove 1 of 2 things:
        - i. that the debtor is generally not paying such debtor's debts as they become due
            1. i.e. equitable insolvency → debtor may have money, but not paying
                - a. as opposed to balance sheet insolvency
        - ii. OR if a custodian was appointed or took possession within 120 days before date of this involuntary petition filing
            1. Note: assignment for benefit of creditors in state court is an express grounds for granting order for relief in an involuntary case

- ii. **303(i) → judge can award debtor costs and reasonable attorneys' fees if petition is dismissed**
    1. creditors and lawyers must be very careful when they try to launch such a bankruptcy
    2. involuntary bankruptcy is usually used for Ch.11/business, but be very careful → it can seriously damage the business's reputation and could result a huge judgment against creditors if case is dismissed, i.e. significant fees and damages
- iii. a creditor can gain back actual/necessary expenses as postpetition claims/administrative expenses for such a case under § 503(b)(3)(A), this is also a priority claim under 507(a)(2)

c. this type of case is obviously **very rare**

IX. CH. 11 BANKRUPTCY

a. Individual can file Ch. 11
  - i. But mostly it is corporations and other businesses!
  - ii. 1129(a)(15) requires Ch. 13 means test to be used in Ch. 11 with a natural person

b. <u>Basic Idea and Overview</u> → allow reorganization and restructuring of business with DIP as trustee
  - i. Why file Ch. 7?
    - 1. automatic stay stops everything which is especially useful for businesses
      - a. can't repossess airplanes etc.
      - b. can stop judgment creditors from attaching
    - 2. **to stay in business**
  - ii. Why not to file?
    - 1. incredibly expensive to file by the time everything is done
    - 2. business stigma and reputation; customer uncertainty
    - 3. suppliers stop supplying
    - 4. no more goods on credit

c. **Ch. 11 Timeline**
  - i. Ch. 11 → similar to ch. 13
    - 1. 341 meeting is between 20-40 days
    - 2. **In first 120 days, debtor has exclusive right to file a plan of reorganization and then get an additional 60 days to get it confirmed**
    - 3. and anyone can file a plan of reorganization including creditors
    - 4. **discharge is upon confirmation in corporate cases**
      - a. different than individual 13s
      - b. for individuals in Ch. 11, get discharge upon plan completion (not confirmation)

d. <u>Differences b/t Ch. 11 and other types of bankruptcies, and other overview provisions:</u>
  - i. **No trustee, Debtor in Possession (DIP) here, see § 1107**
    - 1. very important distinction
    - 2. **DIP exercises the power of a trustee, 1107(a) → DIP and Trustee used interchangeably in this section of the outline (IX)**
      - a. DIP can sue under the bankruptcy
    - 3. DIP keeps the property unlike Ch. 7

4. DIP/Trustee can operate the business, 1108

ii. **US Trustee shall appoint a committee of unsecured creditors**
   1. 7 largest unsecured creditors
   2. committee can hire counsel → represent interests of all unsecured creditors
      a. can hire attorneys, accountants, professionals, and they get paid out of debtor's pockets
         i. fees are a 503(b)(4) administrative expense postpetition → is a priority claims under 507(a)(2)

iii. **Proof of Claim → 1111(a) says claims are deemed filed by operation of law as scheduled on the debtor's schedule**
   1. but creditor still has ability to file a proof of claim and you should always do so in case the debtor fudges it on the schedules
   2. if case is converted to Ch. 7, then file a proof of claim like in Ch. 7

iv. **Objectives and Procedures:**
   1. confirm a plan of reorganization under §§ 1129 & 1141
      a. this becomes a binding contract b/t debtor and all of their creditors
   2. debtor has an exclusive period to file plan → 120 days from date of petition date filing, 1121(b)
      a. plus another 60 days for confirmation
      b. so 180 days total
      c. this is very helpful and important b/c you want to file before creditors do
   3. plans are voted on (unlike Ch. 13)
      a. you can file an objection or vote against a plan
         i. involves a lot of strategy and negotiation
   4. votes are solicited by means of a disclosure statement approved by the court, 1125
      a. so you get a disclosure statement and a plan
         i. disclosure statement is just a lot of info about the case
         ii. plan tells you how everything will be implemented and worked out

1. how and when creditors get paid and how much
5. to confirm a plan, must conform to requirements in § 1129
   a. equivalent to 1325 in Ch. 13
   b. need affirmative vote of the creditors
   c. also, make sure that either each class of creditors accepts the plan or is not impaired under it
   d. BIOCT – 1129(a)(7)
6. debtor is discharged from all prepetition debts except as provided in the PLAN!
   a. Different than Ch. 13 where discharge does not occur until completion of plan

e. **Debtor's Most Important Concerns/Operating in Ch. 11**
   i. Use of cash → 363(c)(1)
   ii. Use of property → 1107, 1108, 362(c)
   iii. 362(a) provides a lot of cover and 362(c) allows the business to operate under DIP
   iv. § 364 allows further financing and other credit to be obtained by the DIP after bankruptcy starts
      1. (a) → can go get money without permission for "ordinary course of business"
      2. otherwise, for other stuff, DIP must get special court permission
      3. to get more secured debt, debtor needs a court order
      4. unsecured creditors may object to some stuff → if you give 2nd liens to already encumbered property then that results in loss of equity that is coming from unsecured creditor's pockets (no equity left)
         a. *Garland* → unsecured creditors are SOL, no adequate protection for them and unencumbered property can be used as collateral to secure postpetition debt
   v. 1112(b) → allows for conversion or dismissal of Ch. 11 case
   vi. 1104(a)(1) & (2) allow for a trustee to be put in place if necessary
      1. (a)(1) → for cause, fraud, mismanagement, etc.
      2. (a)(2) → mushy std, appointment if it's in the interest of the creditors

3. (a)(3) → if grounds exist to convert or dismiss under 1112, the ct can than instead appoint a trustee
4. *Sharon Steel Case* → DIP was not suing anyone including for preferences and fraud conveyances (went way over the line with these transfers), so the ct appointed a trustee

f. **Concerns of Secured Creditors in Ch. 11**
   i. Collateral protection → adequate protection
   ii. plus worried about soft collateral such as inventory (being sold), accounts receivables, cash, etc.
   iii. Rights of Secured Creditors
      1. still have all the powers under 506(b) to allow interest, fees to grow up to the value of the collateral
      2. Want **lifting of stay under 362(d)**, OR, **Adequate protection** (payments) under 362(d)
         a. § 361 provides definition for **adequate protection**:
            i. cash payments,
            ii. additional/replacement liens,
            iii. other relief fashioned by the court such as giving assurance through an equity cushion in other property
         b. Adequate protection basically keeps secured creditor in same position had case not been filed
         c. Under 362(g), party requesting relief has burden of proof on issue of debtor's equity in the property
            i. Party opposing relief has burden of proof on all other issues
         d. *Seitles* → 2 part case with 2 issues
            i. Automatic stay prevents US from pursuing false claims act claim because this is not a regulatory power, but a pecuniary action
            ii. Should the stay in a corporate case be extended to protect the president and sole remaining shareholder of the debtor?

1. ct used leeway under § 105, under exceptional circumstances, to protect the shareholder here
2. ct looked at 2 things, both equitable principles:
    a. irreparable harm
    b. likelihood of success (big equitable test)
3. so here stay was extended to nondebtor codefendant

iii. Note: 1301 is one exception for codebtor under Ch. 13

e. *Rogers Development Corp.*

i. Facts: creditor was oversecured, property had FMV of 750K, debt is 548K, so equity cushion of over 200K
1. creditor lent more money postpetition
2. then bank filed motion to lift the stay under 362(d)

ii. Ct tosses 362(d)(2) action b/c the property is needed for an effective reorganization
1. Ct made an error of law here b/c 362(g) requires debtor to have burden of proof as to property needed for effective reorganization and they made creditor show it

2. ct holds there is no equity in property even with equity cushion b/c there is other liens on it

iii. 362(d)(1) argument to lift stay is tougher

1. and ct says that they are oversecured and have an equity cushion that provides adequate protection

iv. but the SC's interest in the property continues to grow up to FMV, 506(b)

f. *Timbers*, Sup Ct: the automatic stay and the delay it causes in and of itself is not enough by itself to lift the stay or get adequate protection of payments

i. Prof says to note that collateral here was real estate that was going up in value so secured creditor would be fine later on

3. **Cash collateral → prohibition on use without consent of the court, 363(c)(2)**

a. Sec creditors worry about cash b/t it's very fungible

i. As long as sec creditor made allowance for proceeds arising from collateral under the sec agreement, then debtor can't use that cash collateral which is proceeds up to the value of the secured debt

b. If debtor uses cash collateral without consent, then there are penalties

i. Unauthorized use of cash collateral is grounds for **conversion** (to Ch.7) or dismissal, 1112(b)

c. *Earthlite* → cash collateral is special

- **i.** Adequate protection does not apply to cash collateral
  - **1.** cash is special → does not go up or down in nominal value
  - **2.** fungibility of cash and steady value is enough for adequate protection
  - **3.** debtors have to pay some adequate protection if cash collateral is to be used

4. *Polk* → prepetition waiver of automatic stay in the security agreement is not enforceable
- **a.** These are against public policy and stay protection is part of the Code and helps the debtor with a fresh start
- **b.** Ct notes that if you have a waiver supported by some special consideration, then it might be allowed → i.e. if creditor had given extra money

g. **Concerns of Unsecured Creditors**
- **i.** They don't want a loss of unencumbered property
  - **1.** especially when FMV of property is going down and debt going up, GUSC can go unpaid
- **ii.** they don't want a loss of going concern value
  - **1.** value of the business name, customer lists, goodwill, etc.
- **iii.** plus, they don't want 2nd liens on already encumbered property under 364 (more financing)
  - **1.** but the ct will force this over objections if need be

h. **Preferences**
- **i.** Basic Idea → although outside of bankruptcy, you can pay whichever creditors you want (subject to time limits of other money owed), in bankruptcy these payments may be avoided as "preferences"
- **ii.** **What is a preference?** → it is a cause of action only available under § 547 of the Bankruptcy Code

1. it's a legal transaction outside of bankruptcy, but it's a voidable transaction in bankruptcy if it meets the elements of a preference (and if there are no defenses to it

iii. Trustee or DIP sues for return of a preference → DIP sues its own business

iv. POLICY → all creditors in a category should be treated equally
   1. Congress chose the 90 day and 1 year periods

v. **§ 547(b), Preferences → Elements:** (b) The trustee may avoid any
   1. transfer (see § 101(54) → very broad)
   2. of an interest of the debtor, § 541
   3. in property, § 541
   4. to or for the benefit of a creditor
   5. on account of an **antecedent debt** owed by the debtor before such transfer was made
   6. made while the debtor was **insolvent**
      a. 547(f) → presumption of insolvency within a certain period of time, i.e. within 90 days preceding petition date (does not matter if it's an insider or not for the 90 day period)
         i. this just means that this needs to be rebutted by the transferee → must prove debtor was solvent at time of transfer
      b. For INSIDERS, from 90 days back to a year, then you have to prove insolvency
   7. within 90 days prepetition OR between 90 days and one year prepetition if recipient is an INSIDER (see § 101(30))
   8. **transfer enables the such creditor to receive more than such creditor would receive in a Ch. 7 case**
      a. must figure out what an unsecured cred would get in a Ch. 7 liquidation
         i. somewhat similar to best interests of creditors test
      b. **always determine what debtor would get in Ch. 7**
      c. ***fully secured creditor can never have a preference against them***

- vi. HYPO: mortgage payment to mortgage company prior to bankruptcy is NOT a preference → lien flows through unaffected in Ch. 7 so no advantage to creditor here
    1. Granting SI in second asset meets the elements of a preference, but there may be a defense...
- vii. **Defenses to Preferences, § 547(c) →** to the extent such transfer was –
    1. (c)(1) a Contemporaneous Exchange for new value given to the debtor
    2. (2) incurred by the debtor in the ordinary course of business or financial affairs of debtor
    3. a security interest in property acquired by the debtor to the extent that such SI secures new value (purchase-money exception)
    4. was made with new value given by the creditor for the benefit of the debtor
        - a. Note: up to the new value, it's a defense, the rest remains a preference
    5. made for a DSO
    6. consumer debt for less than 600 dollars
    7. non consumer debt for less than $5000 dollars
- viii. **Transfers w/ Checks → Checks and Float**
    1. when does transfer occur for purposes of timing when done with a check?
        - a. ANSWER: When the check actually gets credited from payor's bank to payee's bank (could be the same thing as clearing the account)
        - b. Date of transfer → when payor's bank honors the payee bank's request for payment
        - c. *Barneville v. Johnson*, SC Case
            - i. Key is when the money leaves the debtor's account → that's when we have a transfer for a Preference Analysis
- ix. Indirect Preference → people other than the transferee who benefit from such a transfer

i. **Executory Contracts**

- i. <u>What is an Executory Contract?</u>
    1. basically on that has not been consummated just yet, it is ongoing
    2. Law Review Prof's article definition that has been adopted by the courts:

a. **Material Breach Test: "A contract under which the obligation of both the bankrupt and the counterparty to the contract are so far unperformed that the failure of either to complete performance would constitute a material breach excusing the performance of the other."**

3. so if performance of one party is so far completed (further along), then he/she can't breach and it is not an exec K
4. complex K's lead to problems and more complexities
    a. MUST ASK whether we are at a point where there has been enough performance
    b. *Riodizio, Inc.* → dealt with option Ks
        i. One party had competed perf and they were done (they paid for their option), and under Prof's test, it wouldn't be executory
        ii. But there is another test courts use: **Functional Analysis**
            1. here, ct held that since each party must perform to obtain the benefits of the option K, it is still an exec K

ii. **§ 365, Executory Contracts (and unexpired leases)**
1. if K is not executory, then this section does not apply
2. (a) → trustee, subject to court's approval, may assume or reject any exec K or unexpired lease of the debtor
    a. assume → means to take on that K
    b. reject → means to default on the K and cease performance
    c. **remember, it's UNEXPIRED leases, not expired ones!!**
3. <u>(b)(1) → provides mechanism for DIP or trustee to assume a K under which they had a prior breach, 3 ways:</u>

- a. 1) trustee cures, OR provides adequate assurance that the trustee will promptly cure (i.e. cure over time)
  - i. some more info here on nonmonetary breaches (i.e. mowing the lawn), but don't worry for our class prof says
- b. 2) trustee compensates, OR provides adequate assurance that the trustee will promptly compensate, a nondebtor party to such a K or lease for any actual pecuniary loss to such party resulting from such default
- c. 3) trustee provides adequate assurance of future performance under such K or lease
- d. Trustee will file a motion here and then go talk to other contracting party → usually is resolved through a stipulation here
- e. **Ct will give deference to the debtor's "sound business judgment" here when trying to assume or reject a K**

4. (b)(3) → special shopping center provisions added in by the lobby for shopping ctr landlords
5. (c) → **restrictions on assuming or assigning certain Ks, <u>cannot</u> assume IF:**
   - a. (1)(A) → applicable law excuses a party, other than the debtor, to such K or lease from accepting performance from or rendering perf to an entity other than the debtor or DIP
     - i. i.e. with a personal services K → cannot assume if it's assignment is forbidden under applicable nonbankruptcy law
   - b. (2) → if the K is to make a loan, or to issue a security of debtor, then not assumable
   - c. (3) → cannot assume a nonresidential lease that has been terminated prior to the bankruptcy case
6. (d) → provides deadlines for trustees to assume or reject from petition date forward, and if they

don't it will be deemed rejected by operation of law:

- **a.** with a K or unexpired lease of nonresidential real estate
  - **i.** in Ch. 7 – 120 days
  - **ii.** Ch. 11/13 – 120 days
- **b.** With a K or unexpired lease of Residential real estate and personal property:
  - **i.** Ch. 7 – 60 days
  - **ii.** Ch. 11/13 – confirmation of plan

7. (f)(1) → deals with trustees **assigning exec Ks, only if:**

- **a.** (2)(B) requires adequate assurance of future perfection by the assignee of such K or lease, whether or not there has been a default
  - **i.** how do you do this? → prove this to the judge by having the assignee testify along with admitting into evidence his/her financial records/books
- **b.** (3) certain restrictions on parties to exec Ks to assign stuff
  - **i.** cannot allow have termination or modification of K as a result of such assignment or assumption
  - **ii.** *Jamesway* → ct allowed DIP to assign lease and invalidated certain lease provisions that debtor objected to
    - **1.** if a clause in the lease creates an anti-assignment effect, ct will not look favorably upon it
    - **2.** i.e. clause requiring debtor to pay a landlord a profit

upon assignment was unenforceable

8. *Krystal Cadillac* → ct held that under state law, franchise agreement could not be terminated
    a. **Must focus on whether or not agreement is even alive before you can terminate it**
    b. Ct held that termination was invalid b/c automatic stay stops it in bankruptcy
    c. So it let the debtor/DIP be able to cure, assign, and assume the franchise for the benefit of all the creditors

iii. If other party from a rejected exec K has a loss or claim, it becomes GUSC, see 502(g) → makes the claim a prepetition claim

iv. If debtor cannot perform, but contract still has a lot of value, assume it and then ASSIGN it!!

v. Policy with Exec Ks → if were to force debtors to perform bad Ks, ultimately one unsecured creditor gets paid at the expense of all the other GUSC
    1. treat like creditors alike → so force this contracting party to share pro rata with GUSC

j. **Avoiding Powers of Trustee; Use of State Avoiding Laws; and Fraudulent Conveyances**

i. **Strong Arm Power of the Trustee or DIP, § 544**
    1. Basically, trustee can stand in the shoes of a 3rd party bonafide purchaser for value without notice of SI (Hypothetically)
    2. Trustee gains these hypothetical powers on date of bankruptcy filing → i.e. rights and powers of, or may avoid any transfer of property of the debtor that is voidable by...
    3. **(a)(1) → trustee becomes a judicial lien creditor on the date of filing, whether or not such a creditor exists**
        a. if this judgment creditor executes on property, then, for example, the judgment creditor gains priority over any unperfected SIs/liens on the property
    4. **(a)(2)** → makes trustee an execution creditor also (not that important)

5. **(a)(3) → trustee is BFP with regard to real property, whether or not such a purchaser exists**
    a. **BFP gives even more power than just being a lien creditor**
    b. if SC is unperfected, then trustee can take property without SC's lien
    c. i.e. over anyone who fails to record land mortgages/liens in the land records
6. this can in essence make a SC into and unsecured creditor
    a. unperfected SCs are basically unsecured creditors in bankruptcy → they must perfect!
7. there are some EXCEPTIONS where SCs are allowed to perfect their interest in a certain time period into bankruptcy, i.e. after petition date, like 20-30 days
    a. PMSIs, ordinary course of business exceptions
    b. And 362 allows an exception to the stay to this (i.e. to allow these SCs to "perfect")
8. *Bowling* → case where trustee is using 544(a)(3) power
    a. was trustee a BFP on real property?
        i. Split in the courts; either:
        ii. Stand in the shoes of the debtor
        iii. OR no knowledge for trustee based on day of filing
    b. Here, must show mortgage was not notarized → here, ct said evidence shows it was not, so trustee wins

ii. **Fraudulent Conveyances**
1. **§ 548** of the code brings this into bankruptcy
    a. very similar to MD provisions, fed one:
        i. has an **actual intent** to hinder portion
        ii. receiving less than **reasonably equiv value in exchange** AND

1. debtor was **insolvent** or became insolvent due to conveyance
2. debtor had **unreasonably small capital** for transaction
3. debtor intended to incur or believed that the debt would incur **debts that would be beyond debtor's ability to pay as they matured**
4. debtor made transfer for benefit of INSIDER under an employment contract and not in the ordinary course of business

iii. **Congress carved out some charitable contributions**

b. fraud conveyance must be within 2 yrs of filing date

2. MD Fraudulent Conveyance
   a. Use this for 2-3 yrs before petition date (normal SOL in MD is 3 yrs)
   b. Trustee looks to **544(b)(1)** to gain these powers
      i. "trustee may avoid any transfer of an interest of the debtor in property" that is voidable under applicable law by a creditor holding an unsecured claim under 502
      ii. i.e. if there is an unsecured creditor in the case that could have sued under state law (e.g. under fraud conveyance state law), **then the trustee can stand in the shoes of that unsecured creditor → so here trustee needs a creditor to stand in the shoes of!!!**

c. thus, all the MD fraud conveyance provisions become relevant in bankruptcy

3. *In re Image Worldwide* → case about reasonably equivalent value in big Ch. 11 cases
   a. Sets for a functional approach to what is reasonably equivalent value
      i. Must look at the whole corporate structure; can't just look at corporation 2, i.e. lower corporation
      ii. In this case, ct said corp 2 did not get enough value so it's fraud conveyance

k. **Plan of Reorganization and Conf of Plan in Ch. 11**
   i. § 1129 → confirmation list of requirements for the debtor
      1. equivalent to 1325 in Ch. 13
      2. (a)(3) → must be in good faith
      3. (a)(7) → must meet BIOCT with respect to each claim
         a. OR a class must accept the plan in spite of it failing BIOCT
      4. (a)(8) → each class or claims of interest must accept the plan, OR they cannot be impaired under the plan
         a. i.e. they must accept or pay them in full
         b. ***if a debtor can't meet a8 requirements, there is an alternative difficult process for securing a plan → **a Ch. 11 cramdown**
            i. different than Ch. 13 cramdown
            ii. cramming down the plan of reorg on creditors that haven't accepted and are impaired under it
      5. (a)(9) → all 507 priority claims must be paid in full on effective date of plan
      6. (a)(10) → if a class of claims is impaired (not paid in full), then you have to have once class of claims accepting the plan
      7. (a)(11) → plan must be feasible
   ii. § 1126 → provides for voting in Ch. 11
      1. disclosure statement is approved by the ct

a. send this out with the plan
b. must have solicitation of votes of creditors

2. Voting is done based on class: have to have 2/3 dollar amount and ½ in number voting in favor **of those creditors who actually vote in a class (so don't look at whole class, just the ones who voted)**
   a. HYPO: 100K debt, and 30 creditors
      i. 20 vote representing 90K of debt
         1. of 20 votes, 11 must approve; and of 90K, 60K must be approving
   b. many creditors don't vote and this moves things along

iii. § 1141 → Effect of confirmation
   1. new plan is a binding K b/t debtor and creditors
      a. it's enforceable in state court
      b. this plan comprises ALL the future obligations b/t the parties

I. Chapter Choice
   i. If debtor cannot meet Ch. 13 debt limits in 109(e), then may have to file Ch. 11 reorganization for individual
   ii. New law in 2005 for Ch. 11 → postpetition earnings from personal services of an individual **are property of the estate,** § 1115
      1. just like Ch. 13
      2. may deter debtors from filing a Ch. 11

X. JURISDICTION AND VENUE

Jurisdiction to Bankruptcy Court

Venue → is controlled by 28 U.S.C. 1408

- Court's procedure title of US Code
- 1408(1) Venue is proper for bankruptcy case where corporate debtor is domiciled (i.e. incorporated), and something else for individuals...

1408

Except as provided in section 1410 of this title, a case under title 11 may be commenced in the district court for the district—

(1) in which the domicile, residence, principal place of business in the United States, or principal assets in the United States, of the person or entity that is the subject of such case have been located for the one hundred and eighty days immediately preceding such commencement, or for a longer portion of such one-hundred-and-eighty-day period than the domicile, residence, or principal place of business, in the United States, or principal assets in the United States, of such person were located in any other district; or

(2) in which there is pending a case under title 11 concerning such person's affiliate, general partner, or partnership.

- *Northern Pipeline v. Marathon*, 102 s ct 1958
    - Problems with bankruptcy jurisdiction
    - Bankruptcy judges are Art. I judges, not Art. III judges
    - Sup Ct found that Congress's grant to bankruptcy judges was so broad that they overstepped their bounds and basically made Art. I judges into Art. III judges
        - Art III judges have life tenure; Art I bankruptcy 14 yrs
        - Art III can only be impeached; Art I bankruptcy can be removed easily
        - Pay differences

Congress made bankruptcy court the adjunct of the District court

- jurisdiction is in an Art III court and then referred to the bankruptcy court
- there are local rules also → automatically refers all bankruptcy cases to bankruptcy courts
- results in tons of conflicting case law at the District Court level

NOTE: you can't contract away your right to file bankruptcy; courts hold this to protect unsecured creditors who are not part of the sec agreement

RULES FOR LAWYERS IN BANKRUPTCY

- in a consumer bankruptcy case, the debtor is the client
    - this is who the attorney represents
- debtor-attorney
    - ch. 7 : businesses or industry
    - ch. 13 : individuals
- what rules do lawyers have to comply with, consumer cases, ch. 7 + ch.13 ? → **§ 329**
    - file with the court compensation agreement if after one year before petition date
    - part b allows a refund of the fee if excessive
    - why do they have to do this?
        - Protects individuals under financial stress
        - Debtor loses nonexempt assets as liquidated to creditors
            - Need debtors to care about representation
    - MUST FILE THESE DISCLOSURES
        - Rule 2016b statement
    - DRAs – defined under § 101(12A) → debt relief agency

- If you are a DRA, then you have to comply with these other sections of the Code, §§ 526, 527, 528
  - Very complicated new provisions → heated litigation about them, alleging they are unconstitutional
- Problems with a definition → applies to attorneys and non-attorneys
- Anyone who provides bankruptcy assistance to an assisted person for money
- § 526 → uses the term "assisted person" a lot
  - new defined term in § 101(3) → only applies to representing consumers with nonexempt property of less than 150K
  - 526a4 → doesn't allow for taking money????
    - Makes an attorney be fraudulent for taking credit card money
      - See § 727 and 523
        - 523a2 → incurring debt without intention of ever paying that
- § 527 → disclosures = boilerplate when providing assistance
- § 528 → more requirements for DRAs
  - affirmative requirements for disclosures
    - written contract with client
    - explanation of services

- why might you tell a client to go out and get a car before bankruptcy?
  - Because you can fully deduct payments on means test
  - Practical reason is because you needed one
  - And you are not going to cramdown later
  - But bankruptcy code says you can't do this!!!!!!!!

For a full catalog of our books,

please visit our website

www.mclarenpublishing.com